LOCUST

LOCUST

The Devastating Rise and Mysterious Disappearance of the Insect That Shaped the American Frontier

JEFFREY A. LOCKWOOD

BASIC
BOOKS

A Member of the Perseus Books Group
New York

Published by Basic Books,
A Member of the Perseus Books Group

Books published by Basic Books are available at special discounts for
bulk purchases in the United States by corporations, institutions, and
other organizations. For more information, please contact the Special
Markets Department at the Perseus Books Group, 11 Cambridge
Center, Cambridge MA 02142, or call (617) 252-5298, (800) 255-1514
or e-mail special.markets@perseusbooks.com.

Library of Congress Cataloging-in-Publication Data
Lockwood, Jeffrey Alan, 1960–
    Locust : the devastating rise and mysterious disappearance of the
insect that shaped the American frontier / Jeffrey A. Lockwood.—
1st ed.
        p.   cm.
    Includes bibliographical references.
    ISBN 0–7382–0894–9
    1. Rocky Mountain locust—West (U.S.)—History.   I. Title.
SB945.R7L63   2004
632'.726—dc22
                                                            2003025538

Text design by Brent Wilcox
Set in 11-point Sabon by Perseus Books Group

First Edition

1 2 3 4 5 6 7 8 9 10—06 05 04

To
THEODORE J. COHN,
ROBERT E. PFADT, *and*
DAVID C. F. RENTZ
*a modern entomological triumvirate
exemplifying traditional scientific virtues
—and comprising the finest scholars,
gentlemen, and orthopterists
that it has been my true pleasure and
good fortune to have known*

CONTENTS

Nothing tends so much to the corruption of science than to suffer it to stagnate; these waters must be troubled, before they can exert their virtues.

FROM EDMUND BURKE,
ON THE SUBLIME AND BEAUTIFUL

ACKNOWLEDGMENTS

This book represents my own synthetic efforts, but the support, work, and ideas of many people made the project possible. I would like to thank my friends and associates at the University of Wyoming who lent their energy and expertise to the making of this book. Scott Schell, Spencer Schell, and Doug Smith provided valuable research on a spectacular range of historical, political, and biological matters. Alexandre Latchininsky was an invaluable source of insights on the biology and ecology of locusts and the life of Sir Boris Uvarov. Untangling elements of taxonomic rules and their arcane exceptions was made possible through discussions with Scott Shaw. Tom Parish provided key meteorological information allowing me to make sense of "Albert's Swarm." Tom Foulke offered valuable insights as to methods for converting nineteenth-century locust damage estimates into modern terms.

I must also extend my sincere gratitude to a wide range of colleagues from other institutions. Peter Adler of Clemson University generously tracked down information on M. P. Somes. The Nebraska State Historical Society's Ann Billsbach and the Lincoln (Nebraska) City Libraries' Robert Boyce provided original source material regarding the life of Samuel Aughey, which augmented the biography written by the University of Nebraska State Museum's Margaret R. Bollick. Bill Chapco of the University of Regina shared valuable information on the molecular biology of grasshoppers and locusts. Key historical insights on insect biochemistry were provided by Dave Carlson of the USDA's Agricultural Research Service. Ted Cohn, adjunct

curator at the University of Michigan's Museum of Zoology, offered
important insights into the history of acridology and the nature of
the Rocky Mountain locust. Clarence Collison and Barbara Perrigin
of Mississippi State University were kind enough to provide historical information on early entomologists. The National Park Service's
historian, Bill Gwaltney, managed to provide details of nineteenth-
century characters that were well beyond my research capabilities.
Mike Ivie of the Montana State University shared his unique ideas
concerning the relationship between the Rocky Mountain locust and
the Eskimo curlew. Ian McRae (University of Minnesota) and John
Luhman (Minnesota Department of Agriculture) aided my efforts to
uncover the course of M. P. Somes's life. Jon Muller of Southern Illinois University provided particularly intriguing details on the life of
Cyrus Thomas. Key taxonomic and biologic insights were generously
offered by Dan Otte of the Philadelphia's Academy of Natural Sciences. Bob Randell of the University of Saskatchewan provided
unique insights on Ashley Gurney and other acridological luminaries.
Hillary L. Robison (University of Nevada at Reno) generously shared
insect remains collected with Jonathan Ratner from Knife Point Glacier.
Colorado State University entomologists Jason Schmidt and Boris
Kondratieff took time to track down details of early work on
grasshoppers at their institution. Carol Sheppard (Washington State
University) and Richard Weinzierl (University of Illinois) allowed use
of their research findings concerning the Walsh-Klippart debate. Beth
Simmons of Metro State College generously shared her research on
early expeditions to Rocky Mountain glaciers and early grasshopper
infestations in Colorado. Kim Smith of the University of Arkansas
provided expertise on ornithology. Charles Warwick and Dwight Divine of the Illinois Natural History Survey provided novel perspectives
on the work of Cyrus Thomas.

I should also thank those people who provided some of the impetus
and encouragement for me to turn my work with the Rocky Mountain locust into a book-length project. Jay McPherson of Southern Illinois University at Carbondale originally provoked me into writing an
article for *American Entomologist* on the story and meaning of the locust's demise. This work was adapted for the readers of *Orion, Wild*

Earth, and *High Country News*—and the essay received the 2002 John Burroughs Award. From there, Rob Robertson—a literary agent with a gift for authentic collaboration and a profound knowledge of the publishing world—convinced me that there was a book lurking within these shorter pieces. My editor, Amanda Cook, was remarkably creative, attentive, and helpful. Together, Rob and Amanda countered every horror story that authors tell about agents and editors, and I cannot exaggerate my sincere gratitude for their assistance and support. Of course, the project would not have been possible without my department head, Tom Thurow, allowing me the freedom to pursue this dream. And last but not least, I thank my family—Nan, Erin, and Ethan—for valuing my work, reading my early draft, and understanding why this project was important to me. I apologize to anyone whose contribution to this project I may have overlooked.

Finally, I must also thank readers and disciplinary experts in advance for their willingness to pardon my occasional oversights and overreaches. Any project that hopes to integrate science and natural history with elements of politics, sociology, history, and religion is destined to simplify certain aspects of the story and perhaps even introduce blatant, if hopefully forgivable, errors.

INTRODUCTION

JULY 1875, DODGE COUNTY, NEBRASKA

It could have been a dust storm rolling in from the west—except the July breeze wasn't enough to rustle the cornstalks, let alone lift a yellow-brown cloud of soil. In all likelihood, Abram McNeal, like the other settlers in eastern Nebraska, could not fathom what he was seeing on that fateful day. He pulled on the reins of the plough horse, bringing the rig to a stop. The smell of fresh-cut grass perfumed the summer air. Setting the reins over his thigh, he pushed back the brim of his tattered hat and wiped the sweat from his eyes. He could just make out the tops of the cottonwoods along Maple Creek, where John and Arthur Bloomer had staked the first claims in the county just eighteen years before. Not far beyond that, the eerie cloud drew closer, glints of sunlight flickering along its edges. The horse nickered and shook her mane. Abram might not have understood what was coming, but he knew that he had to get back to the homestead.

By the time he could see his wife in the garden, she had stopped weeding and was standing stock-still. Dropping the hand that had been shading her eyes, she gripped the handle of the hoe and her knuckles whitened. She tried to conceal her growing fear from their twin daughters, who were hidden between the rows, filling a basket with green beans and humming a ditty from Sunday school. The county's first agricultural fair was in another week, and it seemed that everyone in the county—4,200 men, women, and children—would be in Centerville. As the shimmering wave seemed to wash over the hills on the other side of the Platte River, she scooped up the girls and headed to the house.

As Abram unhitched the horse, the first one hit him in the cheek and clung to his beard. He swiped at the insect, and it leapt to the ground. As it fluttered back into the air, he knew—although he'd never before seen—what formed the cloud that was now filling the horizon. We can readily imagine his growing fear as another ten insects pelted him, then hundreds fell like living hail, driven by papery wings rather than a howling wind. This much we know from newspaper accounts: The sunlight dimmed, and the air took on the thick veil that he associated with the smoke of a prairie fire. The roaring crackle of a million wings sounded like a horrific blaze.

Abram panicked at first, frightened in a way he'd never been by blizzards, fevers, and cougars. These other invaders could be managed by knowledge, planning, and courage. But as the swarm descended, Abram felt as if he was suffocating. Locusts filled the air. They were clinging to him, their spiny legs tangled in his hair. He flailed as the insects worked their way down his shirt collar and up his pant legs. He seemed to be at the tip of a tornado, sucked into a demented whirlwind.

The scream of his daughters broke the grip of his own terror. His wife and the twins hadn't made it to the house, and now the locusts were crawling into the folds of their dresses. The insects clung like giant burs in his daughters' silken hair. His wife had set the girls down and buried her face in her hands, paralyzed with fear.

He swept the girls into one arm, wrapping the other around his wife's shoulders and guiding her to the cabin. At the door, he brushed the horrid insects from their hair and clothing, stomping the locusts that fell at their feet. Shoving his family through the doorway, he started to follow—and then he heard the panicked whinny. The horse, still hitched to the cutting rig, reared up, locusts matted in its mane and chewing on its sweaty hide in search of moisture. Abram slammed the door and headed back into the swarm. The horse bolted, dragging the scythe through the length of the garden and racing alongside the cornfield beyond.

Like a dog that suddenly turns on his antagonist, Abram ran into the garden, grabbing the hoe that his wife had dropped. He swung in wide, vicious arcs, knocking the locusts from the plants, grinding them into the soil. After long, futile minutes his chest was heaving, his anger spent. He dropped the hoe and plodded back to the house, its walls now seething with a living blanket of locusts.

In the doorway, he crushed one locust after another underfoot, until the ground was slick with their ruptured bodies. Behind him, the garden was in shreds and the limbs of the willow tree by the house nearly bent to the ground under the weight of the insects. Beyond that, the corn was being stripped bare, he could see a dozen rows into the field. His gaze lifted to the horizon—as thousands of insects continued to drop onto the land, millions more streamed overhead. He fell to his knees, the yellowish grease of the crushed locusts staining his overalls. Through the door, he heard his wife sobbing, his daughters whimpering.

We can only partially reconstruct that terrifying afternoon in 1875 because Abram McNeal left no journal telling of his life on the prairie. But we know from the accounts of other settlers that Abram McNeal was surely overwhelmed—and perhaps for the first time in his life he despaired. Every Sunday, the scattered families in the valley made the bone-jarring trek over dirt roads to the Congregational church in Fremont to listen to the Reverend Isaac E. Heaton explain the blessings that came to the faithful. Like so many of his fellow homesteaders, Abram was likely a devout man condemned to watching his farm be consumed by the locust plague—the same terror that God used to punish the pharaoh of Egypt. Like so many of his neighbors in Dodge County that blistering July, Abram McNeal had to wonder what had made the Creator so unfairly curse his children.

Throughout the nineteenth century, swarms of locusts regularly swept across the North American continent, turning noon into dusk, devastating farm communities, and bringing trains to a halt as the crushed bodies of the insects greased the rails. The U.S. Entomological Commission estimated that during the outbreaks of 1874–1877 the Rocky Mountain locust inflicted a staggering $200 million in damage on agriculture west of the Mississippi (this is equivalent to a loss of $116 billion in today's money, with annual agricultural production in the United States being valued at $217 billion). The commission, formed by Congress to assess and redress the devastation, was a brilliant and eccentric trio of scientists: Charles Valentine Riley (the Missouri State Entomologist, who would one day become known as the Father of Economic Entomology), Cyrus Thomas (the Illinois State Entomologist, who abandoned his Evangelical Lutheran ministry to pursue science and eventually serve as a director in the Smithsonian Institution), and Alpheus Spring Packard, Jr. (a Harvard-educated zoologist, who founded the *American Naturalist* and headed the Peabody Academy of Science). Not only did the locust shape the cultural history of the West, but this creature also profoundly affected the lives and work of the most important and influential entomologists in history.

Pioneers and government agencies tried every imaginable method of control. They prayed for deliverance, organized bounty systems, conscripted able-bodied men into "grasshopper armies," and provided food aid for starving communities. Farmers tried to burn and beat the invaders—or, failing this, they turned to drowning and plowing the eggs or crushing and poisoning the hatching locusts. Elaborate horse-drawn devices were invented to destroy locusts, and the most desperate farmers resorted to using dynamite to blast the egg beds of the insects. This approach surely decimated local pockets of the pest and provided a hearty sense of revenge, but pulverizing thousands of acres with explosives was hardly a viable strategy. And so, as courageous and creative as these methods were, the locusts kept coming.

The swarms continued to pummel America's heartland into the 1880s, moving and settling with the caprice of tornadoes. Their devastation was like that of a living wildfire, consuming fifty tons of vegetation per day to fuel a typical swarm. Finally, in the 1890s, to the relief of a beleaguered nation, the locust outbreaks subsided. But such remissions had occurred before, only to have the locusts return with a fury. When a small swarm was reported in Manitoba in 1902 people wondered if another period of devastation was at hand. The specter of an outbreak loomed and there were still no reliable methods to defend the land.

Nobody could have guessed that this would be the last swarm of locusts to be seen in North America. Suddenly—and mysteriously—the Rocky Mountain locust had disappeared. For a decade nobody noticed, as more urgent matters of a world at war occupied the nation. Later, a few state entomologists remarked on the absence of their former nemesis. But soon another ecological and economic crisis captured the attention of the country. The Dust Bowl of the 1930s displaced both soil and people. This disaster was aggravated by horrific outbreaks of grasshoppers—renewing the memories of locust plagues. But the stories would eventually fade in a culture that looked to the future, rather than the past. Nine decades would pass before the Rocky Mountain locust made its next appearance. And this time it would be found in a most remarkable place.

AUGUST 1995, KNIFE POINT GLACIER, WIND RIVER RANGE, WYOMING

"Goddamn! Jeff, come check this out!" Larry cried, dropping to his knees, the frigid water soaking into his pants. Although swearing was not entirely out of character, such ebullience was unexpected—particularly given how cold and tired he must have been. Two days earlier, Larry had hiked the twenty-three miles to Indian Pass in the Wind River Range of Wyoming. The other members of the scientific team, including me, had ridden two-thirds of the way, until our horses started slipping and stumbling on the steep, wet path, after which we scrambled over the rocky trail on foot.

It was our second day on the glacier, and the previous day had been cruelly disappointing; we had found no evidence of insects in the ice. We had good reason to believe that this expedition was going to pay off: Geologists collecting ice cores from this glacier earlier in the season had heard of our work and told us they'd found what looked like rotting insects. Besides, Larry argued, after years of searching we had finally earned enough karma (his term for suffering of any sort, especially when undeserved) to score the "big one." The previous night's dinner of undercooked macaroni with powdered cheese had been punctuated with fewer jibes and jokes than our usual camp meals.

Larry DeBrey had been my first graduate student and had worked as my research associate for the last three years. Before coming to the University of Wyoming, he had operated his own logging company, worked highway construction, and fought forest fires. Only a few pounds heavier than I, he carried twice the weight of ropes, carabiners, ice screws, and collecting bottles that I hauled. Seeing Larry on his knees was not surprising. He'd suffered from scoliosis—and between childhood surgeries and metal rods he couldn't bend over very well, which also explained why he preferred hiking to riding a horse. But he was not prone to outbursts of excitement; dry witticisms were his standard fare.

"Come over here. Look, they're everywhere," he said, waving his hand toward a boulder incongruously perched in the center of the ice flow. The glacial ice crunched under my crampons as I hurried from the edge of the moraine, where I'd been jotting notes.

"What's everywhere?" I asked.

Before he could answer, it was my turn to drop to my hands and knees. The surface of the rotting ice was like a frozen cheese grater. In a tiny cavity, soaked in meltwater, lay a crumpled form about an inch and a half long. Its legs were missing, but the bulbous head, powerful thorax, tapered abdomen, and straight wings left no doubt that this was the body of a grasshopper—or a locust. In the intense sunlight that cuts through the thin air of 12,000 feet, the dark remains had melted out of the surrounding ice.

For five years I had waited for this. At other sites we had discovered ancient fragments that could be tentatively ascribed to the Rocky Mountain locust, and we had found intriguing deposits of modern-day grasshoppers. But we had yet to find an intact body of the locust, the definitive evidence that our quest had not been a foolhardy venture. Could these soggy bodies be the bizarre treasure that might prove to be a window into the last days of the Rocky Mountain locust?

Larry's ruddy face split into a grin at the prospect of having struck entomological gold. He'd stuck with me through August snowstorms, lung-searing climbs, and horrifically bad advice from local guides. Scattered across the surface of the glacier, either in water-soaked pockets or just beneath the ice, were dozens of these mummified insects. The afternoon passed quickly with tedious but hopeful labor, as we gently placed the limp and sodden bodies in numbered vials. That night, as Larry brought water up from the stream and Craig and

Charlie fixed dinner, I laid out a couple dozen of the better-preserved specimens under the harsh, white light of a Coleman lantern. Gently turning the limp bodies onto their sides, I finally found a male. Within seconds of lifting the first body from its watery grave, I knew that it was in the genus *Melanoplus*, to which the Rocky Mountain locust belonged—but the only way to be certain of the species was to examine the internal genitalia of a male. Dismembering the body would effectively destroy a rare and valuable specimen, but I had to know if we had found what we had been looking for.

I didn't know what I was going to tell Larry if the specimen wasn't the Rocky Mountain locust. But then, we'd grown used to disappointment, almost inured to failure. We'd come to love the hunt, the companionship, the quixotic search for buried treasure. I had no doubt that if the species was something other than the locust, Larry would pause from his well-earned meal, nod knowingly, and declare that, by God, tomorrow we'd find the bastards. And if not, then we'd go back to the yellowing reports of the early geologists and the topographic filigree of modern maps. That is, if we could garner endorsements from increasingly dubious colleagues and eke out funding from correspondingly impatient sources. But I'd begun to harbor misgivings of a different sort.

Seeking the physical remains of the once glorious Rocky Mountain locust was both thrilling and saddening. The North American continent had never seen a life form with greater fecundity. Swarms of these insects swept across the prairies, at one time reaching from southern Canada to the Mexican border and from California to Iowa. They were the leitmotif of the Great Plains, as powerful a life force as the great herds of bison. To touch a creature that had shaped the folktales, culture, and history of the West would be worth years of frustration. Or so I had believed.

After searching so long and hard, I began to wonder whether it was right to disturb the icy tombs secreted in the Rockies. Even if the glaciers would one day yield the remains of the locust, maybe this most magnificent of species should be allowed to rest in peace amid one of the country's most spectacular settings. As I began to tease apart the mushy abdomen I didn't know whether we had finally succeeded.

Finding the tiny, diagnostic structures within the decomposing soft tissues was a slow and delicate process that gave me time to contemplate what I did know. I understood that I had transcended the bounds of science. I was coming to realize that my intention to rob the graves of this long-lost creature imposed a deep obligation, the nature of which I was only beginning to discern.

The extinction of the Rocky Mountain locust is the quintessential ecological mystery of the North American continent—a century-old homicide on a continental scale. How could an animal whose swarms numbered in the tens or hundreds of billions simply vanish within a decade? Coming to terms with this species and its lessons has meant seeking leads among the daily journals and tragic stories of the early settlers, returning to the formative years of American entomology through the lives of its most influential practitioners, and searching for new evidence in icy graves and on musty bookshelves. For fifteen years I worked on this case, sometimes for only a few days at a time, sometimes for months. It is a tale of people, egos, values, and insects colliding to generate a remarkable series of events—along with a few false leads.

A brilliant Russian entomologist, Boris Petrovich Uvarov, laid the foundation for what seemed to be the solution to the locust's vanishing act. He showed how these insects can transmogrify into incredibly divergent forms between their solitary and migratory phases. Following on his work, Jacobus Faure, a South African specialist, "proved" that the Rocky Mountain locust was still alive in its solitary form, except that his data belied his proof. Soon thereafter, an entomologist from Oklahoma, Charles Brett, made a similar claim with even less evidence, but a peripheral experiment of his provided a critical clue that was overlooked, even derided, for decades.

The bizarre anatomical work by the great American entomologist Theodore Huntington Hubble, on the genitalia of male grasshoppers, provided the definitive method for determining whether the Rocky Mountain locust had truly disappeared. The Smithsonian Institution's Ashley Gurney used Hubble's discovery to finally declare that the creature had been a true species—and that it was extinct (a finding that was confirmed half a century later in a Canadian laboratory through the wonders of molecular genetics). And so, a case that had been closed for decades based on the contention that the victim was still alive, albeit in another form, was reopened—only to be summarily closed. To explain the locust's extinction, entomologists alluded to a discordant and sometimes contradictory set of large-scale changes in the West.

As an entomologist, I was initially drawn to the mystery of the Rocky Mountain locust's disappearance as a scientific problem. Although superficially satisfying, the explanations for the extinction were ecologically implausible. When I again reopened the case, my interests were objective and my approach was purely professional. But such scientific mysteries are charged with controversy, and I found myself oddly allying with the case's most apparently misguided investigator, Charles Brett. Engaging in fiery debates, spending weeks and months looking for evidence in shadowy museums and on vast grasslands, and digging through frozen mud and crumbling maps turns a scientific riddle into a personal quest. Solving the mystery of the Rocky Mountain locust has taught me a great deal about the life of the locust, the history of the West, the ways of science—and myself. In the end, perhaps I simply rediscovered a century-old insight of America's greatest entomologist, Charles Riley, who came to understand that "in libraries and museums, the entomologist may find the dry bones of knowledge, but only in Nature's own museum can he clothe those dry bones with beauty and life."

The Third Horseman
of the Apocalypse

FOR MOST OF US, INSECTS ARE MERELY A SOURCE OF annoyance. Our panicked response to the mosquito-borne West Nile virus is the exception that proves the rule. We've become so used to insects being a marginal nuisance that when these creatures are transformed into vectors of disease (however mild in most cases), we panic. Compared to the total number of human deaths from West Nile virus in the United States in 2002, ten times more Americans died as a result of talking on their cell phones while driving, and influenza killed more than a hundred times as many people. But in the nineteenth century, insects were more than an inconvenience. During the Civil War, half of the white troops and fourth-fifths of the black soldiers in the Union Army contracted malaria and several thousand died. By the 1870s, the country had suffered the ravages of two of the Four Horsemen of the Apocalypse—war and disease.

Although many of the settlers had evaded the devastation of war, nearly all were agonizingly familiar with disease. Their journeys were shaped by the reality of pathogenic microbes and crippling parasites. Beating the other pioneers to an early start in the spring meant risking exposure to blizzards, but it also meant minimizing exposure to contaminated water that would accumulate as waves of migrants trekked westward later in the year. Encountering the chill of hypothermia was worth avoiding the scourge of cholera. This bean-shaped bacterium with a long whiplike tail was the primary killer on the Oregon Trail. Thousands of graves strung along the route attested to the power of this horrible disease, which killed half of its victims and wiped out entire wagon trains. Infections could take a person from good spirits in the morning to agony by noon and death by evening. Intense stomach pain would be quickly followed by devastating bouts of bacteria-laden diarrhea, draining the wretch of a quart of fluid every hour. Such a loss rapidly dehydrated the exhausted sufferer—and assured the pathogen of finding another victim through the vile trailside conditions. The only hope for a wagon train was to move ahead of the dying pioneers, leaving the blight to fall on the next travelers to come along.

There was another good reason for departing early in the spring, although the settlers were not fully cognizant of this advantage. The sooner a wagon train got under way, the less time the pioneers spent in the filthy conditions at the trail head. Many of the migrants acquired body lice in the crowded riverboats and rundown boarding-houses while heading to, or waiting at, the "jump-off" points for the overland migration. Like six-legged grains of rice, these bloodthirsty insects caused a tormenting itch, but far worse was their ability to transmit disease. An infected person would suddenly come down with a headache, chills, and fever perhaps a week or so into the journey. Soon, a faint, rose-colored rash would spread over the body and the victim would be unable to keep pace with the rest of the party. Lucky patients might be laid on some quilts on the floor of the prairie schooner. The rattling sickbed would aggravate the pain in their muscles and joints, but at least the wagon's canvas bonnet would keep the sunlight from hurting their eyes. And if they were truly fortunate, in a couple of weeks they'd have recovered enough to walk alongside the wagon. But nearly a third of pioneers who climbed weakly into a prairie schooner with the raging fever of typhus would not step back down from the wagon alive.

The settlers often hosted other, less lethal but perhaps more loathsome stowaways within their bodies. Abdominal pains were common ailments, and the lucky individuals were only suffering from thread-like pinworms. The less fortunate harbored earthworm-sized parasites in their intestines. These roundworms would cycle through a person's body every few months. The adult worms laid eggs in their host's small intestine, and the offspring bored through the bowels and traveled through blood and lymph. This ghastly process would culminate with the worms' penetrating the lungs, working their way up the bronchial tree, and being reswallowed to continue the cycle. The hideous hitchhikers managed to extract their modest meals from their host's bowels, leaving the human's vital organs largely unscathed.

For the settlers who avoided or survived the brutality of war and the ravages of disease, the arrival of locusts brought the frontier to the brink of the Third Horseman of the Apocalypse, famine.

Hunger was pervasive in locust-afflicted lands. In addition to devastating crops, gardens, pastures, and orchards, the masses of locusts inevitably contaminated surface waters that the settlers and their livestock required. Farmers in Utah reported skimming six bushels of locusts an hour from streams after swarms had settled on the region. Although there were allusions to the water being "poisoned," the locusts were not directly toxic. However, the putrefying bodies of the insects surely turned ponds, streams, and wells into undrinkable stews.

The strangest but least serious causes of food losses during locust invasions had nothing to do with the insects' consuming farm products—indeed, quite the opposite. Poultry were an important source of protein for many homesteaders, and to the initial delight of the settlers their birds stuffed themselves on the locusts. Although the insects had no defensive chemicals in their bodies, a diet saturated with locusts rendered the eggs and flesh of chickens inedible. Studies at the time found that the locusts were remarkably rich in a "reddish-brown oil of very pungent and penetrating odor," and perhaps this accounts for the tainted meat. There were several reports of turkeys, never considered the brightest animals, gorging themselves to death amid the more-than-you-can-eat banquet of locusts. Farmers eventually discovered that feeding the birds some grain before their gluttonous splurge prevented lethal overeating.

The clearest and most strident warnings of impending famine were issued by military posts in the locust-afflicted region during the 1870s. The concerns of General Edward Otho Cresap Ord were substantiated by detailed surveys and heartrending accounts by other officers. After one of his staff, Major N.A.M. Dudley, toured portions of Nebraska in October and November of 1874, he wrote to the Secretary of War warning of impending disaster:

> The other [locust victim interviewed in one township], J. V. Ferguson, who was sick, has a wife and two children; he had only ten pounds of flour, remnant of a sack received from the aid society, and about two pounds of fresh pork, given him by a neighbor. With quivering lips and moistened eye he said he did not know where he was to obtain a further supply. Both of these families have most excellent claims; one owns a horse and the other a pair of oxen. To sell either is out of the question, as there is little or no money in the country, and then, as they stated, they would be without the means to haul fuel to their homes during the winter, and in the spring they would have no means of cultivating their crops. . . . A young man by the name of Warren, who lives on Muddy Creek [served] through the war in the Union Army. He said his wife had a babe only ten days old; that he had four other children in the house; that they had not had anything to eat for nearly two days until that morning, when he got fifteen pounds of potatoes from the aid society. I gave him a sack of flour and a little pork. I took down the statements of most of the gentlemen; all agree to the main fact that suffering existed now; that it would increase, and unless other and more extended supplies were furnished than those now counted on, people must either leave or suffer the pangs of starvation.

The officer's firsthand descriptions are compelling, but he also interviewed community leaders for their assessment of the broader situation. These testimonials told a consistent tale:

Mr. Burton is reputed to be a gentleman of unquestionable integrity. He said, "I do not like to believe anybody will starve in the valley, yet I do not know how they are to avoid it, unless they receive a greater assistance than any yet contemplated; some, no doubt, will go out of the country to avoid suffering; some have not the means to get out, and no place to go if they leave."

Being uncertain that his evocative stories of individual families and the testimonials of local authorities would be sufficiently convincing, Dudley attempted to quantify the dire conditions prevailing in the region. His systematic approach revealed that in the most desperate precincts, four out of every five families were at risk of starvation in the coming winter. In the best of circumstances, one-third of the people required assistance. Although he was a veteran of the atrocious suffering of the Civil War, Dudley was clearly moved by the plight of the settlers. He could not resist concluding his report with a plea for immediate action on the part of the government:

Great suffering exists in all five of these extreme frontier counties to a fearful extent. The settlers are, in most instances, scattered over a large extent of country; a large portion of them living far up the numerous streams flowing into the Republican. If the winter should be as severe as that of seventy and seventy-one, and as deep snows fall, beyond a doubt hundreds will starve unless a supply of provisions sufficient to last them through the winter is thrown into the valley and they are provisioned for an emergency of this character, for it would be out of the question for any aid society, or the Government even, to reach anything like a majority of them in deep snows.

Although recent homesteaders were extremely vulnerable to the depredations of locusts, hunger was not limited to the leading edge of the frontier. Far to the east, rural communities were struggling to feed themselves following the arrival of swarms. From Missouri's St. Clair County came this distraught call for help:

We have seen within the past week families which had not a meal of victuals in their house; families that had nothing to eat save what their neighbors gave them, and what game could be caught in traps, since last fall. In one case a family of six died within six days of each other from the want of food to keep body and soul together. But it is but justice to say that the neighbors and citizens were unaware of the facts of the case and were not, therefore, responsible for the terrible death which overtook these poor pilgrims on their journey to the better land. This is, we believe, the first case of the kind which has transpired in this county; but, from present indications, the future four months will make many graves, marked with a simple piece of wood with the inscription "Starved to death," painted on it.

The pioneers were accustomed to physical privation, having experienced so much thirst, cold, heat, pain, and exhaustion to reach the frontier. One of every seventeen people—and by some estimates nearly one in ten—who headed west along the Oregon Trail would die on the way, leaving an average of ten gravesites along every mile of trail. Accidental gunshots, drowning, wagon accidents, hostile Indians, hypothermia, cholera, typhus, measles, smallpox, and whooping cough took a terrible toll and hardened the pioneers to bodily suffering. Numb to physical pain and deprivation, the settlers' lasting images of the locust invasions were not so much visceral as mental. The psychological effects of a natural disaster can persist for a lifetime— or more. From the frontier farmers our culture inherited the images of devastation that were etched in their memories, rather than the pangs of hunger that settled in their bellies.

LOCUST INVASION TACTICS

The homesteaders embodied a powerful and particular combination of immense pragmatism and tremendous idealism. As Willa Cather described in O Pioneers!—her classic story of life on the frontier—"A pioneer should have imagination, should be able to enjoy the idea of things more than the things themselves." Even so, the rugged folks who weathered such trials in search of a better life were not prepared for the onslaught of locusts. Perhaps Minnesotan historian Annette Atkins most effectively captured the utter disbelief of these insects' power in her recounting of the *Gentleman from England,* a historical novel about life on the frontier written by her fellow Minnesotans Maud Hart Lovelace and Delos Lovelace:

> [Richard Chalmers] had heard persistent rumors for over a month but "could not yield to grasshopper stories even a measure of alarm." The tales seemed too exaggerated. A "vast ravenous army of insects . . . eating every growing thing and leaving desolation in its wake," he thought to himself; "Whoever had heard of such a visitation outside the pages of the Bible?" Chalmers, like many settlers, employed a hierarchy of defenses. First he ignored the stories, then denied them, and then told himself that even if the rumors were true, the pests could never reach Crockett [fictional] County. Finally, even if the grasshoppers did come, he argued, they could not destroy whole fields. He was wrong. Chalmers became only slightly alarmed when he heard that the insects had crossed into his county. For sport and to quell their slightly nagging fears, Chalmers and several neighbors rode west to see for themselves. They were "incredulously silent" when they first spotted the grasshopper cloud. Those outrageously exaggerated rumors had been neither outrageous nor exaggerated.

The sight of an arriving locust swarm was an unforgettable sensory experience. The settlers tried to force the strange vision into a familiar category. And the imagery that was most frequently reported was that of an impending storm. A letter from E. Snyder of Highland, Kansas describes the sensation of a summertime blizzard transforming into a swarm of locusts:

> At our place they commenced coming down about 1 o'clock in the afternoon, at first only one at a time, here and there, looking a little like flakes of snow, but acting more like the advance skirmishers of an advancing army; soon they commenced coming thicker and faster, and they again were followed by vast columns, or bodies looking almost like clouds in the atmosphere. They came rattling and pattering on the houses, and against the windows, falling in the fields, on the prairies and in the waters—everywhere and on everything. By about

4 o'clock in the afternoon, every tree and bush, buildings, fences, fields, roads, and everything, except animated beings, was completely covered with grasshoppers.

The perception of the locusts as being some manifestation of the weather was the mind's effort to reconcile the physical scale of a swarm with experience of the natural world. A looming thunderstorm had the commensurate capacity to grow ominously and sweep across the land. Insect populations might envelope a tree or a pasture, but only a change in the weather could fill the horizon—at least until the settlers witnessed their first locust swarm. Even the natural scientists of the nineteenth century resorted to meteorological similes to describe these phenomena: "On the horizon they often appear as a dust tornado, riding upon the wind like an ominous hail storm, eddying and whirling about like the wild dead leaves in an autumn storm, and finally sweeping up to and past you, with a power that is irresistible."

The swarms had an unnerving similarity to tornadoes in terms of their damage as well. When the locusts settled they invariably denuded the land, but where they chose to touch down seemed as capricious as the track of a twister. A complex set of factors, probably including falling light, wind speed, and temperature, along with rising atmospheric pressure, conspired to bring a swarm to the ground. These factors are beyond the ability of modern entomologists to untangle in forecasting where contemporary locust swarms will settle. So it is no wonder that for the homesteaders, the arrival of locusts defied explanation. And just as a tornado might pulverize one house and leave the next one unscathed, a locust swarm could shred one part of a county and leave the neighboring precinct untouched. This apparent randomness only added to the sense of helplessness and anxiety during outbreaks.

Perhaps even more unforgettable than the sight of a swarm was the sound of the locusts as they arrived. A whirring buzz compared to "a distant threshing machine" initially heralded their coming, but this smothering hum soon gave way to the sound of their feeding and seething in the fields. The settlers struggled for words to adequately describe this sensation, most often drawing a parallel to a grass fire. A scientist who witnessed many swarms described the sound in vivid terms: "The noise their myriad jaws make when engaged in their work of destruction, can be realized by any one who has 'fought' a prairie fire, or heard the flames passing along before a brisk wind: the low crackling and rasping—the general effect of the two sounds, are very similar."

Even the bands of nymphs could produce dramatic sounds moving across the landscape. Surely one of the most fantastic events involving immature locusts unfolded at the confluence of the Big and Little Blues, tributaries of the Missouri River. Witnesses recounted the incredible events that transpired along these 100-foot-wide waterways:

> [The rivers were] crossed at numerous places by the moving armies, which would march down to the water's edge and commence jumping in, one upon another, till they would pontoon the streams, so as to effect a crossing. Two of these mighty armies also met, one moving east and the other west, on the river bluff, in the same locality, and each turning their course north and down the bluff, and coming to a perpendicular ledge of rock 25 or 30 feet high, passed over in a sheet apparently 6 or 7 inches thick, and causing a roaring noise similar to a cataract of water.

Psychologists tell us that odors are the most deep-seated of sensory memories, capable of evoking events from our past with an intensity beyond that elicited by our other senses. If so, then the stench of rotting locusts in the waning days of an invasion must surely have become a potent trigger for nightmarish memories among the settlers. The vividness with which the odor of decaying locusts is described attests to the power of the experience. Consider the recollections of Milando Pratt, a Mormon farmer-turned-railroad-grader:

> The Great Salt Lake pickled them in its briny waters by the hundreds of thousands of tons then cast their carcasses ashore until a great wall of these inanimate pests was formed for miles along the lake's shore. [They put forth a] great stench . . . and cast the aroma of this slowly

melting putrid wall upon the windward breezes to be wafted earthward toward our suffering camp.

Such a mass of decay seems implausible, but this was by no means the first or only such account of locusts amassed along the lakeshore. A few years earlier a "notable mathematician," most likely Mormon Apostle Orson Pratt, estimated that 1.5 million bushels of locusts were deposited along the shores of the Great Salt Lake in piles six feet high and two miles long. The state entomologist from Missouri reported:

> I spent some time in this county, and the gloomy outlook toward the end of May could not well be exaggerated. The stench from the immense numbers destroyed around Kansas City, was at one time unendurable, and lest it should breed pestilence the authorities of Westport took measures to deodorize and disinfect the atmosphere on a large scale. Fifteen barrels of locusts were one evening shoveled up and hauled from the base of the courthouse at Independence, each barrel weighing 220 pounds.

The reek of decomposing locusts had long been associated, however erroneously, with the onset of disease among humans. Paulus Orosius, a historian and Christian theologian, recounted a swarm that was blown from the coast of Africa and drowned in the sea in about 380 C.E. The locusts emitted a stench greater than that "produced by the carcasses of one hundred thousand men" and purportedly induced an epidemic among the populace. The connection between the odor of decay and the onset of disease is sensible, given that piles of dead bodies can surely be the result of epidemics and corpses are not particularly healthy to have lying around. At the time that locusts were invading homesteads in America, a French doctor was making the discovery that microscopic organisms were the cause of malaria, rather than "bad air" (*mal aria* in Italian), for which the disease had been named. And so, there was a deep-seated evolutionary and experiential basis for nineteenth-century pioneers, like fourth-century observers, to link foul odor to illness.

The raw sensations that the locust swarms induced among the settlers evoked a feeling of being overwhelmed by a force beyond compare. They were awed by the voraciousness of the insects, the sheer capacity of a swarm to transform a farmstead into a wasteland before their eyes. Many of the journals and letters simply say that it would be futile to attempt to describe the rapacious power of the locusts. Some tried to capture the event by means of simile:

> The voracity of these insects can hardly be imagined by those who have not witnessed them, in solid phalanx, falling upon a cornfield and converting, in a few hours, the green and promising acres into a desolate stretch of bare, spindling stalks and stubs. Covering each hill by hundreds; scrambling from row to row like a lot of young famished pigs let out to their trough; insignificant individually, but mighty collectively—they sweep clean a field quicker than would a whole herd of hungry steers. Imagine hundreds of square miles covered with such a ravenous horde, and you can get some realization of the picture presented last year in many parts of Kansas.

Others tried to quantify the intensity of invasions. After a swarm had departed, one Minnesota farmer went into his fields to see how many eggs had been left behind. Digging into the loose soil the poor fellow was flabbergasted to find that no matter where he dug the ground was packed with egg pods. Turning over a shovelful of soil and making a careful count, he found that there were 150 eggs per square inch. Perhaps he'd been an accountant before becoming a farmer because he determined, "At this rate there will be 940,896,000 eggs to the acre, or the nice little pile of 6,586,272,000 on seven acres of my farm."

We might be tempted to discount this exercise in rural mathematics, except that twenty years earlier a similar calculation had been made during the locust invasions of Utah. Two of the settlers, Taylor Heninger and John Ivie of Sanpete County, made their estimates with painstaking precision, noting that "by actual count and careful average we found 118-28/54th eggs to the square inch of ground; making a total of 743,424,000 eggs to the acre, or a total of 2,973,696,000 to the four acre piece." Certainly not all of these eggs yielded locusts and not all of the hatchlings survived the course of development, but even if 1 in 100 reached adulthood their four-football-field-sized farm would have produced 30 million locusts—about the human population of the country at that time.

The settlers were perhaps as stunned by the indiscriminate gluttony of the locusts as by their rate of destruction. We expect grasshoppers and locusts to consume our gardens and fields, but when these insects begin to feed on fabric and flesh something seems demonically amiss. In Nebraska, a pioneer recounted that "At first some of the settlers made vain attempts to scare the pests from their fields, but this was usually rewarded by having the clothes literally eaten from off their limbs." And a Missourian reported truly sinister feeding habits: "They do not refuse even dead animals, but have been seen feasting on dead bats and birds."

From Utah came stories that the locusts devoured everything, "right down to window blinds and green paint." The insects gnawed on decayed fence posts and wooden siding, but their gourmet delight was the wooden handles of tools. Shovels, rakes, and hoes were routinely covered in a bristling blanket of locusts. The traces of salts and amino acids that had soaked into the wood from the farmer's sweat were delectable to the insects. Scraping loose the fine fibers of wood, the locusts slowly polished the handles as if they had been buffed by the finest sandpaper.

Although the settlers may have been astonished by the locusts' voracity, they were appalled by the insects' fierce cannibalism. By flailing at the locusts, the farmers unwittingly created a grisly buffet. The surviving insects greedily consumed the corpses of their brethren, with a dozen locusts descending on a carcass and jostling for position as they tore into the mangled body. Injured locusts were often eviscerated and dismembered while still alive. The locusts were driven not by a macabre lust but by a need for protein and fat—valuable sources of energy, essential nutrients for egg development, and substances that were in short supply on the prairies. Perhaps the settlers' repulsion reflected a powerful subliminal association between the locusts' gruesome propensities and the tales of human cannibalism on the frontier.

Seeing the insects gorge on their own kind may well have evoked images of their fellow pioneers stranded on mountain passes in the high Sierras or lost in desert crossings of the Great Basin and driven by hunger to the most depraved acts of desperation.

If the locusts' consumption of their own dead and dying was not sufficiently unnerving, the account of General Alfred Sully, encamped between the Missouri and Yellowstone Rivers in the summer of 1864, was absolutely chilling. A single locust or a single bird is hardly the basis for fear, but a feeding frenzy is horrifying—in history and in cinema. In an entomological version of Alfred Hitchcock's *The Birds*, which scared the bejeezus out of moviegoers a century later, Sully matter-of-factly reported, "A soldier on his way here lay down to sleep on the prairie in the middle of the day—the troop had been marching all night. His comrades noticed him covered with grasshoppers and awakened him. His throat and wrists were bleeding from the bites of the insects."

The fate of the soldier had he been left to the locusts can not be known, nor can the veracity of the story itself, as there were no similar accounts of locusts feeding on live humans. However, such accounts leave no doubt of the terrifying nature of these insects in the minds of the pioneers. The psychological trauma of the locusts—the capriciousness of their arrival, the magnitude of the swarms, and the voracity of their feeding—became embedded in the lives and language of the frontier.

The pioneers came to refer to a long, dry autumn at the end of a hot summer as "grasshopper weather," most likely because these conditions favored the buildup of locusts. And drastically reduced costs of merchandise were not associated with our familiar disaster-laden label of "fire sale" but "grasshopper prices." Not only were these insects converted into adjectives, but locusts were also metamorphosed into verbs. Mattie Oblinger, a Nebraskan whose family had been besieged by locusts, wrote to her relatives in the fall of 1876, "I suppose you would like to know if we have been grasshoppered again."

For some, gallows humor might have provided a moment's respite from the trauma of locust infestations. A standard joke emerged on the frontier.

TEACHER: Where does all our grain go?
STUDENT: Into the hopper.
TEACHER: What hopper?
STUDENT: Grasshopper!

The locusts worked their way into the lives and ultimately the literature of the pioneers. What modern Americans know of the locusts that decimated the settlers is gleaned from literary accounts of life on the frontier. One of the best recent examples is Larry McMurtry's Western saga *Lonesome Dove*, which includes a striking account of a locust swarm. The insects saturate the air with stunning swiftness:

> Newt's first fear when the cloud hit was that he would suffocate. In a second the grasshoppers covered every inch of his hands, his face, his clothes, his saddle. A hundred were stuck in Mouse's mane. Newt was afraid to draw a breath for fear he'd suck them into his mouth and nose. The air was so dense with them that he couldn't see the cattle and could barely see the ground.

But the ultimate account of a locust invasion is surely Laura Ingalls Wilder's description in her fourth book of the *Little House on the Prairie* series, *On the Banks of Plum Creek*. After a bucolic set of chapters, the reader finds Laura's father regaling the family with the fertility of the country, the abundance of their crop, and the rosiness of their future—and then the locusts arrive. The insects' arrival is presaged by a strange foreboding:

> The light was queer. It was not like the changed light before a storm. The air did not press down as it did before a storm. Laura was frightened, she did not know why.
>
> She ran outdoors, where Pa stood looking up at the sky. Ma and Mary came out, too, and Pa asked, "What do you make of that, Caroline?"
>
> A cloud was over the sun. It was not like any cloud they had ever seen before. It was a cloud of something like snowflakes, but they

were larger than snowflakes, and thin and glittering. Light shone through each flickering particle.

There was no wind. The grasses were still and the hot air did not stir, but the edge of the cloud came on across the sky faster than wind. The hair stood up on Jack's neck. All at once he made a frightful sound up at that cloud, a growl and a whine.

Within moments, the eeriness gives way to terror as the locusts begin to descend on the family's homestead:

Then huge brown grasshoppers were hitting the ground all around her, hitting her head and her face and her arms. They came thudding down like hail.

The cloud was hailing grasshoppers. The cloud *was* grasshoppers. Their bodies hid the sun and made darkness. Their thin, large wings gleamed and glittered. The rasping whirring of their wings filled the whole air and they hit the ground and the house with the noise of a hailstorm.

Laura tried to beat them off. Their claws clung to her skin and her dress. They looked at her with bulging eyes, turning their heads this way and that. Mary ran screaming into the house. Grasshoppers covered the ground, there was not one bare bit to step on. Laura had to step on grasshoppers and they smashed squirming and slimy under her feet.

The locusts are not only frightening and disgusting, they are devastating to the family's farm. But perhaps their greatest damage in the mind of young Laura is to nature's garden, the fruit trees along the creek from which the title of the book is taken:

Pa was not downstairs next morning. All night he had been working to keep the smoke over the wheat, and he did not come to breakfast. He was still working.

The whole prairie was changed. The grasses did not wave; they had fallen in ridges. The rising sun made all the prairie rough with shadows where the tall grass had sunk against each other.

The willow trees were bare. In the plum thickets only a few plumpits hung to the leafless branches. The nipping, clicking, gnawing sound of the grasshoppers' eating was still going on.

At noon Pa came driving the wagon out of the smoke. He put Sam and David into the stable, and slowly came to the house. His face was black with smoke and his eyeballs were red. He hung his hat on the nail behind and sat down at the table.

"It's no use, Caroline," he said. "Smoke won't stop them. They keep dropping down through it and hopping in from all sides. The wheat is falling now. They're cutting off like a scythe. And eating it, straw and all."

In desperation, Pa leaves his family behind to search for work. His journey echoes our culture's canonical story of a people wandering in the wilderness seeking the promised land. Laura learns from her mother's reading of Scripture that locusts played a pivotal role in the time of the Egyptian pharaohs. And so the tale of the pioneers became interwoven with Western culture's most deep and abiding literary account of locusts. Perhaps the Wilders sensed that they were part of a great human migration—an American exodus—across the continent. But what they did not know while watching their farm disappear under a blanket of locusts that summer of 1875 was that no people on earth, not even a pharaoh, had ever witnessed a swarm of such immensity.

Albert's Swarm

[Fig. 6.]

ROCKY MOUNTAIN LOCUST:— *a, a, a,* female in different positions, ovipositing; *b,* egg-pod extracted from ground, with the
end broken open; *c,* a few eggs lying loose on the ground; *d, e,*
show the earth partially removed, to illustrate an egg-mass
already in place, and one being placed; *f,* shows where such a
mass has been covered up.

ISAAC CLINE WILL FOREVER BE REMEMBERED FOR HIS
tragic hubris. He was the chief meteorologist of Texas when Galveston was hit by the deadliest weather disaster in U.S. history. He had
claimed that the city was immune to tropical cyclones, but the hurricane that struck on September 8, 1900, took the lives of more than
10,000 people. At that time, hurricanes were not being named, but
this lethal tempest was called Isaac's Storm by Erik Larson in his grip-
ping book by that title. What few people will ever recall about Isaac
Cline is how he began his career in the U. S. Army Signal Corps (the
predecessor of today's National Weather Service). Cline's first assignment did not involve monitoring hurricanes, tornadoes, or any other
atmospheric events. Rather, he began by tracking the Rocky Mountain locust.

The Army Signal Corps was a logical birthplace for a weather service, as the corps had the capacity to collect and rapidly transmit in-

formation regarding storms and their movements. For the first time, people could be warned of impending disaster and perhaps avoid the worst of the maelstrom. When General William B. Hazen wrote to colleges across the country to recruit graduates into the nascent weather service, Cline's name was submitted by the president of Hiwassee College. After completing a demanding training program and passing a rigorous exam (only the sixteen passing with the highest scores were assigned to the field, and Cline scored sixteenth in his class), he was asked his preference for a duty station. Cline requested to be given an opportunity for research that would benefit humanity. Investigating the link between weather and the Rocky Mountain locust's outbreaks and movements was deemed to be one of the most urgent missions of meteorology. As such, Cline was assigned to Little Rock, Arkansas, with orders to determine the relationship between weather patterns and locust swarms.

Unfortunately, Arkansas was at the eastern margin of the insect's distribution, so Cline made little progress in this line of study. Instead, he found medicine most pertinent to his humanitarian interests. Cline earned his medical degree and was drawn into the nascent field of medical climatology, the study of how weather affects human health. He then became the officer-in-charge at the weather station in Abilene, Texas, and was then given the responsibility of organizing the Texas Section of the U.S. Weather Service and establishing the Galveston weather station. And so it was that his life collided with the deadliest storm in U.S. history—a story eerily reminiscent of another Signal Corps observer who was fated to witness a locust swarm of even greater force.

Like Isaac Cline, Albert Lyman Child was born in the East, earned a degree in medicine, and served in the Army Signal Corps. But unlike Isaac Cline, Albert Child was remembered by no one. Perhaps this is because there was nothing that Dr. Child could have done to avert the natural disaster that he meticulously recorded in his duties as a meteorological observer. Dr. Child made no claims that his community of Plattsmouth, Nebraska, was immune to the ravages of locusts. There was no tone of arrogance in his report, only a sense of near disbelief in what he had witnessed.

Albert Child was a renaissance man on the frontier. After practicing medicine and serving as a school superintendent in Ohio, he moved to Cedar Creek in Cass County, Nebraska, to try his hand at farming. If Cline had been a meteorologist who wanted to be a doctor, then it seems that Child was a doctor who wanted to be a meteorologist. As soon as he arrived in Nebraska in 1857, Dr. Child began keeping weather records. In 1861, he began providing reports to the Smithsonian Institution, and his work was transferred to the U.S. Signal Corps when it took over as the country's weather service in 1873. By then, he'd been elected county judge and moved to Plattsmouth, but his passion for meteorology was unabated. This is how Albert Child came to be the right man, in the right place, at the right time to provide a definitive report of the most immense swarm of locusts in recorded history. He began his account with the objective tone of a trained and experienced observer:

> The extent of the swarm is difficult to ascertain, as the observer can only see a small belt. They may extend indefinitely right or left. During the flight from June 15 to 25 of 1875, I telegraphed east and west. I found a continuous line moving northward of 110 miles, and then somewhat broken 40 miles farther. The movements of the winds for five days (15th to 20th) averaged about 10 miles per hour; and the locust evidently moved considerably faster than the wind, at least 15 miles per hour.

To determine the height of the swarm, Dr. Child used a rather clever approach. He focused his telescope on various objects of similar size to a locust placed at known distances across the rolling hills. Then, he aimed the instrument into the sky, and if the locusts were in focus he'd conclude that the swarm must be at least as high as the horizontal focal distance that he'd just determined. The method only yielded coarse approximations, so Dr. Child was cautious in his estimates. But in his accounts of these observations, his awe at the scale of the phenomenon began to sneak into the technical report:

The swarm I estimated from one-quarter to one-half mile deep. It seemed like piercing the milky-way of the heavens; my glass found no limits to them. They might have been a mile or more in depth.

Like any good scientist, Dr. Child took his data and transformed the raw numbers into a complete picture of what he had witnessed. The mathematics were simple, but the results were nearly beyond imagination. When Dr. Child presented his straightforward calculations of the aggregate size of the locust swarm that was passing over Nebraska, he was incredulous of his own findings:

They were visible from six to seven hours of each of the successive five days, and I can see no reason to suppose that their flight was checked during the whole five days. If so, the army in the line of advance would be 120 hours by 15 miles per hour = 1,800 miles in length, and say at even 110 miles in width, an area of 198,000 square miles! and then from one-quarter to one-half mile deep. This is utterly incredible, yet how can we put it aside?

An area of 198,000 square miles would encompass the combined areas of Connecticut, Delaware, Maine, Maryland, Massachusetts, New Hampshire, New Jersey, New York, Pennsylvania, Rhode Island, and Vermont. The swarm was probably an elongated stream of insects, but if it had been configured in a more familiar geometric shape, it would have comprised a square 450 miles on a side. The frontier of the New World was revealing marvels and terrors of a scale unparalleled in written history. The largest swarm of locusts outside of North America was reported in 1954, when fewer than a hundred square miles were covered by the notorious Desert locust in Kenya. No insect outbreak has ever approached the magnitude of the Rocky Mountain locust.

Trying to estimate the number of locusts in Albert's Swarm is quite a challenge, but we can use some values from the scientific literature to approximate the size of the population. We might safely assume a settled density similar to that of the famed locust swarms in Africa (which involve a larger locust and likely have fewer individuals packed into each square yard). If so, then the 1875 swarm that passed over North America had 3.5 trillion locusts, outnumbering the current human population on earth by a factor of 600 to 1. The swarm outweighed a man to the same degree that the biomass of a whale exceeds that of a mouse. Such quantities are unfathomable, but newspaper reports of damage from neighboring townships clearly substantiate Dr. Child's account.

Although Isaac Cline never managed to associate weather patterns with locust outbreaks, we can now deduce the biological and meteorological conditions that conspired to create Albert's Swarm. Scientists of the nineteenth century had begun to piece together the life cycle of the Rocky Mountain locust, and it appears that Albert's swarm was qualitatively typical of the species. In an outbreak cycle, the locust swarms descended from the northern Rockies in early June. Carried by prevailing winds, these insects swept across the countryside, settling wherever there was abundant food. As the locusts advanced to the south and east, they began to mate, and soon after, females began laying eggs. Cylindrical clusters or "pods" of about thirty eggs were buried in the soil, and so the swarms left behind denuded fields riddled with eggs. The adult locusts would live for perhaps a couple of months, seeding the countryside with the next generation. The embryos would mature through the summer and then hibernate—a physiological state called *diapause* in insects—for the winter. The following spring, the ground would appear to boil as the nymphs hatched on warm days. Forming into immense aggregations or "bands" these immature locusts would march across the land, stripping the vegetation to fuel their development. The nymphs would molt five times, shedding their old outer cuticle and growing in size. On the final molt, the stubby wing buds were replaced with fully developed wings, the reproductive system was functional, and the adult locust was ready to swarm.

This next generation would typically continue the plague, riding the winds further into the heartland of the continent. After a buildup over the course of three or four years—and an equal number of generations—the outbreak would enter its final stage. Stretched to its southern and eastern limits, a portion of the population would stream back to the Northwest in an apparent effort to return to its mountainous homeland. Scientists were unsure of whether this return migration was necessary to restock the founding population or whether a portion of the original population was always left behind in the Rockies to ensure the "seed bank" necessary to produce the next outbreak. In either case, they knew that the locust managed to sustain itself somewhere in the mountains, biding its time between irruptions.

The periodic outpouring of insect life from the West was intimately linked to weather, as Cline and the Weather Service suspected. The locusts flourished during droughts, which we can now infer to have provided several critical catalysts for population growth. The hot, dry weather weakened plant defenses and actually increased the nutritional value of the vegetation as sugars and other nutrients concentrated in the leaves. The dry conditions also suppressed fungal diseases, which could reach epidemic proportions and devastate locust populations in wet years. Furthermore, the heat accelerated the locusts' maturation—and development was a race against predators that inflicted a constant mortality on the dense bands of nymphs. So, the faster the young locusts made it to adulthood, the greater the proportion of the population that would survive to reproduce. Finally, in times of drought lush vegetation was restricted to swales (and well-tended agricultural fields), so the locusts were forced to aggregate in these habitats, a behavior that initially generated and then sustained the coherence of both nymphal bands and adult swarms.

In the years immediately preceding Albert's Swarm, a terrific drought had settled over the central United States. In 1873, just seven and a half inches of rain fell on Wallace, Kansas—the driest year on record. Dodge City experienced its third driest year in history in 1875. Missouri farmers reported that in 1874 "it stopped raining in April and didn't rain again till late October." The twelve months from May 1874 to April 1875 comprised the eighth driest period in 150 years of Ohio weather records. The heat and dryness were devastating for farmers and ideal for locusts.

Although drought conditions fostered population growth in the locusts, a second climatic factor was necessary to create a locust swarm of such incredible magnitude. There had to be a constant, southerly wind to unite the insects over an immense area and maintain the coherence of the swarm for days on end during its northward migration. The monsoon weather that arises from the Gulf of Mexico might be suspected in this regard, but this meteorological event generally lacks essential elements of a June weather pattern. Not only does the monsoon typically develop later in the summer, but it also fails to sustain winds across a geographic scale necessary to propel a locust swarm from Texas to Minnesota. However, in the 1950s meteorologists discovered another annual event with the potential to have carried history's greatest swarm: the Great Plains low-level jet.

This wind stream forms in late spring or early summer and extends into autumn. The 200-mile-wide flow of air is centered on Oklahoma and Kansas but stretches from the Gulf Coast to the Canadian border. This conveyor belt of air averages perhaps 10 miles per hour in the day and rises to 30 during the night—parameters that are consistent with those reported by Albert Child. The winds peak at about a thousand feet above the ground, again fitting with the scale of Child's swarm. If no frontal systems move through the region, the Great Plains low-level jet blows for days on end. Furthermore, this wind system is strengthened by heat, as during a drought. Migrating birds are known to exploit this airstream in their northward journeys, and it seems nearly certain that the locusts did so as well.

So we can infer that the drought of 1874–1875 both fostered the buildup of locust populations and strengthened the jet that scientists call "one of the most prominent meteorological phenomena of the central United States." Crowded into jittery populations spread across tens of thousands of square miles, the locusts almost certainly arose in separate swarms that were then coalesced by a wind stream that swept them into the perfect swarm.

By the 1870s, the nation was coming to realize that the Rocky Mountain locust was a tempestuous hurricane of insect life—that when these storm clouds shimmered on the horizon, a hail of hungry insects was coming. Although Albert's Swarm was the greatest cyclone of locusts to sweep across the continent, Americans and Canadians had been painfully aware of this creature's devastating capacity for some time.

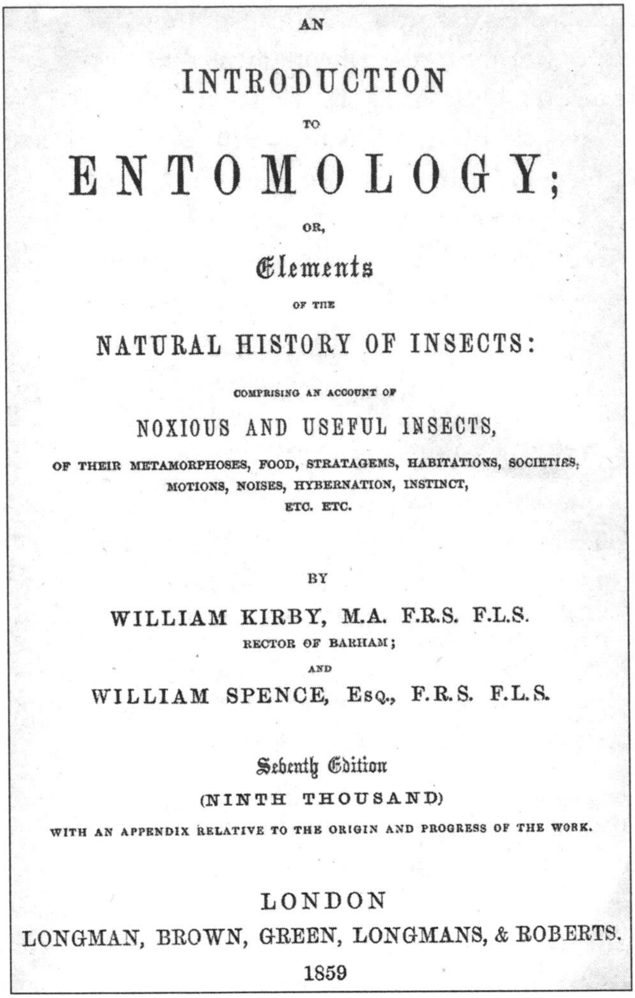

AN

INTRODUCTION

TO

ENTOMOLOGY;

OR,

Elements

OF THE

NATURAL HISTORY OF INSECTS:

COMPRISING AN ACCOUNT OF

NOXIOUS AND USEFUL INSECTS,

OF THEIR METAMORPHOSES, FOOD, STRATAGEMS, HABITATIONS, SOCIETIES,
MOTIONS, NOISES, HYBERNATION, INSTINCT,
ETC. ETC.

BY

WILLIAM KIRBY, M.A. F.R.S. F.L.S.
RECTOR OF BARHAM;

AND

WILLIAM SPENCE, Esq., F.R.S. F.L.S.

Seventh Edition
(NINTH THOUSAND)
WITH AN APPENDIX RELATIVE TO THE ORIGIN AND PROGRESS OF THE WORK.

LONDON

LONGMAN, BROWN, GREEN, LONGMANS, & ROBERTS.
1859

Figure 2.1 *An Introduction to Entomology* by
William Kirby and William Spence, 1859

WHAT'S IN A NAME?

The first popular book of entomology to be published in English was
an imposing series of five volumes beginning in 1815. By the time of
the seventh edition in 1859, this comprehensive text had been mercifully reduced to a single volume that retained the luxuriant language
and engaging prose of the earlier formulations. And the title was no
less opulent (Figure 2.1).

In this definitive coverage of insect biology, William Kirby (sometimes called the Father of Entomology) and William Spence (a renowned beetle collector in his own right, but second fiddle to Kirby) had not yet learned of the locust outbreaks in the New World. However, they devoted a considerable portion of their book to these insects' depredations in the Old World. They took pains to convince the reader that although a single locust was hardly intimidating, in the collective these creatures had rightfully earned their rapacious reputation:

> To look at a *locust* in a cabinet of insects, you would not, at first sight, deem it capable of being the source of so much evil to mankind as stands on record against it. "This is but a small creature," you would say, "and the mischief which it causes cannot be far beyond the proportion of its bulk. The locusts so celebrated in history must surely be of the Indian kind mentioned by Pliny, which were three feet in length, with legs so strong that the women used them as saws. I see, indeed, some resemblance to the horse's head, but where are the eyes of the elephant, the neck of the bull, the horns of the stag, the chest of the lion, the belly of the scorpion, the wings of the eagle, the thighs of the camel, the legs of the ostrich, and the tail of the serpent, all of which the Arabians mention as attributes of this widely-dreaded insect destroyer; but of which in the insect before me I discern little or no likeness?" Yet, although this animal be not very tremendous for its size, not very terrific in its appearance, it is the very same whose ravages have been the theme of naturalists and historians in all ages, and upon a close examination you will find it to be particularly fitted and furnished for the execution of its office.

These early British scientists were not duped by the extraordinary accounts of the ancient Romans, but they were convinced that the emanations of dead locusts could induce epidemics. They faithfully reported Saint Augustine's assertion that rotting locusts had caused plagues that killed 800,000 people in the kingdom of Masanissa 2,000 years earlier and nearly a million in Italy in 591 C.E. Although heaps of decaying locusts are not a source of human disease, Kirby

and Spence's accounts of famine are rather more convincing. They recounted the swarms that led to the deaths of 30,000 Venetians in
1478. To drive home the seriousness of locust plagues in their own
time, they described how Yusuf Karamanli, the bashaw of Tripoli,
raised a force of 4,000 soldiers to fight locusts (at about the same time
that he was battling the U.S. Navy, which President Jefferson had sent
in retaliation against the piracy that was humiliating his new nation
and undermining its commerce). If the reader doubted Kirby and
Spence's implication that the gravity of a locust outbreak could justify
mobilizing an army, so did some of the bashaw's soldiers. But the authors explained that Karamanli was deadly serious about the situation
"and very summarily ordered all to be hanged who, thinking it beneath them to waste their valour upon such pigmy foes, refused to
join the party."

Locust outbreaks have occurred on every inhabited continent. Euro-
peans periodically suffered the invasions of several locust species into
the last century, some of which were homegrown and others of which
immigrated from Africa and Asia. However, modern pest management methods and conversion of natural habitats have largely amelio-
rated locust outbreaks in Europe. Africa, Asia, and Australia are still
commonly plagued by various species of these insects, with outbreaks
in Central Asia encompassing more than 6,000 square miles in 1999.
Although the Australians have the most sophisticated locust management program in the world, the vast, uninhabited landscape makes
finding and suppressing these outbreaks an immense challenge. South
America is less frequently beset by locusts, but the grasslands of Ar-
gentina, Brazil, and Peru are prone to occasional infestations.
Whereas parts of Mexico are sometimes overrun with a tropical locust related to those on other continents, the rest of North America
hosted just a single, unique species of these insects, the Rocky Mountain locust.

The term *locust* is derived from the Latin, *locus ustus,* meaning
"burnt place"—an allusion to the denuded landscape left in the wake
of a ravenous swarm. If we think of life being sustained by oxidative
metabolism, the slow burn of biochemistry, then perhaps associating

locusts with conflagrations is remarkably appropriate. In a very real sense, a swarm of locusts is a metabolic wildfire burning tons of vegetation every day to fuel its migration. The family to which all locusts belong, the Acrididae, may also derive its name from this sense of acrid corrosion that was associated with the damage caused by these insects.

Locusts were then—and still are—mysterious creatures, whose sudden irruptions are their defining attribute. In biological terms, a locust is a type of highly mobile grasshopper with the capacity to attain enormous population densities and a proclivity for aggregating and traveling in bands (as immature nymphs) and swarms (as winged adults). Aside from belonging to the family Acrididae, which has 10,000 species worldwide, the 10 species of locusts are not taxonomically related. The locust's survival strategy has evolved within several subfamilies around the world, although only North America was blessed with just a single species of locust—along with several hundred species of grasshoppers.

Not only are locusts haphazardly scattered throughout the evolutionary lineages within the Acrididae, they are also frustratingly difficult to define in discrete, ecological terms. In a sense, locusts are to grasshoppers as athletes are to humans. Nobody would doubt that a professional basketball player is an athlete, but what about a professional golfer or bowler? What about the dedicated amateur training for the Olympic curling team? And what about the weekend warrior on the softball field? Rather like being an athlete, being a locust is a matter of degree. Some creatures exhibit weak tendencies toward aggregating as nymphs or adults and others manifest the full-blown locust syndrome—the Rocky Mountain locust and the Desert locust of the Old Testament being classic cases at the extreme end of the locust spectrum. At the other end are the various garden-variety grasshoppers that placidly masticate our lettuce patches and bask in abandoned lots (the short antennae of these creatures distinguish them from related families of insects commonly found in pastures and fields—the katydids and crickets).

Locusts may not be readily classified, but entomologists are strident in their contention that this term should not be—as it often is—applied to cicadas. Cicadas are the stumpy, clear-winged insects that resemble gargantuan aphids and belong to the same order as their tiny cousins. Thus cicadas are in an entirely different insect order from the grasshoppers or locusts (Homoptera versus Orthoptera). This might seem a hairsplitting exercise, but consider that in mammals, elephants and shrews are also in different orders. The misnaming of cicadas as locusts originated in the late 1600s and has continued to the present day in some areas of the United States. The confusion is understandable from an ecological, if not a taxonomic, perspective. After all, the periodical cicadas emerge from the ground in staggering numbers and fill the forests with their incessant buzzing. If being a locust were simply a matter of being an insect herbivore that could suddenly attain incredible populations, then perhaps cicadas would qualify. But as opposed to true locusts, cicadas lay their eggs on plants (rather than in the soil), live underground as root-feeding nymphs for up to seventeen years (rather than living above ground and eating leaves and stems while maturing in a few weeks), feed sparingly as adults by piercing a plant with their elongated stylets (rather than feeding voraciously by biting and chewing their food), and remain in the vicinity where they emerged (rather than migrating in swarms).

The officially sanctioned, scientific name of the Rocky Mountain locust is *Melanoplus spretus*. This approved name was chosen by Benjamin Walsh in 1866, although entomologists had been variously referring to this creature for some time. The locust had been unofficially named a few years earlier by Philip Uhler, a Harvard-educated entomologist who was deemed America's greatest hemipterist (Hemiptera being the order of insects comprising the true bugs—a group that might not leap to one's mind as being associated with scientific greatness, but entomologists are a proud, if quirky, lot). He called the insect *Acridium spretus* (the genus *Acridium* was later changed to *Caloptenus* and finally to *Melanoplus*, which is the currently accepted name). In the twisted course of taxonomic history, this name was subsequently and rather surprisingly misprinted by another entomologist as *A. spretis* and later as *A. spretum*. Biologists take the scientific names of organisms very seriously, so the lackadaisical approach to the spelling of this species is unusual. Although Walsh used Uhler's original spelling, the credit for naming the species goes to Walsh. As opposed to his predecessor, Walsh's publication included a full description of the creature along with the name: A detailed characterization of an organism's appearance is considered one of the essential components in creating a valid scientific name for a new species.

All scientific names must take a Latinized form, which facilitates international communication, keeps an otherwise dead language alive, and makes for interesting translations. In the case of the Rocky Mountain locust, the genus *Melanoplus* came from the Latin meaning "black armor." Although the adult locust was more of an olive green, other species in the genus are decidedly darker, and all of these creatures are encased in a sturdy exoskeleton, so the name is quite appropriate. As for *spretus,* it derives from *spretum:* "to scorn, despise, or spurn." And so, the Rocky Mountain locust was the despicable black knight of the continent—an abhorrent creature clad in dark armor that besieged the pioneers: a sort of eighteenth-century insect Darth Vader.

There was some debate as to the most appropriate common name for *M. spretus.* Early American entomologists, having a bone to pick with various grasshoppers in the United States, had already coopted the names "Detestable locust" and "Devastating locust" for other species (which were actually grasshoppers, but adding *locust* made them sound more formidable). Otto Lugger, the first entomologist of the Minnesota Agricultural Experiment Station, advocated the "Hateful grasshopper" (or locust) for *M. spretus.* However, the less evocative but more biogeographically informative name of "Rocky Mountain locust" came into widespread use and general acceptance. This name associated the creature with the apparent origin of its outbreaks—the imposing range of peaks that protruded from the fertile prairies like the exposed skeletal backbone of the continent. What better place than these brooding, mysterious mountains from which to launch the hated armored legions that descended upon the vulnerable frontier farms and homesteads?

For millennia, humans had perceived locusts as invading armies from far-off lands. The arrival of swarms appeared otherworldly, and their scope of destruction seemed godlike. Such a sense of unearthly foreboding and divine malevolence resonates throughout the Exodus account of the sixth plague of Egypt:

> Then the Lord said to Moses, "Stretch out your hand over the land of Egypt for the locusts, that they may come upon the land of Egypt, and eat every plant in the land, all that the hail has left." So Moses stretched forth his rod over the land of Egypt, and the Lord brought an east wind upon the land all that day and that night; and when it was morning the east wind had brought the locusts. And the locusts came up over all the land of Egypt, such a dense swarm of locusts as had never been before, nor ever shall be again. For they covered the face of the whole land, so that the land was darkened, and they ate all the plants in the land and all the fruit of the trees which the hail had left; not a green thing remained, neither tree nor plant of the field, through all the land of Egypt.

So deeply rooted were these insects in the consciousness of Western culture, that the European settlers of America were destined to interpret the Rocky Mountain locust in profoundly religious terms. But making theological sense of such horrendous power was no simple matter—understanding the locust would be as difficult for ministers as it had been for scientists.

The Sixth Plague

IN THE EYES OF A YOUNG AMERICA, THE FARMER WAS the angel of growth. Thomas Jefferson had idealized the virtues of taming the profligate land and planting gardens in the wilderness. But how could the goodness of agriculture be reconciled with the destruction caused by the locusts? At a deep cultural level, the resolution of this conflict was found in religion. When faced with overwhelming loss, especially when wrought by nature, people often draw upon their faith for comfort and answers. And so, for the nineteenth-century Christian pilgrims battling the forces of nature in the American wilderness, the Bible was a powerful source of insight. However, its message concerning locusts and the suffering that followed the swarms was frustratingly ambiguous.

In ancient times, interpreting the cause of a natural disaster was a vitally important task for theologians. In early cultures, locust swarms were most often understood to be a form of divine punishment, and so the most appropriate response was to submit in penitence, pray for forgiveness, and make offerings. According to Pliny, this approach worked in the first century, when appeals to Jupiter produced flocks of rose-colored starlings that destroyed the locusts in Asia Minor. The early Muslims also saw locusts as the apocalyptic agents of God. Even the good Christian entomologists, Kirby and Spence, were well aware of the Islamic perspective: "So well do the Arabians know their power, that they make a locust say to Mahomet, 'We are the army of the great God; we produced ninety-nine eggs; if the hundred were completed, we should consume the whole earth and all that is in it.'" And in 1864, when American farmers were besieged by locusts, pious Muslims in Syria exorcised and ostracized locusts by reading the Koran aloud in ravaged fields on the other side of the world.

The Christian response to locust invasions was most thoroughly documented in Edward P. Evans's bizarre and authoritative treatise, *The Criminal Prosecution and Capital Punishment of Animals*. Amid incredible accounts of legal proceedings against unruly pets and homicidal livestock can be found the strangest of all human-animal legal conflicts that played out in the ecclesiastical courts of Europe—locusts on trial. The earliest involvement of the Church as an extermination agency appears to be in 880, when Roman authorities sought help from Pope Stephan VI. The Holy Father provided a huge volume of holy water, which was apparently used in the course of exorcising the swarm. But exorcism became viewed as a drastic intervention, so a more subtle strategy emerged.

During the reign of Charles the Bold, Duke of Burgundy, the Church took a different tack in dealing with troublesome locusts: excommunication. This approach was applied to a swarm that settled in the northern Italian province of Mantua. In this case, as in many previous instances, the locusts dutifully dispersed not long after the Church's proclamation. Of course, locust swarms tend to move about even when they are not the subjects of religious persecution, but this entomological pattern did nothing to diminish people's faith in the ef-

ficacy of religious interventions. The use of excommunication, however, raised a thorny theological issue. To be excommunicated one
needs to be a communicant in the first place. That is, if an insect is not
part of the Church and able to partake in communion, then it is,
strictly speaking, nonsensical to excommunicate the creature, no matter how destructive it might be. The only legitimate recourse was to
anathematize, or curse, the beasts. But this raised an even more troublesome religious problem.

A locust swarm could mean one of two things. The insects might
be the work of godless nature or even the devil. If plowing and planting were noble labor, even a higher calling, then the locusts could be
seen as the diabolical work of Satan. In this case, calling upon the
Church to deliver a searing curse might be just the thing to drive
them away. On the other hand, the creatures could be emissaries of
God sent to punish the people for their sins. If the farmers had wandered from the straight and narrow, then the locusts could be viewed
as the servants of an angry God. In this case, the proper response
would be humility and repentance to placate the angry deity, who
might then send the swarm on its way. The last thing a cleric wanted
to do was to pronounce an anathema on the Lord's messengers. So,
how could the Church know whether a locust swarm originated demonically or divinely?

On St. Bartholomew's Day in 1338, locusts began to decimate the
farming region around Botzen in the Tyrol of modern-day Austria. To
determine the proper course of events—repentance or curse—the
church convened a trial of the insects before the ecclesiastical court at
Kaltern. The trial followed what had become a standard sequence of
events. First came a petition from those seeking redress. If the petition
was accepted, the proceedings next involved a declaration or plea on
behalf of the inhabitants. This was a flowery speech concerning the
horrors of hunger with loads of classic citations, historical allusions,
irrelevant digressions, and literary discourses. The meandering series
of accusations was followed by the defense's allegation or plea for the
insects. As the locusts could not speak for themselves, they were given
legal counsel, who was no less officious in his rejoinder.

These phases were followed by the presentation of substantive arguments for and against the locusts. The defense invoked the entomological equivalent of the modern insanity plea to contend that the locusts lacked reason and volition and were thus immune from condemnation. After all, the insects were simply exercising their innate and God-given rights to swarm and feed. The prosecution rebutted this claim by acknowledging that the law cannot punish the irrational or insane for crimes already committed but pointed out that it can intervene to prevent further harm. So, the anathema should not be seen as punishing the locusts but as a means of driving them away before they did more damage. Then, the prosecutor played theological hardball, noting that Jesus cursed the fig tree, an entirely irrational organism—and was it the defense counsel's intention to question the Son of God's judgment?

As things started looking bad for the locusts, their counsel resorted to the ecclesiastical version of the "race card" in the O. J. Simpson trial. He proposed that his clients were actually agents sent by the Almighty to punish the farmers for their sinful ways—and to curse these messengers would be to fight against God himself. But the prosecution was unshakable. With righteous indignation he asserted that the pious and near-saintly villagers were God's people and the insects were surely diabolical. Indeed, for the besieged people to appeal to the Church for assistance was an act of authentic religiosity and abiding faith, not resistance to God.

The resolution of the trial was up to the bishop's proctor, with a sentence pronounced solemnly in Latin by the ecclesiastical judge. In the Kaltern court, the proctor began by expressing his serious reservations that a misfired curse would become a boomerang, "being a weapon of such peculiar energy and activity that, if it fails to strike the object against which it is hurled, it returns to smite him, who hurled it." Then, perhaps to provide himself with an alibi if the Almighty cross-examined him on Judgment Day, he claimed to be muddled by the complexity of the case, saying, "We cannot tell why God has sent these animals to devour the fruits of the earth; this is for us a sealed book." The official next pontificated on what sins might have induced such a plague, which seemed to suggest that the judgment would be in favor of the insects. However, in the end he set aside these arguments and ordered the swarm to vacate the countryside within six days or else suffer anathematization. The proctor's declaration included one final recommendation aimed at the petitioners.

The court strongly suggested that the farmers avail themselves of prayers and penances. The former were left to the congregants' discretion, but the latter were clearly specified. As was customary, the plaintiffs were instructed to manifest their penance in the form of tithes to the Church. It was widely known—although it bore repeating by the proctor—that abstinence from sin and payment of tithes, particularly the latter, enhanced the efficacy of anathema. In fact, the province had the option of shortcutting the legal system entirely and purchasing an anathema directly from the pope. But an end run of the ecclesiastical courts via the Vatican was not cheap. Although Kaltern was an affluent market town, famous for its wines, and lying just ten miles south of the locust infestation, the Botzen villagers were rather less wealthy, and so they settled on simply putting the locusts on trial. The procedural delay was problematical, what with the locusts busily chomping on their crops while the court's officers pontificated. But the outcome of the trial was not in jeopardy, as there don't appear to have been any cases that went the locusts' way. And between the legal delays and the judge's verdict—their relative contributions being left to the reader's interpretation of biology and theology—the locusts left the region not long after the trial concluded.

GOD'S SERVANTS OR GREEN IMPS OF SATAN?

The possibility that the Rocky Mountain locusts were God-sent was implicit in the most common biblical allusions used by the settlers in their letters and journals. These God-fearing people often made reference to the plagues of Egypt, although it was not always clear whether this was a theological analogy or literary device, as seen in this vivid recollection of a Nebraska homesteader:

> The summer of '74 was blessed with an abundance of rain and warm weather. Corn grew rank and was surprisingly forward for the sea-

son of the year. The small grain too gave promise of exceptional yield. Farmers in the Valley were beginning to make preparations for harvesting and housing the crop which should at once place them in easy circumstances, when a calamity as complete as it was unexpected with one fell stroke destroyed all their calculations and for a time left them stunned and almost broken in spirit. It came in the shape of one of the plagues of ancient Egypt. . . . They move not so much in sheets as in great columns from one to five thousand feet thick, resembling great fleecy clouds propelled onward by some strong but hidden agency.

A Minnesota homesteader, on seeing the whirling, glittering cloud of insects descending on her family's farm, sank to her knees and wailed, "The locusts! God help us!" We have to wonder whether she was appealing to the Almighty for deliverance from his wrath or from evil. And remember Richard Chalmers, the character in *Gentleman from England,* who was unable to fathom the tales he'd been hearing of the locusts? Well, seeing is believing, and Annette Atkins recounts, "Watching the creatures at work, Chalmers remembered a Bible passage: 'The land is as the garden of Eden before them, and behind them a desolate wilderness.' At last he believed." But, we might ask, what exactly did Chalmers come to believe?

According to a historical review of locust outbreaks in Missouri by George Jones, the settlers looked upon swarms as punishment for some moral shortcoming or evildoing. The biblical allusions by the settlers were not merely literary ploys; they were direct parallels to the Old Testament—and God was angry. This interpretation of the locust plagues was evinced in sermons to the people and in discussions among the clergy. A letter from Reverend August Kenter to Reverend J. H. Sieker in 1874 begins with some compassionate ambiguity as to God's intention in having sent a swarm of locusts into his Minnesota community:

Dear Brother,
    On the 12th of June I arrived, thanks to God, in good health and spirits and renewed vigor, at my dear home and found wife and chil-

dren well. But what a destruction! had the army of God completed meanwhile. Nothing remained of my forty acre wheat field. . . . At the commencement, it seemed as if God in his infinite grace would make an exception with some; but visiting my congregations a few days afterwards, to look after families, of whom I expected that they were suffering; I found enough of them, who had no bread and I divided what I had on hand amongst 12 families to whom it came like a Godsend.

The reverend portrayed himself as a compassionate shepherd, providing for his congregants. And although he leaves little doubt as to the locusts having been sent by the Almighty, we might suppose that this disaster was simply a trial of the people's faith. Maybe God was testing his flock, as he had done with Job. But the rest of Reverend Kenter's angst-filled letter, although failing to explain what sins warranted such cosmic retribution, leaves no doubt that this disaster was a divine punishment:

But the dear Lord did not want to make any exceptions . . . we at once saw our hopes destroyed, for the Lord ordered them to swallow up also the few fields in our neighborhood, which had been spared up to this time. . . . So has the Lord overlooked not one in his punishment. . . . All the 60 families in my two congregations, of whom the greater part are here, 1–2 & 3 years, without means, yea many of them who came here poor with many little children have not had one harvest yet, but have made their living by working for others.

If the locust invasions were deserved by those who suffered from the consequent hunger and poverty, then the social reaction to the besieged farmers was at least largely consistent. The victims were widely viewed as impoverished mendicants, whose situation—even if not a result of having angered God—was evidence of a sinful lack of character.

The less widely held theological interpretation of the locust invasions was that the swarms were of demonic origin. Perhaps the most impassioned case for this view came from a Minnesota pioneer who lamented, "The Lord only knows which harmed the poor settlers more, the prowling Red-skins who were wont to sally forth from the hills and uplands or the green imps of satan the grasshoppers, which pounced upon us in bewildering hordes—both literally took the bread out of our mouths." In this view, the godless natives along with the locusts (and presumably the wolves and other creatures that menaced the settlers) were all part of a diabolical plot. The wilderness was often perceived as a dark and foreboding place, so it was sensible to assert that the swarms were an outpouring of evil from this depraved land. The homesteader was something of an agrarian missionary, converting the heathen wilderness into an orderly garden. If the homesteaders lost their land to the locusts, then they were simply unfortunate victims of satanic forces.

This religious view was consistent with the social interpretation of the locust-besieged settlers as deserving of assistance. These bedraggled farmers were victims of evildoers, as opposed to the unworthy poor who parasitized the hardworking sectors of American society. After all, the poor, hungry settlers were the salt of the earth, yeoman farmers building the nation from the ground up. The locusts had destroyed their crops but not their virtue. Such an appeal was made on behalf of the Kansas homesteaders:

> With emphasis we assert, that our suffering people are not wanting in enterprise nor courage, nor in any of the elements of true manhood. The uncomplaining patience with which even women and children are enduring the misfortunes that have fallen upon them, is nothing short of heroic. Our people have not lost faith in themselves, nor in the resources and prospects of the State in which they live, nor in Him without whom not a sparrow falls to the ground.

But during the peak of the locust outbreaks in the 1870s, the nation was in the grip of an economic depression. There was plenty of suffering concentrated in the cities, so there was not much sympathy to spare for the scattered farmers. Factories were fast replacing farms as the financial heart and cultural soul of the growing nation. Moreover, the homesteaders had already been offered free land:

How much more public largess could they expect? The hardships of the frontier—including blizzards, droughts, loneliness, Indians, and locusts—were viewed as "part of the deal." But if providing physical assistance was a matter of intense debate and social reluctance, spiritual aid was rather less costly and somewhat more graciously given.

CHURCH AND STATE

Whether deserved or gratuitous, divine or demonic, the locust outbreaks required some response from religious leaders. The churches played a very limited role in providing physical aid, although it should be said that their capacity in this regard was rather nominal. Moreover, a tough-love minister might rationalize that withholding material handouts would foster moral growth, self-reliance, and responsibility—but refusing to offer prayers was beyond even the most harshly judgmental preachers. So religious leaders attempted to intercede with God on behalf of the suffering farmers.

For the most part, the clergy walked the careful line that had been drawn six centuries earlier based on the contention of Thomas Aquinas that animals, including locusts, were not culpable for their misdeeds. From here, Christian orthodoxy had eventually come to the standard position that the proper response to a troublesome swarm was to call upon the populace to repent and humbly entreat an angry God to remove the scourge. Although there are few records of what was said in church services about the Rocky Mountain locust, the prayers offered by state officials likely reflect the cautiously compassionate tone of the religious leaders.

Under pressure from the churches, Missouri's governor was the first to seize on the political and theological advantages of a call for public prayer on behalf of the farmers. He managed to allude to the locusts without specifically mentioning these creatures. Perhaps the seeming absurdity of setting aside a day of prayer concerning an insect outbreak was deemed inconsistent with the dignity of the governor's office. And so, in May of 1875, Charles H. Hardin somewhat obliquely proclaimed:

Whereas, owing to the failure and losses of our crops much suffering
has been endured by many . . . and if not abated will eventuate in sore
distress and famine; Wherefore be it known that the 3rd day of June
proximo is hereby appointed and set apart as a day of fasting and
prayer that Almighty God may be invoked to remove from our midst
those impending calamities and to grant instead the blessings of
abundance and plenty; and the people and all the officers of the state
are hereby requested to desist during that day, from their usual em-
ployments, and to assemble at their places of worship for humble and
devout prayer, and to otherwise observe the day as one of fasting and
prayer.

Many years later, Leland Ossian Howard, the fourth chief entomologist to the U.S. Department of Agriculture, revealed that the timing of Hardin's "day of fasting and prayer" was not arbitrarily chosen. Rather, the governor had consulted with the state entomologist,
who advised Hardin that the locusts would begin to fly from the infested regions in early June. So Hardin's timing for an appeal to divine
intervention was rather more ecologically sophisticated and politically
cynical than the merely fortuitous delays of the ecclesiastical courts in
earlier centuries. And this locust prosecution didn't have the grinding
officiousness of an ecclesiastical trial. Whether through the power of
science or that of religion, within a few days of the time dedicated to
prayer the swarms departed. Not since Saint Magnus, Abbot of
Füssen (Germany), repulsed a locust swarm using the staff of Saint
Columba in 666 had the Church been able to lay claim to such stunning and immediate entomological efficacy. And just as locusts bred
more locusts, the people hoped that success—even if miraculous—
might breed further success.

Following the locust invasions of 1876, various groups had pressured the governor of Minnesota to issue an official call for a day of
prayer. In March 1877, churches turned up the political and theological heat. Urgent requests poured into the capital from religious leaders across the afflicted counties. Some took matters into their own
hands: Catholics near Cold Springs pledged to offer prayers to the
Blessed Virgin for fifteen years and to construct a chapel in her honor

if she would intervene with the Almighty to lift the scourge. A few pragmatic petitioners advocated that the governor declare a "day of work," with the attendant wages going to alleviate the suffering of the farmers left destitute by the locusts. But demands for spiritual supplication were more common and conventional—and, in politically pragmatic terms, more likely to be accepted by the citizens. Offering up prayers was one thing—giving up wages was quite another.

Minnesota's governor John S. Pillsbury declared April 26, 1877, as "a day of fasting, humiliation and prayer" to deliver the people from the locusts and to comfort the afflicted. On the appointed day, Pillsbury closed his own flour mills in Minneapolis, perhaps to avoid the appearance of hypocrisy or to attract the attention of the national press, which enthusiastically covered the day's events. However, not everyone was happy with the governor's unusual merger of church and state. The Liberal League publicly denounced their government's plea for divine intervention, stating, "We hold that this belief in the power of prayer is palpably untrue, its influence pernicious and in this day a marked discredit to the intelligence of Minnesotans."

But the skeptics' objections would be empirically refuted. According to a pamphlet published by the American Tract Society, "A very remarkable change in the weather occurred" the day after the prayers were offered. Historians affirm than an April snowstorm was followed by two days of hard frost—and the land was delivered from the scourge. Although there is no evidence that Pillsbury was in cahoots with meteorologists, given the Missouri governor's conspiracy we have to at least ponder the possibility.

Although crop losses still occurred in 1877, relative to previous years the locust damage in Minnesota was markedly diminished. That fall, religious leaders were touting the efficacy of Christian faith, while the farmers were putting up their crops and the governor was making political hay. Pillsbury issued a proclamation of thanksgiving for the plague having been lifted, although he had the good grace not to explicitly credit himself and his statewide day of prayer with the turn of fortune. And in Cold Springs, the faithful made good on their vow and built a chapel to the Virgin Mary under the direction of Reverend Leo Winter. Whether or not the people offered words of thanks for fifteen years is not known, but the chapel itself only survived a bit longer than the promised period of prayers. The wooden structure was destroyed by a tornado in 1894 and not rebuilt until 1951. Although the granite structure was officially renamed Assumption Chapel in honor of Mary, it is still commonly called the Grasshopper Chapel in recognition of its origin.

In May 1877, the Dakota Territory joined the gubernatorial rush to religiosity. Although the governor dismissed the severity of the situation and contended that financial aid would "demoralize the people and make mendicancy honorable among some classes," religiosity apparently was within the scope of his leadership. Not to be outdone by his eastern neighbor, Governor John L. Pennington proclaimed May 4 as his own territory's day of fasting, humiliation, and prayer. Perhaps impressed by previous successes in Missouri and Minnesota, but more likely because of piety and empathy, the residents generally observed the special day. Banks closed and merchants suspended business in recognition of what might now seem to be a constitutionally problematical unification of church and state.

Kansans took a different tack regarding the role of religion. There were apparently few appeals from the churches for state-sanctioned prayers beseeching God to remove his six-legged servants from the fields. At least within some religious communities, direct action was favored over divine intervention. The Newton *Kansan* praised the devout and pragmatic settlers, saying, "The Mennonites are not afraid of the grasshopper. He is an old acquaintance of theirs; and they kill him at once without holding mass meetings or writing complaining letters to the newspapers."

These glimpses of religious responses to the Rocky Mountain locust provide some insight into the pioneer communities' view of themselves and their relation to God. Although a few people favored the bold interpretation that locusts were Satan's minions, the general response appears to have reflected the caution of the ecclesiastical courts centuries earlier. Most settlers assumed a position of self-admonition with the hope that through humility, repentance, sacrifice, and prayer the Almighty could be persuaded to deliver them from their suffering. However, we have to infer this religious reaction from social snippets and historical hints—with one remarkable exception. The Mormons were the West's most fastidious historiographers. And not only did these pious people keep abundant records, but they also had plenty of locusts.

TESTS OF FAITH

Having headed to Utah on a religious quest for a homeland, the Mormons were accustomed to seeing their experiences as part of a divine plan. Their trek into the wilderness of North America was the nineteenth-century version of the Israelites' journey into the deserts of the Middle East. And just as Canaan was the promised land of the latter people, the Great Salt Lake Valley was the holy land of the former. Both pilgrimages were fraught with difficulties, although the Israelites were headed away from the land of the locusts and the Mormons were headed into swarms. Being inured to physical trials, the Mormons initially viewed the locusts as yet another test of their faith and devotion imposed by Providence.

The leaders of the Church of Jesus Christ of Latter Day Saints assured their flock that the swarms were a means by which God reminded his children of their dependence on him. Like the flood sent by God to cleanse the world from its depravity, the physical privation wrought by the locusts was the Creator's way of calling the settlers back from their materialism, worldliness, and self-sufficiency. Just as a parent uses punishment to teach a child a valuable lesson, the church leaders reminded the people that "the Lord chasteneth those he loveth." And the Almighty was a strict father.

The Mormons were inundated with locusts in the 1850s. A correspondent from Pleasant Grove wrote, "I do not think there were any more in Egypt in the time of Moses than there are now on my place, for the ground is literally the color of grasshoppers." As if the swarms were not difficult enough, the responsibility for this invasion was placed squarely upon the Mormon settlers. Their leaders scolded them for having flagrantly violated the will of God and avowed that the plague had been sent as a punishment for having failed to observe the Sabbath.

For most Christians, the Sabbath is the day of rest that comes at the end of a week. And by all accounts, the Mormon people had faithfully observed their Sunday obligations. But the Sabbath also occurs on another temporal scale. Mormon theologians explain that when the Israelites prepared to enter Canaan the Lord revealed to Moses a plan for storing food to ensure that the people would have full larders during the difficult times that would inevitably come. According to the twenty-fifth chapter of Leviticus:

> The Lord commanded that "the seventh year shall be a sabbath of rest unto the land, a sabbath for the Lord: thou shalt neither sow thy field, nor prune thy vineyard." . . . After the seven Sabbath years the Lord further commanded that a "jubilee shall that fiftieth year be unto you: ye shall not sow, neither reap that which groweth of itself in it, nor gather the grapes in it of thy vine undressed. For it is the jubilee; it shall be holy unto you."

Strict observation of Sabbath and Jubilee years is vitally important in Mormon theology. In this case, religious restraint complemented physical prudence. Farmers in the desert—either Canaan or Utah— where droughts and locusts could destroy a year's harvest, were well advised to lay away a supply of food. Moreover, good agricultural practice suggests that periodically resting or fallowing the land fosters a more sustainable production system. As bad luck or divine providence would have it, the locusts began to arrive the year that the Mormon farmers failed to observe a Sabbath, and the insects bred prolifically and continued their devastations into the following year. On July 13, 1855, a prominent church official, Heber C. Kimball, issued his harsh critique of the farmers' failure to heed President Brigham Young's instructions:

> Perhaps many feel a little sober because our bread is cut off, but I am glad of it, because it will be a warning to us, and teach us to lay it up in future, as we have been told. How many times have you been told to store up your wheat against the hard times that are coming upon the nations of the earth? When we first came into these valleys our

President told us to lay up stores of all kinds of grain, that the earth might rest, and it is right that it should. It only requires a few grasshoppers to make the earth rest, they can soon clear it. This is the seventh year, did you ever think of it?

Mormon historians note that if the farmers had obeyed Brigham Young and observed 1854 as a Sabbath year, the land might not have been so conducive to the locusts—and the hardworking pioneers would have had a time of rest. The insects would have found only fallow fields and moved on after leaving only a few eggs. Instead, the swarms arrived to find the desert converted into a banquet, and the pests proliferated. To make matters worse, the Mormons had also failed to put up stores of food, so not only did they lose three-quarters of their grain but they also had little in reserve. The theologians add that God would surely have provided a compliant people with a bumper crop before a Sabbath year, so the Mormon farmers were thrice punished for their disobedience. Insubordination, faithlessness, and greed—no wonder the locusts came to Utah.

In a community rooted in a single religion, the church leaders can count on civic support and affirmation of their views. The *Deseret News* echoed the theological interpretation of the locusts, proclaiming, "The destroying angels are abroad! They are coming this way. They are armed and legged and winged—as orthodox angels should be— and fully equipped for war. The maneuvers are not exactly according to the manual, but they act in concert and their march is irresistible."*

The army of destroying angels that arrived in the 1860s presented a profound challenge to the Mormon faithful. The locusts' arrival did not seem to correspond to any great misdeed on the part of the settlers, so how should the swarms be interpreted and what should be

---

*Although the metaphor of angels was biblical, there is an interesting biological homology between heavenly beings and lowly locusts. Unlike all other winged creatures (birds, bats, pterodactyls, etc.), insects did not exchange limbs for wings in the course of evolution. Their wings arose from thoracic plates, without having to modify their legs. Interestingly, the only other winged creatures that retained all of their limbs are mythical beings—the griffin, Pegasus, and the angel. So, locusts and angels both have wings and their full complement of limbs and, at least according to the *Deseret News,* they both are heaven-sent.

done about them? Here is where the great Mormon leader, Brigham Young, exhibited his powerful capacity for religiosity and practicality in providing answers to his people.

On the one hand, his message was deeply spiritual. In reply to a letter from a Mormon farmer battling locusts in Kansas, Young replied, "The only remedy that we know for them out here, is to exercise faith and pray the Lord to bless our land and our crops and not suffer them to fall prey to the devourer, and to overrule circumstances that His purposes may be accomplished." In this manner, he sustained the core of religious faith that was at the heart of Mormon life. But Young took the "lesson of the locusts" one step further, using the invasion of this menace to affirm the validity of Mormon practices and the importance of community. In a sermon at Tooele, Utah, in 1867, Young told his followers:

> According to present appearances, next year we may expect grasshoppers to eat up nearly all our crops. But if we have provisions enough to last us another year, we can say to the grasshoppers— these creatures of God—you are welcome. I have never yet had a feeling to drive them from one plant in my garden; but I look upon them as the armies of the Lord, and with them it is easy for Him to consume a great nation. We had better lay up bread instead of selling it to strangers, and thus avoid a great calamity that otherwise might overtake us.

And so, the Mormon leader continued to teach that all of the world, even the locusts, was the work of the Almighty. And if the Mormons were attentive to their faith's edicts regarding the maintenance of a well-stocked larder, then they should have no reason to fear the handiwork of the Creator. Thus, the locusts were not God's curse but his way of testing whether the Mormons had been obedient. On those who had been greedy and exchanged their food for the money of strangers, rather than keeping their bread within the family as commanded, the locusts would inflict well-deserved punishment. Fundamentally, Young's view of God and the locusts was consistent with the tenets of modern parenting. Their heavenly Father was simply delivering a lesson in "logical consequences": His children had been told what would happen if they disobeyed the church, and now those who chose to ignore a holy decree would suffer.

Brigham Young was, however, much more than a theologian with a capacity to put a spiritual spin on the natural world. He was an eminently practical man who understood that faith did not put food in the hungry bellies of Mormon farmers and communities besieged by locusts. Submission to divine will was laudable, and welcoming God's creatures into the garden was virtuous, but in 1868 the crops were fast disappearing under a blanket of voracious insects. Having seen fields and orchards stripped near Provo and his people depending on prayer to combat the locusts, he was ready to mix in a bit of pioneer pragmatism with his religious rhetoric. It was true that just twenty years earlier flocks of seagulls had miraculously saved the faithful from Mormon crickets (which were named for this event and are actually not crickets at all but a bizarre, coffee-colored, wingless katydid that aggregates and marches in dense bands). However, relying on miracles is a risky strategy for a beleaguered religious community, living in a desert, with no reason to expect help from outsiders or the government. And so in a sermon given at Mill Creek the Mormon leader preached:

> Those who manifest by their works that they seek to do the will of the Lord are more acceptable before Him than those who live by faith alone. . . . Have I any good reason to say to my Father in heaven, "Fight my battles," when He has given me the sword to wield, the arm and the brain that I can fight for myself? Can I ask Him to fight my battles and sit quietly down waiting for Him to do so? I cannot.

He went on to remonstrate that had the people been properly storing food in anticipation of the Sabbath, the ravages of the locust might have been negligible. But the core of his message was that God helps those who help themselves. Brigham Young heartily endorsed the admonition found in James 2:26: "For as the body apart from the spirit is dead, so faith apart from works is dead."

For all of their unusual religious beliefs, the Mormons were ultimately much like the other pioneers. In the end, they were pious prag-
matists who understood Oliver Cromwell's sage advice to his troops:
"Put your trust in God, my boys, and keep your powder dry." In this
sense, their story is probably representative of how many of the settlers viewed religion on the frontier. They would not be content with
praying for divine deliverance from the locusts; they would wield their
own swords. And it was in this realm of direct confrontation that the
settlers showed the great American penchant for innovation, practicality, and industry. Prayer was fine, but what the West really needed
was a good horse-drawn locust harvester.

4

Humans Strike Back

WHEN THE ROCKY MOUNTAIN LOCUSTS INITIALLY invaded homesteads and farms, the settlers' immediate reaction was to retaliate with whatever implements were at hand. If only they could keep the insects from alighting and establishing a beachhead, then perhaps the invasion could be repulsed. The desperate settlers fired guns into the swarms, clanged pots and tin cans, and raised their arms and voices in a vain effort to keep the locusts from descending. Others burned smudge pots or piles of straw to create smoke screens, but the insects kept coming through the choking haze. The dismal failure of such attempts convinced even the most stalwart homesteader that the locusts could not be kept from landing in the fields.

Once the swarms had settled, the farmers tried to drive them back into the air. In Utah, the people turned out in droves with brush whips to lash at the insects. Elsewhere, farmers traversed their fields while swinging ropes and shaking plants to dislodge the locusts. While the men flailed at the invaders, the women tried to protect valuable plantings by cloaking them with carpets, blankets, and quilts. The insects merely chewed through the flimsy coverings, leaving shredded remnants draped over the ravaged gardens.

When the locusts finally left of their own accord, the settlers told one another that surely such disasters were like lightning strikes. There were plenty of confident declarations that the plague was a passing storm, devastating yet fleeting. But hope gave way to despair when the locusts returned, either arriving as swarms or, far more often, boiling from the ground upon hatching. Still, there was always the local self-appointed authority asserting that "this was most assuredly the last year of the plague." Such Pollyanna pronouncements were soon dismissed, and the settlers came to realize that the locusts were not ephemeral enemies. This opponent would return again and again. Along with this realization came the understanding that once a swarm appeared on the horizon, there was no hope of either repelling or displacing it, but this did not condemn the farmers to utter hopelessness. Maybe the amassed adults on the wing were invincible, but their offspring might be defeated with a bit of ingenuity and a lot of hard work.

SMASHING, SCOOPING, AND SUCKING LOCUSTS

The invention of lethal machinery was the pinnacle of pioneer technology in the battle against locusts. The devices were intended to kill the hatchlings in the fields before they developed into more damaging and mobile adults. The arsenal of human- and horse-drawn implements looked like the result of a creative conspiracy between Rube Goldberg and the Marquis de Sade.

Perhaps the most obvious way to kill an insect is to crush the creature. But fly swatters pale in comparison to the Drum, Hansberry, Hoos, and Simpson Locust-Crushers. Named for their inventors, these heavy, horse-drawn implements used rotating drums, rollers, wheels, or wooden bars to mash the locusts into the soil. Such attempts to squash the nymphs were largely ineffective as success depended on having hard, smooth ground. The machines that drew the locusts into a system of macerating belts and pulleys or fan blades were somewhat more viable. When a wheeled scoop (made of sheet metal or canvas stretched over a wooden frame) was pushed or pulled through the field, the locusts could be flushed into the lethal inner workings of the device and deposited back on the ground. The Peteler Locust-Crushing Machine and the Flory Locust-Machine relied on this principle. The greatest engineering marvel of this type, however, was the King Suction-Machine, which used a revolving fan to vacuum locusts into the death chamber, where they were flung against a wire screen and dropped into removable bags.

The most fantastical weapon for killing locusts was a horse-drawn flamethrower. Imagine a pitch-pine fire burning on an open grate, straddling a pair of runners; then add an arched metal sheet to cover the grate and direct the heat downward. With this device, two men and a team of horses could incinerate ten acres of locust-infested fields in a day. If the fire was kept stoked and aerated, two-thirds of the enemy could be roasted in the process. Less dramatic approaches included various means of dragging kerosene-soaked flaming rags across the fields. And still less pyromaniacal strategies called for simply laying out bundles of straw, which could be set alight on cool mornings to incinerate the sluggish nymphs that had hidden beneath the flammable shelters. But the strangest of all incendiary contraptions was patented by Kimball C. Atwood. This complex and expensive device involved a stove to which was attached a bin for holding sulfur and elaborate bellows and tubes that carried the hot, poisonous fumes to the ground. An apron behind the rear axle was intended to keep the operator from experiencing his own version of Dante's inferno. There are no reports of whether this contraption actually worked—perhaps the machine was never employed or nobody survived to report having used it.

The least complex and most effective devices were designed to gather and poison or bag the young locusts. The Adams, Anderson, and Canfield Pans all depended on dragging a flat pan (ten to fifteen feet wide and two or three feet deep) filled with kerosene or coated with coal tar through an infested field. Panicked locusts hopped over the low lip at the leading edge of the pan and perished in the oil or gunk. The simplest of all these devices came to be known at the Robbins Hopperdozer. This was essentially a modified road scraper with the interior coated in coal-tar.*

In 1877, Minnesota subsidized the purchase and distribution of 56,000 pounds of sheet iron and 3,000 barrels of coal tar for arming the farmers with hopperdozers. The community of Litchfield alone claimed that more than a thousand of these contrivances were in use that year, each collecting 2 to 5 bushels of locusts a day. Later reports placed locust harvest at 200 pounds per hour, or more than 2,500 individuals per minute.

The Benson, Godard, Hutchins, Sylvester, and Wilson-Rhode Locust-Catchers were a bit more varied than the poisoned pans, the former netting, scooping, sweeping, or otherwise depositing locusts in a collection bin to which a removable bag or box was attached. These inventions did away with the problem of disposing of locust-laden kerosene or tar, but they created the problem of burying or otherwise destroying bushels of nymphs. For these locust-catching devices, the best marketing award has to go to John Carlen of Bernadotte, Minnesota, who appears to have been the only inventor clever enough not to name his machine after himself. That said, there is no evidence that Mr. Carlen's "Hero 'Hopper-catcher" caught more than its share of locusts or sales.

An editorial in the *St. Paul Pioneer Press* suggested that the hopperdozer provided "complete efficacy in clearing the land of hoppers [and that] pluck and perseverance meet with their just reward in the saving of their crops by those who exercise it." Such enthusiasm surely boosted the spirits of the struggling farmers. Even if your team is getting trounced, it's still nice to have cheerleaders shouting encour-

---

*Interestingly, the implement was not named after the bulldozer, which did not exist until the 1930s. Prior to the hulking machine, *bulldozer* referred to a person who intimidated by violence. This term had its origin in "bull dose," a slang phrase used on slave plantations for a severe beating that was literally "a dose fit for a bull." In the same year that hopperdozers were being invented, the term *bulldozing* came into popular use to describe the beating of black voters during the presidential election. Hopperdozers, on the other hand, were named for the effects of the coal tar or oil that was applied to the pan. These substances caused the intoxicated insects to stagger sleepily and then appear to doze.

agement. However, Minnesota historian Annette Atkins was probably right in claiming that the real value of inventing, adapting, refining, and using these machines was psychological. The smashing, scooping, and sucking provided the settlers with a sense of doing something, of not being helpless. Through their labor they affirmed the work ethic and honored rural values. But despite the newfangled inventions' having been of limited use in controlling locusts, modifying standard agricultural practices had substantial promise.

FLOODS, FURROWS, AND FARMS

The eggs left behind by the swarms were the one life stage against which the settlers could readily launch a counterattack. These buried pods were highly concentrated, so less labor could yield greater results than trying to battle nymphs or adults. And most obvious and important, the eggs were immobile, unable to evade whatever punishments humans devised. In this regard, the keys were to alter the amount of water and disturb the protective cover of soil.

Females preferred to oviposit in well-drained sandy soil, so the eggs were normally kept dry by virtue of their parents' having carefully chosen a suitable nursery. Although the locusts' eggs were well protected from natural assaults, prolonged and repeated flooding could eventually drown the embryos. With irrigation, the farmers could inundate their fields in the fall or, more commonly, in the spring before the eggs hatched. With good luck and timing, an observant settler could even flood the fields just as the tiny nymphs were emerging from the soil.

Likewise, the buried eggs had no defense against an assault by the plow and harrow. The plow was used to turn the soil and bury the eggs deep in the earth so that the nymphs could not wriggle to the surface. Conversely, the harrow raked the eggs to the surface, exposing them to the elements and hungry scavengers. However, as if suspecting such a counterattack on their offspring, locusts often foiled these strategies by destroying the forage and grain prior to laying their eggs and moving on. This lack of feed translated into a severe shortage of draft animals, and finding horses, mules, or oxen to plow or harrow the infested fields was nearly impossible in many cases. There was one last, spectacularly desperate means of disrupting the soil that harbored the next generation of locusts. A few farmers resorted to dynamiting the egg beds, which surely did far more good to their sense of vengeance than it did harm to the locusts.

Once the nymphs hatched, hand-dug ditches made effective pitfall traps for the little locusts. In this inverted version of trench warfare, the open fields were safe but the trenches were deadly. Trial-and-error revealed the optimal ditch dimensions: eighteen inches wide and two feet deep—too wide for the nymphs to hop across and too deep for them to escape. The depth could be reduced if there was a means of filling the bottom of the trench with water. Conversely, some farmers dug the trenches extra deep so that the trapped insects could be buried once the stench of their decay became overpowering, and the ditch would continue to function. Otherwise, the moldering bodies had to be shoveled out or new trenches had to be dug. In general, the bands of nymphs were simply allowed to wander into the ditches of their own accord, as they seemed to have no hesitancy in tumbling over the edge. Impatient farmers attempted to drive the bands toward the lethal pitfalls using flails, but this was rarely necessary or worth the effort. In at least some cases, the trenches were spectacularly successful. According to the *Nebraska Eagle*:

> Farmers living at Brushy Bend dug a ditch over half a mile long, on the north side of a farm. At the bottom of the trench they made holes about five feet apart, making about four hundred and eighty holes in all. Each of these holes will hold about a bushel, and the 'hoppers traveling south from the sand-ridges will fill them quite full in one day. This would seem incredible, but nevertheless that one ditch is destroying about four hundred and eighty bushels of hoppers per day.

As the swarms continued to plague the settlers, farming practices began to change. The swarms provided some benefits to those people who had the ability to financially absorb the immediate losses. Although most homesteaders relied on hand-to-mouth subsistence, established farmers found that replanting crops with late fall yields could offset some of their losses. One Missourian optimistically noted that after the swarms departed in July, "Root crops do well, and vegetables of all kinds attain immense proportions, owing to the freedom from weeds, and fertility resulting from the dung and bodies of the dead locusts." But the locusts caused much broader and more profound changes in agriculture than such tactical shifts suggest.

Historians credit the repeated invasions by the locusts with reshaping American agriculture west of the Mississippi River into the production patterns that persist today. Admonished by federal entomologists, farmers began to diversify their production systems. Wheat had come to nearly monopolize the Midwest, but this crop was particularly vulnerable to the locusts. For example, nearly two-thirds of the Minnesota farmland was producing wheat in 1873, just before the locusts' most withering offensive. By the last year of the invasions, less than one-sixth of the land was in wheat. The farmers learned that peas and beans were far less vulnerable to the insects, and corn was a more robust grain crop than wheat.*

In addition to planting alternative crops, many farmers turned to animal production. Poultry could exploit the locusts to some degree, but the greater shift was to dairy and beef. Although pastures were often damaged by the locusts, these lands were almost always left in better shape than the crops. In particular, native grasses and rangelands seemed to fare relatively well or at least to recover rather quickly after a swarm departed. Farming the semiarid lands west of the 100th meridian was a marginal venture without the locusts, and these insects were the nail in the coffin for many homesteaders. Ranching, however, relied on the native grasslands. And cattle production became the mainstay of western agriculture. The prairies could be, and frequently were, overgrazed by livestock, but they were often mercifully passed over by the swarms migrating to more fruitful and verdant lands.

---

*In recent years, America's heartland has regressed to more vulnerable expanses of monocultures. The botanically and genetically narrowed base of agriculture remains a serious concern to those who understand both the ecology of pests and the lessons of history. Vast, uniform blankets of crops are highly susceptible to pests, as producers learned in the corn blight of 1970, which destroyed one-seventh of the U.S. crop at a cost of more than $2 billion.

This approach to battling the locust really amounted to conflict avoidance, rather than direct confrontation. As with flooding, plowing, harrowing, and ditching, diversification required no technological sophistication and little capital investment. All of these practices had been available to farmers for centuries. But wasn't America the land of innovation and industry? Where were the chemical and biological weapons that dominate the modern agricultural battlefield?

POISONS, PARASITES, AND PREDATORS

Insecticide chemistry was in its infancy during the Rocky Mountain locust's heyday. Some of the machines invented to assault the insects made use of poisons, such as kerosene, coal tar, and sulfur fumes, but these were incidental to the function of the machine. Any of these lethal substances could be, and were, replaced with devices to crush, bag, or incinerate the locusts. However, various and assorted chemicals were directly applied to the locusts or the plants they were consuming. Salt, saltpeter (potassium nitrate), naphthalene (the active ingredient in mothballs), kerosene, and cresylic acid soap (derived from coal tar) provided little control, and some of these chemicals probably killed more crops than locusts. Plant extracts, such as pyrethrum powder and quassia water, worked no better, but at least these remedies were safer for people and plants. Milo Andrus, a creative but apparently unorthodox Mormon farmer, suggested sprinkling whisky on locust-infested plants. Perhaps this was Milo's way of disposing of a forbidden liquid, but the whisky would have been more effective in drowning his sorrows than in intoxicating locusts.

The most effective insecticides of the day were arsenical compounds—lead and calcium arsenate. These poisons were usually mixed with bran to create an oatmeal-like paste that was applied to the bases of trees or scattered through an infested field. Although there were no reported cases of human poisonings, dead birds were often seen in the treated fields. Rabbits and hares seemed to fare the worst of all creatures. And whereas large numbers of vertebrates were killed by the deadly bait, only a small proportion of the pests were poisoned.

The greatest limitation to waging effective chemical warfare against the locusts was operational. There was simply no way to effectively disperse the insecticides on the necessary spatial scale. Shoveling globs of poisoned mash was a terribly inadequate means of application. Chemical control was logistically impossible without insecticides formulated as liquids or dusts, equipment to deliver the poison efficiently, and vehicles to efficiently move the sprayers through the fields.

An entomologist of the time concluded, "There is yet room here for experiment, though, considering that in all historical times, the resources of many nations have been employed against Locusts without furnishing anything that will protect plants on a large scale—little hope can be entertained of discovering such a substance," and he was right for nearly seventy years. The widespread use of synthetic organic insecticides came with the popularization of DDT in the 1940s, after which a flood of pesticides poured into American agriculture. The 1960s might have risked becoming the era of silent springs, but the 1860s seethed with the whirling cacophony of locust swarms.

The settlers were well aware that natural enemies often thinned the ranks of the locusts. The farmers saw an array of predators and parasites consuming their foe, most often witnessing legions of scarlet mites and swarms of buzzing flies emerging from the fallen locusts. In some cases, they drew erroneous but understandable conclusions regarding their most potent allies. In 1878 and 1879, astute Mormon farmers noticed that the locusts were dying in a most unusual and dramatic manner: "Brother John Dayes, of the 20th Ward, called this morning with a number of pests that had clustered together on the sprig of a currant bush, and were holding each other with a death grip. They were mere shells, the whole internal portion of their bodies having been gnawed away by an insect, which bores its way through the ironclad, outer covering and never leaves its prey until death ensues."

They had observed a fungal epidemic, not the work of an insect parasite. This malady is now known as summit disease, so named for the propensity of the locusts or grasshoppers to climb to the top of vegetation in the terminal stage of infection. But our understanding of microbial pathogens in humans, let alone insects, had barely dawned in the 1870s. The germ theory of disease had been advanced less than a decade earlier by Louis Pasteur, and Robert Koch's first proof of bacteria causing disease (anthrax) did not come until 1876. So it is not surprising that the people of the frontier waged biological warfare against locusts using livestock rather than microbes.

The settlers found that chickens and turkeys could be used to protect gardens from some of the depredations of the locusts, although a full-fledged swarm quickly overwhelmed the domestic fowl. Moreover, tainted meat and lethally overstuffed birds were potential costs of turning the poultry loose on the locusts. After the swarms had moved on, cattle were herded into fields to stomp the buried eggs of the locusts. This pummeling proved quite effective if the soil was moist or friable, but only so much land could be trampled. Even pigs were pressed into service, as they proved to be nearly as enthusiastic about locust eggs as they are about truffles. The hogs happily rooted through the soil to scavenge the delectable egg pods. Again, however, there were not enough pigs in the nation to turn the tide of locusts.

The most potent allies of the farmers were the native birds, many of which reportedly consumed vast numbers of locusts. Indeed, birds were hailed as such effective forces in the battle against the locusts that several states revised game statutes and passed legislation to protect these locust predators. Such laws were necessary in light of the enormous numbers of birds that were being hunted. Although precise numbers are difficult to determine on a national or regional basis, local statistics provide a powerful impression. The records from Bohannon Brothers, a butchering firm in Nebraska, show that the ten meat packers in Lincoln shipped out 50,000 prairie chickens and quail in 1874 and 1875. In eastern Nebraska, Johnson County estimated that 10,000 prairie chickens were exported each year, and neighboring Pawnee County reported twice as many of these birds shipped in 1874. The September 8, 1865, edition of the *Omaha Republican* reported, "On the 6th Captain Hoagland's party bagged 422 prairie-chickens, 4 quails, 6 hawks, 1 duck, 4 snipe, and 1 rabbit; total, 462. Captain Kennedy's party bagged 287 prairie-chickens, 2 quails, 8 hawks, 15 ducks, 6 snipe, and one rabbit; total 353. Excluding the two rabbits, the total number for one day by these two parties was 813 birds."

Across thirty counties in Nebraska, the average number of prairie chickens and quail destroyed each year was placed at nearly half a million. By one estimate, these avian allies would have consumed 486 trillion insects—had the birds been allowed to live. And, of course, the number would be truly astronomical if extrapolated across the western states. But there was good reason that the calculations came out of Nebraska, for this state produced one of the most audacious characters in the story of the Rocky Mountain locust.

Professor Samuel Aughey, Jr., provided the reports that transformed our ecological and legal perspectives concerning the role of birds in suppressing insect outbreaks—and in stemming the flood of locusts across the West. His data were revolutionary, his numbers were startling, and his extrapolations were courageous. Although nobody doubted Aughey's powers of persuasion, his scientific integrity was another matter. This first director of the University of Nebraska State Museum was hailed as a scientific pioneer by some and disparaged as a charlatan by others. Aughey's story reveals a great deal about the lives and times of nineteenth-century scientists in America—revelations that reverberate throughout the tale of the Rocky Mountain locust.

Born in 1832, Aughey grew up in simple conditions in rural Pennsylvania. Through childhood collecting of fossils and Indian artifacts, he became fascinated with natural history. After teaching school for a time, Aughey entered Pennsylvania College, graduating in 1856. Following an itinerant period of teaching and surveying, he entered the Lutheran Theological Seminary in Gettysburg and was ordained in 1858. He married Elizabeth Catherine Welty that year and shortly thereafter accepted a call to serve a church in Lionville, Pennsylvania. Much to his delight, the position allowed him to maintain his dual interests in science and theology. These two passions might have been sustainable, but Aughey was a man of many, sometimes conflicting, desires, which variously proved to be his undoing throughout life.

In this case, he desired to be both a rural minister and a social activist. Aughey apparently adored the public limelight—which was not a quality that sat well with a small Lutheran community. His outspoken abolitionist views put him at odds with members of his congregation, and he resigned after four tumultuous years. He served a few other Pennsylvania churches and then landed a position as an army chaplain. According to the Aughey family story, he was a secret agent for Abraham Lincoln, although there appears to be no substantiating historical evidence of his adventurous role in the Union forces. Indeed, Aughey seemed remarkably adept at inflating his accomplishments. His daughter recounted that her father had been a perilous adventurer and the first explorer of the Niobrara River and the Dakota Badlands—neither claim appears to have any basis in fact.

In 1864, he was called to a congregation in Dakota City, Nebraska, but Aughey could not settle into his pastoral role. Compelled by his childhood love of natural history, he left the ministry to devote himself to science, including the study of evolution. The family history suggests that he worked for the Smithsonian, although once again there are no corroborating records. Whether by his self-aggrandizement or his serendipitous combination of credentials, Aughey managed to convince the University of Nebraska to hire him as a professor of natural science. Religious orthodoxy was the primary requirement of faculty at the two-year-old university. Aughey could legitimately point to his theological training, his orthodoxy being rather dubitable in light of his liberal politics and advocacy of Darwinism. But in 1871, there could not have been an abundance of ordained ministers with aptitude in the natural sciences on the Nebraska frontier.

University records clearly show that Aughey had a heavy workload of teaching biology, botany, zoology, chemistry, geology, and German. What is less evident is whether Aughey actually taught in proportion to this demanding schedule. Students complained that he missed classes, and this reported absenteeism coincides with other claims that he was in his laboratory from early morning to late night. Evidently, doing science was far more interesting to Aughey than teaching about it. He performed chemical analyses on a remarkably varied but seemingly haphazard assortment of substances, including soil, sugar beets, and patent medicines. The professor even performed autopsies, apparently undeterred by a lack of formal medical training.

Aughey was eventually named the first curator of the Nebraska State Museum, a position from which he was able to recapture the spotlight. In this capacity he could effectively advance the cause of avian conservation as vital to suppressing outbreaks of the Rocky Mountain locust. Much of what scientists and legislators came to believe about the role of birds as keystone predators of locusts was the result of Aughey's work and writing. His passion for this subject led him to make—or at least to report—observations on the locust-eating habits of 250 species of birds, including the dissection of stomach contents from more than 600 individuals. Aughey reported that virtually all of these birds ate locusts, including various finches and grosbeaks, which are normally considered seed-eating. Such records are far-fetched but conceivable. However, the integrity of Aughey's science was clearly compromised by his report of finding four locusts in the stomach of a ruby-throated hummingbird, a creature that is anatomically and behaviorally incapable of such feeding.

Nevertheless, Aughey's authoritative presentation of observations and fastidious tabulation of data persuaded state and federal officials of the veracity of his work. He organized his report using a faulty taxonomic framework, rich in supercilious terms but lacking in scientific rigor. The credibility of his fifty-page discourse that was sent to and printed by the U.S. Department of the Interior might well have been called into question when the nomenclature of the birds had to be revised by an expert in Washington, D.C. But the federal commissioners presumably believed that Aughey's muddled taxonomy did not negate his ecology. If doing the right thing for the wrong reason is cause for admiration, then Aughey can be heartily commended for instigating legal protection for birds across the West. Birds surely were of some benefit during locust outbreaks, but their actual efficacy was a mere fraction of what Aughey's imaginative qualitative and quantitative estimates suggested.

One might forgive Aughey's passion for birds as the well-meaning efforts of a devoted conservationist. But, alas, his creativity in the realm of science was not limited to the ecology of birds and locusts. As befits academic understatement, a later museum director described Aughey's record keeping as being "of little use." Aughey's botanical catalog for Nebraska apparently bordered on scientific fraud, being based on work from other authors rather than actual specimens from his museum. The university's historian diplomatically described him as "a loveable personality [but] the enormous burden laid upon his shoulders by the University did not tend to foster scientific precision." Aughey was unquestionably devoted to service and had a strong public following even though his replies to various queries were "based upon a minimal amount of scientific investigation." The public wanted timely and authoritative answers—accuracy was less important.

Although Aughey's science was shaky—if not fictionalized or even falsified—his politics were robust. He was an ardent booster for the state, claiming that Nebraska soil could miraculously regenerate its own fertility and that "rain follows the plow." And in the end, Aughey's downfall was not scientific malfeasance but administrative misjudgment. The Board of Regents was not pleased with the time Aughey was spending in Wyoming investigating coal deposits, in which officials suspected he had a financial stake. The tensions came to a head in 1883 when Aughey became embroiled in a scandal involving forged endorsements. With four court judgments against him, Aughey resigned while continuing to maintain that he was "innocent as an angel" and that he was being persecuted for his support of Darwin's evolutionary theory.

The minister-turned-scientist became territorial geologist for Wyoming, but four years later tragedy struck again. On a visit to a smelter in Kentucky, Aughey was poisoned by chemical fumes. After five years of convalescence in Hot Springs, Arkansas, Aughey returned to the ministry. The scientist-turned-minister became a pastor in Abner, Alabama, but his multifarious passions were undiminished. This time, his biological urges became his downfall. Aughey had continued to keep in touch with friends in Nebraska, including a married woman. Alas, he was as careless with his love letters as he'd been with his scientific data. Mrs. Aughey discovered his romantic indiscretion and mailed one of her husband's more steamy notes to the Lincoln *Weekly News.*

The editor apparently didn't find the disgraceful conduct of the city's former resident worthy of the front page. But it did rate a big headline on page 3: "Loved Each Other: And Both Are Married but Not to Each Other." The accompanying story began:

> There is a neat bit of gossip current down around the village of Waverly in which two well-known people are involved in a decidedly embarrassing way. . . . Evidence is not wanting to show that, although the former has a husband who enjoys the respect of the community, and the latter an extremely estimable wife, these two parties have been carrying on a clandestine correspondence and telling to each other a great many things that should never be told outside of a family circle.

The paper followed with what were apparently juicy snippets from the intercepted letter, although modern prurient interests would find little titillating in the excerpts.

Apparently shamed by these public revelations, Aughey returned to academics, teaching at a small college in Alabama. Although he died in 1912, scandal lived on. When his daughter offered to endow a scholarship at the University of Nebraska in her father's name seven years after his death, the chancellor politely declined. He suggested, "I am inclined to think that under the circumstances perhaps you would prefer to have the memorial in some other institution where there is no forgotten record that might possibly be brought to light."

The settlers had learned that Christian faith and Yankee ingenuity were not surefire solutions to the locust invasions. And now, if the beleaguered farmers could not count on Aves or academicians, where could they turn for help? There remained one last hope. Even in the nineteenth century, there was one creature that was seemingly more plentiful than birds and surely more powerful than professors: the politician.

The federal government had lured the homesteaders to the West, and the state and territorial governments stood to benefit handsomely from land taxes and commerce if the settlers stayed. Even the railroads, and by association the eastern industrialists, profited from a vibrant agricultural economy on the frontier—every trainload of wheat heading east and every freight car of manufactured goods heading west meant revenue. So, with everyone benefiting from the success of the farmers, how could the government possibly fail in its obligation to them? How, indeed.

Politicians and Pests

THE ROCKY MOUNTAIN LOCUST PRESENTED THE NATION with a set of problems that forced a radical reconsideration of our assumptions regarding natural disasters, agrarian values, and needy people. Perhaps most dramatically, the locusts catalyzed the great social transformation in which the virtue of hard, honest work was supplanted by a new standard of worth. With the decline of agrarianism and the commensurate rise of industrialism, the country began to equate success with money. As wealth became the measure of virtue, poverty became not simply a material failing but evidence of moral turpitude. In short, people who lacked money lacked social worth.

Contrary to the Jeffersonian ideal of self-sufficiency and independence, the needy pioneers were weak in spirit. According to this view, what the impoverished locust victims needed was a strengthening of moral character—with just enough assistance to keep them from starving. These spiritually and materially poor folks would have to learn the harsh lessons of their failed lives. And providing them with excessive handouts would only enable them to become permanently dependent on the virtuous and wealthy.

Today we still struggle with the ethical response to poverty as we debate how to allocate resources to alleviate human suffering. We continue to argue whether the poor are lazy or unfortunate, whether public assistance is a handout or a hand up, and whether welfare deepens the rut of dependence or provides a road to autonomy. Compassionate conservatism is a nineteenth-century notion dressed up in twenty-first-century jargon. But, we might object, at least modern society doesn't blame the victims of natural disasters for their condition. We might question how many times we should pay to rebuild beach houses along hurricane alley, farmhouses in flood plains, or log cabins in fire-climax forests, but we would never suggest that people bring tornadoes or earthquakes on themselves by leading immoral lives— right? Except, in the eyes of at least some segments of contemporary society, the natural disaster of AIDS is viewed as the punishment of sinners by an angry God.

And so it was that the Rocky Mountain locust forced the nation into its earliest confrontation with three of the great issues in American culture. First, this insect brought into sharp relief the conflicting ideals of agrarianism and industrialism, of work and wealth. The existence of the working poor and the lazy rich had to be understood. Next, these creatures compelled us to confront the nature of poverty. As the cities were struggling with the economic depression of the 1870s, the countryside was fighting hunger. Finally, the locusts forced every level of government to come to terms with its obligations to the people in times of suffering and need. The conservatives, liberals, and libertarians had very different notions about the propriety of public assistance. These fundamental questions continue to lie at the center of our society in the twenty-first century: Should we value work and effort or wealth and success? Are poor people indolent beggars or unfortunate victims? And what are the ethical duties of society, community, and family during times of adversity? Perhaps the story of the Rocky Mountain locust holds more lessons for our modern culture than we might initially attribute to the tale of a lowly insect.

CHARITY BEGINS AT HOME

The country found its private and public services woefully unprepared for the locust's ravages. According to the American historian Gilbert C. Fite, "Want and privation were more widespread on the upper Midwest and central prairie frontier in 1874 and 1875 than at any other time during the settlement of that region." However, most social services were based in the cities, where poverty and joblessness had become a serious problem. In urban settings, poverty was generally an acute condition, with only a small portion of families needing help at any time. But the locusts were generating prolonged destitution across entire regions. By all accounts, the rural settings should have been free of such troubles. After all, the people had the raw materials for self-sufficiency. With soil, seed, and labor, the settlers ought to have had everything they needed. Dry years, wet years, hail, frost, and insects were part of farming on the frontier. What destitute homesteaders needed was a stronger moral fiber, not a handout.

In light of sociological conditions, it is not surprising that private charities were the first organizations to provide assistance to families left destitute by the Rocky Mountain locust. The nation was facing hard times, and ironically the scale of the locust infestations was so great that the only conceivable response was homegrown intervention. Local, grassroots aid societies were not logistically or financially well prepared for the disasters, but they were more nimble and empathetic than government agencies. Even so, judgmentalism often trumped compassion.

Parochialism and paternalism undermined an otherwise altruistic effort. Perhaps F. W. Giles spoke for many of his neighbors in complaining, "Even in these frontier counties, the lack of supplies exists chiefly among the immigrants who have come in the State within the last year or so, and who had no dependence for living but the sod crops which the grasshoppers destroyed. Strictly speaking, a large number of the destitute are hardly citizens of Kansas at all." An editorial in the *St. Paul Pioneer Press* expressed anti-immigrant sentiments in even more explicit terms, claiming that providing aid was tantamount to teaching the settlers, "especially those from foreign countries," to be permanent mendicants. Hearing widespread rumors of destitution, a righteous Kansan paternalistically warned, "It was apparent that an indiscriminate and desultory system of begging would be resorted to, and as a consequence an irreparable injury to the moral sentiment of our people, as well as disgrace to the State, would ensue."

Soon, the aid organizations themselves came under fire. People levied strident accusations of favoritism, wastage, stealing, and corruption among the private charities. These unsubstantiated charges led to calls for county-level control over the funds. Integrity aside, charities were completely overwhelmed in locust-afflicted areas, and local governments were soon dragged into the crisis.

The western counties were a vital source of pride, identity, and community as evidenced by an 1875 newspaper editorial that proclaimed, "The counties of the Territory of Dakota are neither bankrupt nor helpless and the publication of such a bill [for state assistance] to the world is a libel and we enter our solemn protest against it. Does anyone pretend that Clay County is unable to care for its poor? Such an idea is simply ludicrous." But throughout the West, counties lacked the finances to meaningfully assist their desperate citizens. Although the states encouraged county commissioners to redirect funds from their treasuries, few had the wherewithal to provide direct aid. The locust-ravaged case of Martin County, Minnesota, serves as an apt example. Officials estimated that 450 families needed help, or about 60 percent of the population. These people required $90,000 for bare-bones subsistence, but the total county revenue in 1874 was $2,488.

State legislatures were fighting a losing battle in trying to keep the counties on the front line. Unfunded legislative mandates for the counties to provide hopperdozers and to coordinate the burning of infested prairies fell on deaf ears and empty palms. Some states granted local governments the ability to levy taxes to offset the costs of digging ditches to trap the locusts, but this power was of little help when the damage done by the swarms had left the residents too impoverished to pay their taxes in the first place—you can't squeeze blood from a turnip. As the situation continued to deteriorate for the desperate settlers, state officials had no choice but to respond.

The states had no way of objectively assessing the extent of human misery caused by the locusts, but the governors and legislators had hard, cold data unambiguously showing that a serious political problem was developing. The number of land claims in Dakota, Kansas, Minnesota, and Nebraska had fallen by more than 50 percent during the locust invasions of the 1870s. Retaining settlers and attracting immigrants were vital to economic growth, but pumping resources into the homesteaders was equivalent to admitting that a major disaster was unfolding—and the national press adored disasters. If a legislature provided aid to retain the populace, the state would be portrayed as a locust-blighted wasteland, and potential immigrants would go elsewhere. Speculators and land boomers pressured the government to keep a low profile, fearing adverse publicity nearly as much as the farmers feared the locusts. But if the states did nothing they'd continue to hemorrhage their economic lifeblood, creating the short-term impression of fine health while succumbing to demographic anemia.

State governments also had to deal with the dueling interpretations of poverty's causes: moral weakness and blameless misfortune. In a classic fence-sitting performance, Minnesota's Governor Cushman K. Davis maintained that humanitarian concern compelled the state to assist the farmers who were beset by circumstances beyond their control. But he balanced this dangerously liberal position with suspicions that the poor were lacking in moral character and might be tempted to exploit public benevolence. To ensure the neediness of recipients, his state-funded assistance programs were intensively overseen by investigatory committees in rather absurd disproportion to the meager funds that were distributed.

Minnesota's next governor was the consummate paternalistic politician. In John Pillsbury's view, the role of the state was to protect the poor from their own weak natures and to bring them to account for their failings. He created a wicked Catch-22 for the locust victims: If they were truly upright and deserving, then they would never deign to grovel for, let alone accept, public assistance. And so, those who asked for aid were surely lacking in moral character and demonstra-

bly unworthy of charity. However, it is not fair to portray Pillsbury or
the other western governors as utterly lacking in compassion. Indeed,
the extent of the efforts by the states to assist their people suggests
that the "tough love" rhetoric was a cover for what turned out to be
rather soft hearts.

The states provided assistance in various forms to locust-ravaged
farms and communities, with direct aid in the form of monetary payments and loans being perhaps the least politically palatable approach. In Kansas, Governor Thomas A. Osborn told the lawmakers
that 32,000 people—5 percent of the state's population in 1875—
needed help. The legislature initially considered selling bonds to fund
relief efforts, but the bill failed because of a conflict over whether the
moneys should be gifts or loans. After lengthy debate, the legislature
authorized $73,000 in state relief bonds and authorized nineteen
counties to issue bonds in specified amounts up to $5,000.

Minnesota legislators were more frugal in their aid, reflecting their
ambivalence as to the legitimacy of government involvement and the
status of the indigents. Although the state was urged to appropriate
$100,000 to locust-ravaged farmers in 1875, lawmakers pared the
amount down to $20,000. Furthermore, they added a harsh means
test to the bill, linking a family's destitution to the degree of funding.
This put farmers in the horrible position of having to sell their last
cow or draft horse—the essential means back to self-sufficiency—to
garner full assistance. Many refused to put themselves in a position of
such complete vulnerability.

Settlers realized the woeful inadequacy and inconsistency of the
state's support and often decided to make do with whatever scraps of
food and shreds of pride they could retain—thereby eroding their
share of public assistance to a pittance but keeping their dignity. Consider, for example, Hiram Clark, his pregnant wife, and their six children, who chose to keep a yoke of oxen and a cow as vestiges—and
hopefully precursors—of autonomy. The state provided this struggling family with $5.95 worth of flour, sugar, dried apples, and tea.
Such niggardly aid reflected the visceral discomfort that welfare
elicited in the nineteenth century. Direct handouts in the form of cash

or food were simply too progressive for the political leaders and electorate of rural America. The agrarian ideal was starting to crack, but the cultural values of hard work and fierce independence had not yet crumbled.

The proverbial injunction regarding the relative merits of feeding a man a fish versus teaching a man to fish was surely on the minds of legislators when they considered ways of assisting their hungry constituents. To help farming communities recover from locusts the states turned to a most obvious and logical form of indirect assistance: seed grants. In 1874 and 1875, the governors of Minnesota, the Dakotas, Nebraska, and Kansas appealed to their legislatures to purchase seed for farmers left destitute by the locusts. At one end of the political spectrum, the same Minnesota legislature that hacked the funding request for direct assistance increased the appropriation for seed from the recommended level of $50,000 to $75,000. At the other end of the spectrum, an odd game of political cat-and-mouse emerged. Dakota lawmakers authorized $25,000 in bonds for direct relief and seed, whereupon the governor vetoed the appropriation to protect the Territory's image while claiming that there was no precedent for issuing bonds for such a purpose. However, the legislature overrode the veto, an act that seemingly would have been the end of a more typical political story. But for reasons that remain somewhat obscure, the bill was never implemented, so the worst of all possible situations was created: The Territory gave the impression of being plagued by locusts to potential homesteaders and gave no assistance to the existing settlers.

Despite the political palatability and moral virtue of providing seed, this program was nearly as underfunded as the efforts to provide direct assistance. For example, Minnesota farmers needed an estimated 60,000 bushels of seed, but the state could provide less than a third of this in 1875. Consequently, the typical allotment of 15 bushels, enough to plant just ten acres, fell far short of what homesteaders needed to get back on their feet. The state's efforts were also criticized on the basis that the program provided seed for only one crop, wheat—the locust's favorite food. In 1876, the legislature appropriated funds for twenty-five dollars worth of seed per grantee, enough for thirteen acres. This acreage was still far below that needed for a viable enterprise. And to rub a bit of salt in the wound, the state required recipients of this meager gift to demonstrate their complete destitution. But conditions had become so dire that 3,000 farmers applied for seed grants within a month of the bill's passage.

Providing farmers with seed solved parts of the problem created by the locusts—hunger and poverty—but this program did nothing to directly combat the enemy. There was, however, an approach that employed people, dead locusts, and political precedent—the bounty system. Just ten years after the first colonists landed at Plymouth Rock, a bounty was offered for wolves. As Americans moved west, bounties for killing unwanted creatures moved with them. Finding legal precedent for seed grants might have been difficult, but locust bounties were a logical extrapolation of a familiar practice. Indeed, providing payments for killing locusts was rooted thousands of years earlier in Western history. Citizens on the Greek island of Lemnos were required to pay a locust tax, each citizen delivering his tribute in the form of dead locusts. Minnesota and Missouri developed less coercive approaches than the Greeks, choosing to pay their citizens for gathering locusts.

The payment systems developed in the 1870s were tailored to deliver the biggest bang for the buck. Missouri offered five dollars per bushel of eggs and no more than a dollar a bushel for nymphs. The logic was twofold: Many more locusts were represented by a fixed volume of eggs than the same volume of nymphs, and excavated eggs represented a complete nullification of damage, whereas captured nymphs had already begun to feed. A sliding scale for nymphs further refined the bounty system. A bushel in March brought a dollar, in April fifty cents, and in May twenty-five cents. To receive payment—the costs being split evenly between the state and the county—a locust hunter had to provide the clerk of the county court with the amassed locusts and swear an oath that the creatures had actually been gathered within the particular jurisdiction making payment. The state didn't care about the source of the bodies, but the counties had no intention of paying residents to collect locusts from neighboring districts. The law also mandated that the clerk ensure that the eggs or nymphs would be destroyed by burning, presumably so that a bushel of locusts did not show up at the courthouse more than once.

For all of its apparent merits in providing meaningful work and honest wages for destitute farmers, the bounty system could not make much of a dent in the locust populations. And there were other grumblings about this strategy. The May 31, 1877, edition of the St. Paul *Pioneer Press* sarcastically articulated a growing concern with the payment-for-locusts approach:

> The 'hoppers being so numerous in Kandiyohi it seems the people, or a portion of them, have concluded it will be more profitable to raise a crop of them under the bounty law than to destroy them. There are lots of such people all over the infested district, and it is one of the disastrous effects of the bounty law that it encourages this easy surrender to the 'hoppers. . . . If anybody chooses to lie down and be eaten by grasshoppers, we don't care much if he is devoured body, boots, and breeches. If he fights and keeps on fighting, the cases will be rare in which he fails; but if he does fail then he is entitled to sympathy, and only then.

The paper's critique of the perverse incentives created by the bounty payments was probably accurate in some districts. However, given the available tools and tactics, there was little basis to contend that failure to defeat the locusts was primarily a result of indolence.

While the Protestant work ethic was being supplanted by the emerging standard of material wealth in the industrial segments of society, this conversion of values came slowly to rural America. And so, if honest labor was the solution to life's trials on the frontier and if folks were reluctant to roll up their sleeves and fight the swarms, then the western legislatures had just the program to induce, even coerce, a bit of hard work. Kansas, Minnesota, and Nebraska passed laws allowing road districts, townships, or counties to conscript able-bodied men, excluding "paupers, idiots, and lunatics," for the purpose of fighting locusts. These locust armies were rarely called up, but the legislation allowing communities to force their residents into unpaid labor demonstrates the severity of the situation and perhaps the desperation of the states. Minnesota sweetened the deal by providing materials for constructing hopperdozers, while the other states primarily relied on the efficacy of digging ditches.

The qualifications for conscription reflected frontier life and demographics: Kansas set the youngest range (between twelve and fifty years of age), and Minnesota established the oldest (twenty-one to sixty years). The term of service amounted to no more than ten days in any case, but the states included fines or even imprisonment for noncompliance. Minnesota and Kansas allowed men to commute their service by paying a dollar per day, an amount preferable to the fine of three dollars per day for desertion. As with bounties, drafting men into battling locusts had an ancient precedent in Western culture. Two thousand years earlier, the Greek colony of Cyrenaica in North Africa adopted laws enjoining the extermination of locusts and punished violators with the brutal severity normally reserved for military deserters.

Ultimately, the states found themselves in the same situation as the private charities, relief societies, and counties—overwhelmed by the scale and intensity of the locust invasions and appealing to the next higher level of government for assistance. The western states tried to cajole, entice, embarrass, and coerce federal involvement in the unfolding disaster. The governors argued that the federal government was already enmeshed in agricultural assistance, spending immense sums to improve transportation systems and strengthen interstate commerce to facilitate the movement of farm products. Given the existing programs and the undeniable value of agriculture to the nation, the expenditure of federal money to save farmers and crops from the locusts was a perfectly logical policy. Congress was unconvinced.

Kansas led the next charge on Washington. If the governors couldn't sway the country's leaders, then perhaps the state legislature could wield some muscle. So the Kansas House and Senate passed a concurrent resolution directed at Congress. They called upon their national counterparts to appropriate federal funds for assistance in the locust disaster. This plea elicited no response.

Minnesota went on the offense with a multistage political assault on the nation's capital. The state's first tack was to ask for permission to beat federal swords into state plowshares. Governor Davis wrote the Secretary of War with a novel request: "Many thousands are now suffering for food, and I am using every public and private source to send immediate supplies for food. This State is entitled to two years quota of arms, estimated at $8,160. I respectfully request to turn over to me, instead of arms, a quantity of rations, equivalent in value." This plea having apparently failed, the legislature turned up the heat.

The state's next approach was a joint resolution by the legislature calling upon their senators and representatives in Washington to "secure, without delay, such legislation by Congress as will furnish a liberal bounty for the destruction of grasshoppers, especially for the destruction of their eggs, under such restrictions as may be necessary to prevent fraud." This appeal was premised on the seemingly plausible but ecologically flawed argument that "this scourge, if not arrested, may extend in time to all parts of the Union [including, by inference, agriculture in the politically powerful South and East], and thus produce disastrous results of national importance." The federal government took no action to subsidize locust bounties, so the state tried one more approach—shame.

Good old Lutheran guilt turned out to be an effective means of persuading Congress to take corresponding action. During what came to be called the Grasshopper Legislature, Minnesota lawmakers voted to extend the state's deadline for payment of property taxes in nine locust-afflicted counties. Setting aside their own acrimonious debate, the legislature issued a joint resolution asking Congress to apply similar Christian compassion to the homesteaders. Chagrined—or perhaps sensing that the political pressure from the West, like the locusts, would be unrelenting—the federal government was drawn into the turbulent mix of insects, agriculture, and politics.

MOBILIZING THE NATION

The locusts had become salt in the wound of the nation as the country nearly bled itself to death during the Civil War and then struggled to heal itself during Reconstruction. And so it is no wonder that the federal government had failed to turn its attention to hardships of the frontier in the 1860s and '70s, when the heart of the nation was suffering so greatly. Confronted by the strife and aftermath of war and the persistent tumult caused by locusts, the U.S. Congress struggled with the nature of its duties to the people. The nation's leadership had to resolve the same issues that the state governments confronted—natural disasters, agrarian values, and needy people—along with some uniquely federal conflicts.

The powers of the federal government are constrained by constitutional limits, and the Congress was more than delighted to accede to President Andrew Johnson's interpretation of the government's role in ameliorating poverty: "A system for the support of indigent persons in the United States was never contemplated by the authors of the Constitution." Although he was not referring to victims of locust outbreaks, Johnson's argument was made in the midst of the swarms in the 1860s, and Congress was happy to extrapolate his sagacious and convenient reasoning to the disastrous situation in the 1870s. But there's a rub: The president had been alluding to the chronically poor, not the accidentally impoverished.

Led by Minnesota's governor, the states were casting the locust-afflicted communities as economic casualties of a natural disaster—not malingering paupers. Whether or not they had actually come to believe this, such an interpretation was politically necessary for there to be any hope of federal assistance. Drawn in by this contention, the federal government created a precedent for policies that would play out through the Dust Bowl, hurricanes, floods, and even the drought that left fields desiccated and cities parched at the turn of the twenty-first century.

As the disaster rose to the highest levels, so too did the sophistication of the attendant arguments. Representative Stephen A. Cobb from Kansas maintained that fundamental principles of justice required Congress to provide aid to the settlers. But how could Washington be blamed for locusts in Kansas or any other state? Simple, argued Cobb: The federal government had lured the homesteaders to the West with promises of free land. By enticing settlement in the locust-ravaged lands, the government had put the farmers in grave risk. The Congress might have been unwitting in bringing farmers into the land of the locusts, but this did not absolve the government of all responsibility. The Homestead Act was tantamount to national complicity in the disaster that had befallen the West.

Others suggested that the government had promised, at least implicitly, that the homesteaders would receive federal assistance in times of crisis if they would remain on the land. After all, the U.S. Cavalry had been assigned to protect frontier communities from Indian attacks. The national defense argument was pushed one step further: The locusts were portrayed as an invading army and the farmers as brave patriots who were battling a fiendish enemy. Just as farmers had been called upon to defend the nation from foreign forces, so the nation now owed the settlers assistance in their conflict. The principles of civil defense, which continue to underpin our modern responses to natural disasters, obligated the citizens in the settled regions to help those on the frontier. The western states and territories contended that this support was not charity or even some sort of laudable—but optional—benevolence. Rather, the afflicted farmers had a right to aid in their time of need, and the American public had a civic duty to provide this assistance.

Whereas poverty aid was politically dicey, federal disaster assistance was on firmer ground. For their part, the farmers fully comprehended the social condemnation of the undeserving poor. They acknowledged that lazy paupers and dishonorable beggars had no moral claim on the generosity of successful businessmen and wealthy landholders. But the settlers' case was put in terms of disaster relief, not poverty. The nation had not dismissed the victims of the Chicago Fire as lowly mendicants. The country had come to the rescue of those who had endured this tragedy, and the suffering caused by the locusts was no different. At least this is the case that the farmers and their representatives tried to make to Congress.

The arguments that carried the day in Washington had nothing to do with compassion or justice but relied on enlightened self-interest.

The expanding nation needed settlers to occupy the West. The powerful railroad and manufacturing industries wanted raw materials moving east and goods flowing west, and society needed citizens working on the land rather than rabble-rousing in the cities. Congress might have ignored the suffering that the locusts brought to the settlers, but it couldn't dismiss the fear of railroaders, promoters, developers, counties, and states that the depopulation of the frontier would mean the end of economic growth. A hungry farmer was one thing, but an angry capitalist was something else indeed. As if to settle any remaining argument, the Department of Interior presented Congress with a report on the Rocky Mountain locust that had this dire introduction:

> No insect has ever occupied a larger share of public attention in North America, or more injuriously affected our greatest national interest, than the subject of this treatise. Especially during the past four years has it brought ruin and destitution to thousands of our Western farmers, and it constitutes to-day the greatest obstacle to the settlement of [the] country between Mississippi and the Rocky Mountains.

The most immediate problem from a political and economic perspective was the abandonment of the frontier by homesteaders. And this is where Congress first focused its legislative attention to mirror the state initiatives. The Homestead Act required settlers to improve and occupy their claims continuously for five years in order to gain title to the 160 acres of land. After just six months a homesteader could gain title through the process of commutation, which amounted to paying the government $1.25 per acre—an economic impossibility for most subsistence farmers. Another version of this occupy-improve-and-pay system was called preemption. But all of these formulations required residency and improvements, both of which had become impossible in the midst of a locust invasion. The insects were forcing families either to split up—as the husband sought work and the wife and children clung to whatever the locusts had left in their wake—or to abandon their homesteads entirely and relinquish any equity in and claim to the land. And so Congress amended the Act in an effort to keep home-steading viable in the course of locust outbreaks.

The initial provision allowed homesteaders in parts of Minnesota and Iowa to vacate their homesteads until May 1, 1875. As the scope of the locust outbreak became apparent, Congress extended the amendment to exempt all farmers "whose crops were destroyed or seriously injured by grasshoppers" from the strict residency requirements. This broader provision was enacted from 1876 to 1878 and set July 1 as the mandatory date by which a homesteader had to return to his or her claim for the year in order to meet the residency requirement. In the mind of Congress, this provision allowed farmers to seek work outside the locust-ravaged districts for six months.

Critics pointed out that a midwinter deadline would have made more sense, allowing the afflicted people to farm elsewhere and then return to their own land. Others sniped that this provision resulted in a cruel cycle that turned settlers into itinerants who were dragged back and forth between wage labor and farming. The result was simply a prolongation of the suffering before the inevitable failure to eke out a living as a human yo-yo. A quick and definitive failure, rather than a lingering struggle, would have allowed families to move on to other opportunities. Despite these criticisms, the amendments were a political success and allowed at least some homesteaders to qualify for final patent after the locusts subsided. The public response was favorable enough that Congress extended this strategy to a lesser-known Act.

The Timber Culture Act allowed farmers to acquire a standard homestead of 160 acres by planting and cultivating trees on 40 acres of land for ten years. On much of the western prairies, creating forests was an ecological impossibility. However, significant tracts of the Midwest could support the growth of trees. The challenge of sustaining 40 acres of new timber for a decade and the consequent loss of this land to more profitable agricultural production led to the Act's being amended to require that there be just ten acres of healthy and growing trees after eight years. But even these lowered standards became impossible to meet after a locust swarm arrived. And so Congress allowed farmers an extra year of residency on homesteads filed under the Timber Culture Act for each year of locust infestation.

These hands-off, legalistic tactics were sensible approaches for senators and representatives living and working at a geographic and emotional distance from the front lines. Amended laws provided broad solutions to a large-scale crisis, but a hungry farmer can't eat the *Congressional Record*. The pressure for direct federal assistance came from a most unexpected quarter: the U.S. Army.

CALLING OUT THE ARMY

He was surely responsible for the deaths of more Indians—and American citizens—than most of his fellow officers, but Brigadier General E. O. C. Ord might also be credited with saving the lives of more western settlers than any other figure in American history. After graduating from West Point, Ord fought against the Seminole Indians in Florida, the Rogue River Indians in Oregon, and the Spokane Indians in Washington. In the Civil War, General Ulysses S. Grant reported that Ord's "forces advanced with unsurpassed gallantry, driving the enemy back across the Hatchie, over ground where it is almost incredible that a superior force should be driven by an inferior, capturing two of the batteries, many hundred small arms, and several hundred prisoners." He was given command of the right wing of General William Tecumseh Sherman's army in the capture of Jackson, Mississippi. Eighteen months later, he led the Army of the James during the assault on Richmond, and General Sherman maintained, "[Ord's] hard march the night before was one of the chief causes of Lee's surrender." Ord's life as a warrior wound down after the Civil War, creating an opportunity for his humanitarian work.

Through a brilliant political maneuver at the state level, General Ord, commanding officer of the U.S. Army Department of the Platte, was named vice chairman of the Nebraska Relief and Aid Association. This appointment placed the general—and thus the federal government—smack in the middle of the human suffering wrought by the locusts. What emerged from this juxtaposition of power and poverty was an intriguing battle of principles and politics. The General's greatest battle began in the fall of 1874.

On October 24, Ord sent a message to Lieutenant General Phillip H. Sheridan, commander of the Military Division of the Missouri, asking permission to distribute surplus army rations and clothing on the locust-ravaged frontier. Although no law permitted such a provision of supplies, Ord knew that the homesteaders decimated by the previous summer's swarms would be in dire straits with the onset of winter. And without his impassioned—and unprecedented—plea to use military stores to alleviate a natural disaster, a horrific famine was looming. Ord's argument was simple and straightforward:

> The report and the inclosed [*sic*] report of Major Dudley show that unless relieved soon many poor frontier people will certainly starve to death, while the Army store-houses within 100 miles are filled with provisions. Though the laws may prohibit the use of soldiers rations for other purposes than that for which they are purchased, yet I do not believe that Congress would hesitate to approve any issue of supplies necessary to save lives of our own people, and recommend that authority to make such issues only be at once granted, until Congress can be applied to provide for them.

Major N. A. M. Dudley, one of Ord's trusted officers, had conducted extensive reconnaissance and reported detailed information on what he had discovered. For example, the Major found that of the 800 residents of Red Willow County, Nebraska, more than two-thirds would require help in the coming winter, and "of these 544 needy people, it was found that 100 had either no food or less than a five day supply." Such details gave credence to Ord's overall assertion:

> There is a famine prevailing in Western Nebraska and Kansas, and . . . probably thirty thousand persons and their animals are in danger of starving unless food be sent them speedily . . . nearly three hundred thousand acres of land are plowed in the district which has been devastated. . . . These people have been largely induced by donations of Government lands to settle where they now are, and have also been promised assistance in their distress if they would remain. With the mercury ranging below zero and their stock in a state of starvation, it

is now impossible for them to leave, even were they so inclined. But their lands are valuable, the country healthy and productive, and with a little aid from the Government in their hour of need they will gladly remain and become useful citizens.

Sheridan's response to Ord's request was immediate but evasive. His letter would warm the cockles of any modern-day, risk-averse administrator with a penchant for ambiguity. He took the bureaucratic tack of acknowledging that Ord's proposal might be appropriate in particular cases but could be risky as a general approach—and completed the obfuscation by throwing in a non sequitur warning that aid would compound suffering:

> It is a little unwise to compromise the Government by the action of its military officers in regard to any general distribution of supplies to the people residing in the section devastated. Existing orders provide for relief of distressed persons in individual cases. There may be a good deal of suffering in portions of Nebraska, but if the Government takes any advanced steps to relieve it, the suffering will be magnified a hundred times more than it really is. While I recommend the approval of what has already been done, I would advise a good deal of caution to be exercised in any issues that may be made in the future.

Ord interpreted Sheridan's reply to be an official, if somewhat cryptic, rejection of his proposal. Undeterred, he pressed his case with the Secretary of War, William W. Belknap. The secretary was sympathetic to the settlers' plight and Ord's logic, but he wasn't about to put his neck on the political chopping block by authorizing the distribution of military property to a civilian relief program. So Belknap passed the buck, suggesting that President Ulysses S. Grant authorize the allocation of clothing and blankets in light of both the crisis and the likelihood, or at least the hope, of subsequent congressional approval. Permission was granted the next day, and the following message was sent by the president to the Senate and House of Representatives in order to affirm his decision: "I have the honor to lay before Congress a communication of the Secretary of War relative to the action taken in issuing certain supplies to the suffering people of Kansas and Nebraska, in consequence of the drought and grasshopper-plague, and to respectfully request that such action be approved."

And so, just a month after Ord's initial request, he and General John Pope at Leavenworth were overseeing the distribution of military supplies throughout Nebraska and Kansas. The army distributed 10,004 heavy infantry coats, 16,184 pairs of shoes, and 8,454 woolen blankets in a desperate effort to relieve the suffering of the blighted homesteaders. But as the winter dragged on, the settlers were forced to consume their scant supplies, including seed that they would need for next year's crop—if they lived until spring. It seemed certain that widespread starvation would arrive before the thaw. Ord knew that handing out surplus clothing was a less delicate matter than passing out stores of perfectly good food that were needed to feed the troops. Reallocating military rations to the locust victims required that Congress be authentically engaged in the matter, rather than being treated as a political afterthought. So, Ord advanced this second prong of his offensive, convincing Nebraska's Senator Phineas W. Hitchcock to propose an allocation of $100,000 worth of army provisions for the besieged settlers. The bill failed in the early winter of 1874.

As temperatures dropped and suffering mounted in early 1875, Congress took up the matter of the pioneers' plight in the bitterly cold days of winter. The previous year's Mississippi flood relief efforts provided something of a precedent, as the federal government had given food and clothing (including some from military stores) to the victims. The flood of locusts pouring out of the Rocky Mountains arguably warranted a commensurate response. Lawmakers appropriated $150,000 in food and clothing, "to prevent starvation and suffering ... to any and all destitute and helpless persons living on the western frontier who have been rendered so destitute and helpless by ravages of grasshoppers." They also took a somewhat longer view of the crisis, earmarking another $30,000 for wheat and vegetable seed distribution in the spring. The president signed the bills into law on February 10, and a massive relief effort was under way.

The Dakota, Missouri, and Platte Departments of the Army shared the appropriation. According to the Commissary-General of Subsistence, 1,957,108 food rations were distributed that winter. The recipients amounted to 107,535 people, including nearly 44,000 children, in Colorado, Dakota, Iowa, Kansas, Minnesota, and Nebraska. Given the army's standard food ration and the number of beneficiaries, we can calculate that the federal program distributed over 700 tons of salted or fresh pork, nearly 1,000 tons of cornmeal, 150 tons of beans and sugar, 100 tons of coffee and tea, and almost 40 tons of salt. Kansas and Nebraska received extensive aid, whereas the Dakota Territory saw the least assistance, not for want of need but because General Alfred Terry considered the crisis exaggerated. In March and April, the worst months of the year because winter larders were at their lowest, 750,000 rations were distributed in Nebraska. How many graves were filled with emaciated victims of the locusts in the winter of 1874–1875 is not known, but perhaps hundreds succumbed to hunger. The number would likely have been in the thousands if the country had not rallied to save the starving settlers.

In March, Ord was transferred to Texas, a move that put an end to the West's most sympathetic and effective spokesman—and the hungry farmer's most powerful political ally. The federal program of seed distribution to beleaguered farmers would continue for another two years, but the outpouring of food and clothing would not be repeated. Other proposals for federal support failed to garner support, such as this recommendation in a report commissioned by Congress: "To many, the idea of employing soldiers to assist the agriculturist in battling with this pest, may seem farcical enough, but though the men might not find glory in the fight, the war—unlike most other wars—would be fraught only with good consequences to mankind." Despite this morally persuasive argument, lawmakers did not mobilize the nation's troops to directly combat the locusts. The federal government would continue to provide logistical support in the war against the locusts, but the farmers were left to do the actual fighting.

THE STAGE IS SET

The federal programs associated with the Rocky Mountain locust and its victims in the 1870s set the stage for the next 125 years of agricultural policies in the United States. In late October 1876, Minnesota's Governor Pillsbury organized a meeting of the leaders from other locust-afflicted states. The governors of Dakota, Iowa, Kansas, Minnesota, Missouri, and Nebraska met in Omaha to devise a comprehensive plan for dealing with the crisis. This distinguished group was joined by a panel of experts consisting of university professors and the state entomologists from Illinois and Missouri.

The convention yielded three substantial, interrelated outcomes. First, the governors unanimously concluded that the locust problem was too sweeping in its scale and complexity for any state to solve. Federal assistance was desperately needed, although the form that aid should take was not immediately evident. However, the second outcome of the convention helped to crystallize the form of assistance that the state leaders would demand from Washington. The governors provided the funds to publish 10,000 copies of a pamphlet outlining methods for controlling the locust. In the course of preparing this document it became evident how little was objectively known about control methods. Between their conviction that the locusts were a national disaster and their realization that they lacked vital scientific knowledge, the third outcome of the convention was formulated.

The governors called on the federal government to form and fund an entomological commission, a group of skilled scientists to address this critical knowledge gap. For the first time in the young nation's history the people were turning to science as a means of solving a national problem. A sense of urgency, even desperation, flowed from the public through the states, to the capital—and then beyond the mechanisms of politics and the machinations of economics to the hallowed halls of science. Perhaps science hadn't been the country's first answer to the crisis, but there was a growing sense that it might be the nation's last hope. Without too much historical hyperbole, this venture can be understood as defining how American society would perceive the value of scientific research. In a very real sense, this was the Manhattan Project of the nineteenth century—the cultural precedent for the value of publicly funded science to the people of the United States.

Those politicians gathered at the convention drafted a charge for the proposed commission that reflected the need for practical science.

The commission was to be charged with "reporting on the depredations of the Rocky Mountain locust and practical means of preventing its recurrence or guarding against invasions." The responsibility to assess and report damage ensured that the states would have reliable surveys of locust populations, both to warn of upsurges and to prove the extent and severity of the problem to Congress. The charge to develop and evaluate control methods meant that scientists might find a way of quashing outbreaks before they started. Or, failing this, qualified experts would provide farmers with the most effective methods possible for suppressing the locusts.

The only question was: Who should comprise the commission? The answer was a turning point in the history of American agriculture and politics. The enormous growth of the U.S. Department of Agriculture—perhaps its very existence—can be linked to the personalities selected for this high-profile mission. The man named to head the U.S. Entomological Commission was present at the Omaha meeting. His scientific acumen permitted him to cleverly direct the course of deliberations toward the formation of the commission, and his political savvy allowed him to be perfectly positioned when discussions turned to the nuts and bolts of appointments to the body. The Missouri state entomologist was a man with a love of power and a romantic name to match—Charles Valentine Riley.

6

Lord of the Locusts

C HARLES VALENTINE RILEY IMPRESSED THE POWER brokers at the governors' convention with his flamboyant confidence, artistic temperament, and captivating presence. As the state entomologist for Missouri, he was an undisputed expert on the Rocky Mountain locust, but his capacity for persuasion went far beyond his formal office. Riley's elegant bearing made him appear much larger than his slender, five-foot ten-inch carriage would have suggested. With his luxuriant wavy hair, prominent eyebrows, and extravagant handlebar mustache, Riley, a colleague once said, looked "much more like an Italian artist than like an American economic entomologist." But Riley might never have pulled off what became the greatest political coup in entomological history without the alliance of Cyrus Thomas, a man whose ambitions were more modest and whose appearance could not have been more different. The heavy-set Illinois state entomologist peered sternly over a beaklike nose—playing the role of wizened owl to Riley's swarthy peacock. The two scientists made an intellectually and politically formidable duo.

Riley was disdainful of the entomological incompetence of those gathered in Omaha, but in this case he chose finesse over his typical lack of tact. Although he'd managed to undermine his own interests in aggravating his superiors in earlier conflicts, he saw that the stakes were high enough at the conference to merit a modicum of diplomacy. Riley had long aspired to raise the status of agricultural entomology in the country. Pest management was mired in outdated practices and erroneous folklore, and he'd made the case that the nation's agriculture desperately needed the scientific foundation that entomology could provide. Five years earlier, in his report as the Missouri state entomologist, he'd laid out his philosophy of the importance of insects, explained the need for converting losses into dollars, and made the argument that farmers could never master the complexity of insect life on their own. His dream for entomology was impassioned as to the future and, as was typical of Riley, caustically reproachful about the present: "Finally, I hope to live to see the day when there will be a corps of well supported economic entomologists scattered throughout the country, instead of the few who are now in the field under crippled conditions." Riley perceived that the proposed entomological commission would be the catalyst for his dream.

After the governors' conference, Riley lamented how difficult it had been to convince the attendees that the locust could not permanently persist throughout its region of invasion, and he mocked the taxonomic ignorance of the politicos. The governors and their aides had considered any large grasshopper a Rocky Mountain locust, and Riley knew that erroneous reports of the locust invading the Southeast were based on such confusion. Even in Illinois, farmers had sounded the alarm of an impending locust outbreak when they came across high densities of leafhoppers, tiny insects whose only real similarity to newly hatched locusts is the capacity to hop. The mocking tone of Riley's later account of the confusion between a large common grasshopper and the locust reveals his contempt: "It [the grasshopper] has a wide range, hibernates in the winged condition, and not only differs in size and habits from the Rocky Mountain Locust, but entomologically is as widely separated from it as a sheep is from a cow."

But at the governors' conference Riley and Thomas understood that public ignorance and confusion were valuable assets. American society was scientifically naive but increasingly enthralled by the power of technology and industry. The states were faced with an overwhelming and bewildering creature—and the entomologists held the key to unlocking the scientific insights that might turn the battle. The governors were convinced of the need to demand that Congress form an entomological commission, but calls by the states for assistance had frequently fallen on deaf ears in Washington. Riley knew that the political maneuvering necessary to garner the power and resources that he sought would require several more allies.

Alpheus Spring Packard, Jr., was the third entomologist to become involved in the scheme to create a federally funded commission. This Harvard-educated medical doctor with a penchant for insects provided a link to the eastern establishment. With a profile resembling that of Charles Darwin, a graceful manner, and immaculate dress, Packard also lent an aura of cultured dignity and academic credibility—he'd been the Curator of the Peabody Academy of Science and had cofounded the *American Naturalist*. And as icing on the cake, his status as state entomologist of Massachusetts provided a grounding in the real world.

Packard had worked with Thomas during an expedition of the U.S. Geological and Geographic Survey of the Territories in the early 1870s. These two scientists were clearly impressed by the leadership of the survey's chief, Ferdinand V. Hayden, and they saw him as a man with the capability and foresight to administer the nascent locust commission. And in this regard, Riley wholeheartedly agreed. He had collaborated with Hayden once before in proposing congressional funding for a study of injurious insects. The bill had failed in committee, but Riley was sure that Hayden was the ally he needed to advance the cause of economic entomology in the country.

With the impetus of the governors' conference for a locust commission, Riley had a fresh piece of bait for his hook. But there were two problems. First, Congress would have to be convinced to fund this venture. And second, the political drive necessary to sell the idea to Washington would need to be cleverly linked to Hayden's agency within the U.S. Department of Interior, rather than the most obviously relevant federal agency: the U.S. Department of Agriculture. The USDA had been established in 1862, so it had no substantive track record and little grassroots support. The department provided very limited service to agriculture other than distributing seed in a largely unappreciated program that was unrelated to locust depredations. If farmers saw nominal value in this agency, Riley and his colleagues viewed it with nothing short of antipathy.

These entomologists favored practical fieldwork and applied studies rather than book knowledge and pure science. But the entomological division of the Department of Agriculture had, since its inception in 1863, emphasized the discovery and naming of new insect species. The division's first and only chief, Townsend Glover, worked with a single assistant in the most humble of programs, aspiring to little and achieving less in the minds of the state entomologists. Glover was a genteel naturalist who accumulated files of interesting facts (but never published because of his insecurity) and masses of poorly preserved insects, believing that well-rendered drawings were as useful as the actual specimens. This approach to taxonomy irritated Riley, who was meticulous in the curation of his collections. Even worse, while Glover was diddling with new species and other dandy curiosities, farmers were facing an ancient plague.

Thomas, however, was perhaps even more annoyed by Glover, whose puttering never took him out of his Washington office and into the fields where farmers were battling insect pests. Thomas expressed his frustration to Hayden and laid the groundwork for allying economic entomology with the Department of Interior's Geological and Geographic Survey rather than the Department of Agriculture's Division of Entomology: "You might as well try to get a prairie dog out of his hole as to get Glover out of his nest. . . . I had to get appointed to the Conference of Governors so as to bring up the matter." And so Thomas had also seen the meeting in Omaha as an opportunity to turn the political tide in favor of applied entomology, rather than ivory-tower diversions of taxonomy.

Thomas took the lead in working to secure congressional support, with Riley lobbying behind the scene. Two bills were introduced in the winter, one proposing to put the commission under the Department of Agriculture and the other to place it within the auspices of the Department of Interior. To the mixed relief and disappointment of the entomologists, neither bill passed. But with some political wrangling the initiative reemerged the following spring, as a single proposal coming from the Senate to provide $25,000 for a five-person entomological commission within the Department of Interior. Political pundits were aghast at the notion of federal support for entomologists to assist farmers. Two weeks after the bill was introduced an editorial in *The Nation* described the legislation in wickedly sarcastic terms:

> The bill provides for an investigator-in-chief at a salary of four thousand dollars a year, the Herculean labors of the head of the Agricultural Bureau preventing that official from giving the necessary time to it. The act, should it pass the House—which seems doubtful—will be a new application of the great principle of division of labor, for in the future the Agricultural Commissioner will scatter the seed broadcast over the land, while the national entomologist will follow closely on his trail and exterminate the various bugs that may attack the ripening grain. We only want now another Commissioner to harvest the crops, and another to see that they get to deep water, and the husbandman will be entirely relieved from grinding toil.

Perhaps embarrassed by such snide analysis but still aware of the political dimensions of the locusts and the human suffering they wrought, the legislators pared down the proposal to a commission of three people and funds of $18,000. In passing the bill, Congress charged the U.S. Entomological Commission with the tasks specified at the governors' conference. In short order, President Rutherford B. Hayes signed the appropriation. Two weeks later the Secretary of Interior appointed Riley, Thomas, and Packard to the commission and deemed that it would operate within Hayden's U.S. Geological and Geographic Survey. Riley was appointed as the chair of the commission, with Thomas as treasurer and Packard as secretary. They set up their headquarters in St. Louis, on Locust Street—named for the tree rather than the insect, but wonderfully apropos nonetheless.

In 1876, this team may have represented the most capable group of scientists ever assembled in the United States. Within three years, the commission would assemble a series of reports on the biology, ecology, and management of the Rocky Mountain locust unrivaled in their depth and extent. Virtually everything known about this species came through the reports of the commission, and well into the twentieth century we had more information about this creature than about any other insect on earth. Riley would compose and edit more than a million words in formulating this insect's biography in a monumental series of works. In complementary fashion, the most extensive biography in *Founders and Leaders of Entomological Science* and in *American Entomologists* belongs to this founding father of economic entomology (the science of managing harmful and beneficial insects for human benefit). And so to fully appreciate the locust's story and how it changed America requires understanding the cornerstone of the commission, the Lord of the Locusts.

Charles Valentine Riley began life in a rather unusual manner, being given a surname that he shared with neither his mother nor his father. Born in 1843 to a beautiful, young Londoner, the infant was intentionally given an obscure name. The deception was necessary because his vivacious mother, Mary Cannon, was not married to his pious father, Charles Edward Fewtrell Wylde—an Anglican clergyman. A year and a half later the couple bore a second son, George, and the family with three different surnames was complete, if somewhat unstable.

When he was three years old, Riley and his brother moved to the English countryside to live with a great aunt. This family stalwart might have provided some grounding for the young lads, but the arrangement lasted only a couple of years. In the meantime, their mother had become occupied with social matters and sufficiently affluent to have the brothers taken in as "nurse children" with a laboring-class family in a semirural district on the outskirts of London. Relegating their children to the care of others was common for the English middle class, and this arrangement turned out to be idyllic for Charles and George.

The boys had the run of the family's gardens and the surrounding fields. During the next eight years, Riley fell in love with the natural world. His insect-collecting romps coincided with the Victorian passion for natural history. Entomology was considered a virtuous, even spiritually uplifting, diversion, as it was a disciplined object lesson in the refulgence and splendor of Creation. The young Riley won the favor of distinguished residents in his district, who admired his "cabinets"—elegantly arranged collections of natural specimens that graced affluent homes. Perhaps more important, during his mother's regular, clandestine visits she shared her own passion for nature with Charles. But these periods of a mother's love were fleeting, as she could not tarry long before returning to her other life as a married woman (with a man other than her boys' wayward father) back in London.

Riley would never outgrow his dual passions for beauty and nature, but his Elysian fields were rudely converted into a typical English boarding school when he turned twelve. Riley was moved back to London and subjected to British discipline, athletics, and scholarship. Two years later, he transferred to Collège Saint Paul in Dieppe. The move may have reflected the incompatibility of the adolescent's élan and the British institution's expectations, although it was not uncommon for the middle class to attend French schools for culture and language. Riley's artistic talent was increasingly evident, so after a couple years in Dieppe, he moved to Bonn, where he was accepted as a student by Christian Hohe, a renowned painter in the realist tradition. Riley settled into his studies in Bonn and impressed his mentor. Hohe urged his student to make Paris the next stop on his artistic journey, but at seventeen Riley moved about as far as possible from the City of Lights. After a seven-week voyage across the Atlantic and into the wilds of America, Riley arrived in Kankakee County, Illinois.

What motivated Riley to select America's agricultural frontier over Europe's cultural capital is not entirely clear. There are some indications of a sudden crisis in family finances (his father died in debtor's prison some years later), but it seemed that the young man was increasingly dissatisfied with the impracticality of a classical education in art. He longed for the insect-filled fields of his past, rather than the people-filled streets of his future. If Riley truly craved earthy realism over the Realism of oils on canvas, then his first days in the New World certainly made sense—the young man became a farmhand.

Riley sought out a family friend, George Edwards, who introduced the frail immigrant to the rigors of agricultural life. What Riley lacked in experience and strength he made up for in tenacity and passion, impressing not only the Edwards family but their friends and neighbors as well. Soon, the perpetually hardworking and trilingually articulate young man emerged as a spokesman and became accepted as a leader within the immigrant community. Amid his farm labors and service, Riley found time to continue his dual passions for science and art, making careful studies and beautiful sketches of the insects he encountered in the fields. A farming life might have been the final chapter in Riley's story, except that his body could not keep pace with his heart. The continual toil of a farmhand wore down his delicate physique.

In the winter of 1863, Riley moved fifty miles north to Chicago. He was possessed by the soul of a romantic—and the commensurate lack of plans or money. Riley took an array of odd jobs: cigar making, pork packing, and portrait painting. But within three months his meager savings and prodigious spirits were depleted. If lives have true turning points, then Riley's came when he managed to land a job with the *Prairie Farmer,* the foremost farm journal in the West. This position allowed him to exploit his experience and talents—who could better express the farming life and insect biology in captivating prose and elegant drawings? Seeing his proficiency, the magazine made him the editor of their entomology department. Over the next five years Riley became immersed in the cultural, social, and intellectual life of the city. His path very nearly crossed those of the entomologists who would one day join him on the Entomological Commission. Thomas published his first article about insects in the *Prairie Farmer* not long before Riley joined the staff. And Riley was well enough respected to be invited to a dinner in honor of the great Louis Agassiz, arguably Harvard's most famous professor of the nineteenth century and Packard's mentor at the time.

Riley had settled into his plum position when disturbing news drew him from the relative comfort of the city. Between learning of friends from Kankakee who were dying on the battlefields of the Civil War and his abhorrence of slavery, Riley felt compelled to join the Union forces. He enlisted with the 134th Regiment of Illinois and was discharged six months later without having seen combat. The time was not wasted, however, as he returned to his post with the *Prairie Farmer* with a rich collection of insects gathered during his otherwise futile hours of guard duty. Before he joined the army, Riley had made the acquaintance of one of the regular contributors to the magazine, Benjamin Dann Walsh, the Illinois state entomologist. Now that he was back on the job, Riley sought out this enchanting figure, whose age and country of birth matched those of the younger man's absent father.

Riley idolized his mentor, who provided his protégé with critical elements of a scientific education that he'd never formally received. The young pupil even aligned with the venerated master's worldviews—and it was not difficult to discern his views. Walsh had been a classmate of Charles Darwin at Trinity College in England, and the entomologist was a loyal friend and staunch advocate of the evolutionist. Like Darwin's, Walsh's parents had planned for his becoming a minister, but he found the extent of religious hypocrisy to be unpalatable. Moreover, the Church's positions did not mesh with Walsh's radical liberalism. Having earned his Master's degree, Walsh married a "woman of his choice, if not that of his people" and emigrated to America in search of a new life. Like Riley, Walsh was classically educated, having authored a pamphlet on university reform and a translation of the comedies of Aristophanes. Walsh intended to settle in Chicago but found the city too swampy and disagreeable, so he moved into the countryside—precisely the opposite path of his disciple.

Walsh was a successful farmer but left his land when the area became malarial because of damming by a nearby Swedish colony. He then moved to Rock Island and started a profitable lumber business, from which he retired at the age of fifty. Walsh constructed a set of well-built tenements that he leased "at a fair price," in accord with his socioeconomic views. This investment gave him the income and time to pursue his first love, entomology. He flung himself into studying and collecting insects, eventually publishing more than 800 articles and amassing a collection of 30,000 specimens. Walsh's passion left little room for social amenities but plenty of time for collaborating with Riley on projects. Together, they coauthored nearly 500 articles and cofounded the *American Entomologist*. In recognition of his growing reputation, Walsh was named an associate editor of the *Practical Entomologist*. In 1866, he published a description of a new species in this journal, a simple taxonomic work that would solidify his place in entomological history—for, in this article, Walsh named the Rocky Mountain locust.

Deeply compassionate with the poor and weak, Walsh could be caustic, even brutal, toward his intellectual opponents, a practice that Riley adopted with panache. In one instance, Walsh engaged in a fiery debate with John Klippart—a mover and shaker on the Ohio State Board of Agriculture and associate editor of the *Ohio Farmer*—regarding the life cycle of the armyworm. Now, the number of generations per year and overwintering stage of an insect might not be considered the basis for impassioned argument today, but at the time such debates were extremely popular reading in the nation's agricultural press. After Klippart published what his opponent considered an egregiously misleading column, Walsh retorted, "There are few writers that are ingenious enough to display within the compass of twelve lines such outrageous garbling of another man's language, combined with such incredible ignorance of facts which are notorious to the merest tyro in entomology."

The fearless jibes of this trenchant fellow extended to those who attempted to dupe farmers with snake oil remedies for insect infestations. For example, Walsh rendered this assessment of a patent remedy's promoter: "We fear greatly that, instead of being a decently good entomologist, tolerably well acquainted with the noxious insects of the United States, you are a mere entomological *quack;* and that, instead of talking, good, common horse sense to us, you are uttering all the time nothing but *bosh.*" Riley would eventually come to match, even surpass, both his mentor's skeptical disposition and his impolitic style.

Not only were bureaucrats and charlatans fair game for the normally good-humored Walsh, but even scientific colleagues were targets of his acerbic pen. In criticizing a taxonomist who insisted on using an older—and perhaps technically more valid—name for a species rather than the commonly accepted name, Walsh could not be accused of subtlety or tact:

> To my mind the naturalist who rakes out of the dust of old libraries some long-forgotten name and demands that it shall take the place of a name of universal acceptance, ought to be indicted before the High Court of Science as a public nuisance, and on conviction sent to a Scientific Penitentiary and fed there for the whole remaining term of his scientific life upon a diet of chinch bugs and formic acid.

Walsh, however, managed to build, as well as burn, bridges with agricultural and political kingpins. At fifty-nine, he was appointed Illinois state entomologist, and a year later, he used his formidable influence to see that Riley was made the first state entomologist of Missouri—only the third state in the nation to create such a post. Riley began to model his career after that of his guru, but just a year and a half later Walsh met a most tragic end. Although his total devotion to the lives of insects created a harmless but quirky demeanor, this utter fascination apparently played a central role in his bizarre death. While returning from the post office, Walsh became so engrossed in reading what we can only surmise to have been an entomological publication that had arrived in his mail that he was oblivious of the warning bell of an oncoming train. At the last moment he dove from the tracks, but his left foot was horribly mangled.

After the requisite amputation, Walsh gaily told his wife, "Why, don't you see what an advantage a cork foot will be to me when I am hunting bugs in the woods: I can make an excellent pincushion of it, and if perchance I lose the cork from one of my bottles, I shall simply have to cut another one out of my foot." Walsh typically wore a long cloak and high-peaked hat lined with cork, into which he pinned insects that were unfortunate enough to cross his meandering path through the countryside. But a hat can only hold so many specimens, so by the reckoning of this devoted entomologist his cork foot would be a further asset. With an irrepressible spirit, he wrote to his young colleague on the day of the amputation, briefly recounting the accident, and then going on at length to carefully explain some matters concerning his next state report. Ever jovial with his young worshiper, Walsh gaily concluded with, "Adieu, Yours ever, the 99th part of a man!"

This would be the last that Riley ever heard from his colleague and hero, as Walsh's condition rapidly declined and he died just six days later. Riley came to Rock Island to offer his condolences—and to take Walsh's insect collection, claiming that his mentor would surely have left it to him and that he needed it to complete a joint publication. The state of Illinois intervened and purchased the collection. By all accounts, however, Walsh's greatest legacy was not his pinned specimens (which were destroyed in the Chicago fire) nor his voluminous publications, but his protégé, C. V. Riley.

The brash young entomologist was in for a rude awakening in his new role as a government employee. In his move to St. Louis, Riley crashed headlong into Missouri politics and bureaucracy. He argued constantly with his superiors, with the most intense quarrels focused on his reports. Riley's background in art, gift for writing, and penchant for perfectionism fueled conflicts over the refinement of illustrations, the quality of paper, the number of pages, and the distribution of the documents. To his irrefutable credit, Riley's annual reports were far superior in their scientific depth and presentation quality to anything else of the day—and, for that matter, to a great deal of modern technical publications. Of course, Riley also left his own irascible stamp on the pages, using the opportunity for spirited attacks on his colleagues and their misguided views. The reports combined the terse professionalism of technical writing with the lyrical elegance of Victorian prose, all illustrated with the finest artwork ever to grace such practical pages. Indeed, these reports were the birth announcements of modern economic entomology. And so, in what was to become a lifelong pattern, Riley had been absolutely right in arguing for his position while managing to do so in the most aggravating manner possible.

Despite these victorious battles, Riley became convinced that written and illustrated text was insufficient to the task of educating agriculturalists. The fiery young scientist increasingly shifted time and energy to lecturing. Riley spoke at the Kansas State Agricultural College and Cornell University, but the center of his newfound academic life was the University of Missouri in Columbia. And given Riley's proclivity for controversy, it's hardly surprising that this institution soon became a source of conflict.

With typical brusqueness, Riley offered his harsh and unsolicited evaluation of the quality of agricultural education at the university. The three-year-old institution was one of the first to offer courses in entomology—which should have elicited Riley's praise—but he chose to alienate the administration. And university administrators can be vindictive. The college charged that as state entomologist Riley was obligated to provide an insect collection as part of his duties. Riley argued that there were no such conditions attached to his work. The ill will escalated and the dean retaliated by canceling Riley's classes, alleging a lack of funds and students. The bitter contention regarding whether or not Riley should provide an insect collection was referred to a university committee. This body adjudicated that the terms of Riley's employment as the state entomologist included the expectation that he would provide a collection for use by the State Board of Agriculture and the Agricultural College. However, the committee ruled that Riley was not obligated to provide two collections, only to ensure that the college had access to the one he'd established in St. Louis. Once again, in characteristic Riley style, his facts were correct and his approach was inflammatory.

Fortunately, university administrators also tend to have limited memories and unlimited crises, so Riley was able to return to his weekly lecturing and eventually to the good graces of the institution. With no experience in the norms of college teaching, he was not a particularly effective lecturer, but he was a mesmerizing illustrator on the blackboard. The entire student body was given the chance to attend his presentations, and many students availed themselves of the opportunity to see the flamboyant teacher render fabulous drawings with both hands at the same time. Over the next few years he became known as Professor Riley, a title that clearly fed his voracious ego and one that he used for the rest of his life. In 1873 he was given an honorary doctorate by the university, which he also conspicuously included in subsequent references to his credentials.

In the midst of professional squabbles and honors, Riley was able to pull off what has become one of the legendary victories in the annals of agriculture's battle against pests. This annoyingly arrogant, unconventionally trained entomologist single-handedly saved the French wine industry. In 1871, France's agriculture was in dire straits. Its cotton industry had declined during our Civil War, its silk industry was in crisis because of a disease wiping out colonies of silkworms, and a new pest was ravaging French vineyards. The grape phylloxera is a minuscule insect that forms tumors on the plant's roots, allowing secondary soil-borne pathogens to infect and kill the vine. Riley suspected that the insect had been accidentally introduced from its native land, the United States—where grape rootstocks had become resistant to the insect. Applying his studies of grape phylloxera in Missouri, Riley collaborated with French scientists in grafting their vines to American roots, and 6 million acres of devastated vineyards were restored to health. In 1873 Riley was awarded a gold medal by a deeply grateful French government.

This narrowly averted disaster presaged much of what would come to be the core of modern pest challenges. With the increasing mobility of people among distant lands came the arrival of stowaway insects, weeds, and pathogens. Riley was at the forefront of applying scientific principles to agricultural problems. He was perhaps the first to fully appreciate that evolution could generate stable ecological relationships and that reestablishing these associations could be the key to solving new pest problems. This insight would allow him to later save the California citrus industry from a foreign insect and would provide the fundamental principle for much of modern pest management. There was no doubt that this young scientist could work wonders for agriculture, if only he could remember that the insects—not his underlings, colleagues, or superiors—were the enemy.

The Triumvirate

RILEY'S CONFLICTS OFTEN INVOLVED MATTERS OF power and control, but he also wrestled with deeper, more philosophical disputes. His was a naturalistic theology, in which humans had the capacity to disturb—and, most important for an economic entomologist, to understand and thereby restore—the balance of an idyllic world. For Riley, there was a creative tension between fact and faith so that our true comprehension of God's work and our purpose came through firsthand experience of the glories of his creation. Riley maintained, "There is no better textbook, however, than that which lies open before us on every hand—the great textbook prepared for our reading by the Creator. There it is, ready to unfold the great truths it contains, to all who earnestly seek them." With the material being a manifestation of the divine, whatever nature revealed had to be consistent with God's will. And so, the process of evolution was the handiwork of the Creator, and Riley became a staunch supporter of Darwin's theory.

Riley had been introduced to Darwin through a letter sent by Walsh in 1868. Encouraged by Darwin's correspondence, Riley sent his annual reports to the great biologist, who replied, "There is a vast number of facts and generalizations of value to me, and I am struck with admiration at your power of observation. The discussion on mimetic insects seems to me particularly good and original." And when he first met Darwin in 1871 at Down House outside of London, Riley was delighted to find his reports well worn and heavily annotated. Between Walsh's rejection of the clergy and Darwin's vilification by the Church, Riley became antagonistic to overt and organized religion while retaining his own, private faith in Natural Theology.

Riley's experience with the grape phylloxera convinced him that understanding natural selection—the American vines had evolved resistance to the insect pest—could provide vital insights for agriculture. In his capacity as state entomologist for Missouri, he also saw how practical entomology could be undermined by misplaced religiosity. Riley published an unusually tempered and diplomatic critique of the governor's religious approach to pest management in the May 19, 1875, edition of the St. Louis *Globe*:

I deeply and sincerely appreciate the sympathy which our worthy Governor manifests for the suffering people of our western counties, through the proclamation which sets apart the 3d of June as a day of fasting and prayer that the great Author of our being may be invoked to remove impending calamities. Yet, without discussing the question as to the efficacy of prayer in affecting the physical world, no one will for a moment doubt that the supplications of the people will more surely be granted if accompanied by well-directed, energetic work. When, in 1853, Lord Palmerston was besought by the Scotch Presbyterians to appoint a day for national fasting, humiliation and prayer, that the cholera might be averted, he suggested that it would be more beneficial to feed the poor, cleanse the cesspools, ventilate the houses and remove the causes and sources of contagion, which, if allowed to remain, will infallibly breed pestilence, "in spite of all the prayers and fastings of a united but inactive nation." We are commanded by the best authority to prove our faith by work. For my part, I would like to see the prayers of the people take on the substantial form of collections, made in the churches throughout the State, for the benefit of the sufferers, and distribution by organized authority: or, what would be still better, the State authorities, if it is in their power, should offer a premium for every bushel of young locusts destroyed.

In recounting events on the day of prayer, Riley later told the tale of having come upon a farm in Warrensburg that had escaped the first waves of locusts. He advised the owner to dig ditches around the field to save his crop. In Riley's words, "[The farmer's] piety exceeded his good sense, however, and instead of genuflecting on a spade he was performing the operation in another way, while his beautiful vineyard was being destroyed at so speedy a rate that it would not show a green leaf by the morrow. I respect every man's faith, but there are instances where I would respect his work a good deal more."

Riley's public opposition to reliance on divine intervention put him at odds with some of the clergy. He was taken to task by Reverend Doctor W. Pope Yeaman of the Third Baptist Church of St. Louis, who accused Riley of ridiculing religion. Riley's limited capacity for tact had apparently been exhausted in his letter to the newspaper, so his retort to Rev. Yeaman was rather more direct:

Though I may not have overmuch piety and faith myself, I at least know how to respect those qualities in others, and however much I believe that the insect which was the remote cause of Dr. Yeaman's sermon, is governed by natural laws, which should guide us in understanding and overcoming it, the reverend gentleman forgot his calling, and made himself ridiculous, in charging, for such reasons, that I took pains to "sneer at Providence."

Riley was even more outraged by the claims of church leaders that the locusts were "a chastisement of the Lord [for] wickedness, fraud, falsehood, and corruption [which] abound in every department of society." Bristling with indignation, he asserted, "The expression of such opinions is a downright insult to the hard-working, industrious and suffering farmers of the Western country, who certainly deserve no more to be thus visited by Divine wrath than the people of other parts of the State and country."

Riley was a complicated man, a mixture of art and science, faith and facts, idealism and pragmatism, ego and altruism. Perhaps the one quality that failed to have a counterpoint was ambition. And so, he did not hesitate to leap at the opportunity to chair the first U.S. Entomological Commission. He knew that he could handle the political conflicts, and he relished public exposure. However, he had never worked as an equal, let alone a superior, to first-rate scientists. Cyrus Thomas and Alpheus Packard were no threat to Riley's ascendancy to power, but they amplified his dreaded companion, the demon of insecurity.

Many scientists are haunted by uncertainty as to their talents, skills, and insights. These insecurities are fed by traditions of elitism based on the status of one's alma mater and mentor. This self-doubt is further exacerbated by the harsh system of peer review, which reached an apogee of nastiness in some of the scientific debates in the 1800s. Although we must here step across the line of historical objectivity (presuming one exists in the first place), what we know of Riley's life, combined with his subtle hints and circumstantial evidence, suggests that the Entomological Commission was a less-than-cordial trio of great minds and strong personalities. For Riley, the tensions seemed most intense with regard to his lifelong efforts to cast himself as both a brilliant scholar grounded in intellectual thought and an expert practitioner rooted in pragmatic experience. The presence of Packard and Thomas threatened to belie these idealized images.

Riley prominently displayed his adopted titles and academic credentials, referring to himself as "Professor" and invariably noting his Doctor of Philosophy degree (dispensing with the "honorary" qualifier). He even listed himself as having a Master of Arts, although the origin of this degree is not evident from the historical record. But this allowed him to create the coveted string of accolades when presenting himself as "Charles V. Riley, M.A., Ph.D., State Entomologist of Missouri; Chief of the U.S. Entomological Commission, Lecturer of Entomological in Various Colleges; Author of 'Potato Pests,' etc." The academic status to which Riley aspired through his constructed pedigree was exemplified by Alpheus Packard.

"Alpha" Packard was born into intellectual privilege. His father held a doctor of divinity degree and was professor of Greek and Latin at Bowdoin College; his mother was the daughter of the college's president. Packard might well have been a threat to Riley's political ambitions, if not for a lifelong reticence in public speech. Packard had been born with a cleft palate, which caused a speech defect and engendered a pattern of shyness. Although the deformity had been corrected by an anesthesia-free operation when he was eighteen, Packard's diffidence was firmly entrenched.

Like Riley, as a teen Packard became a keen collector of natural objects, including shells and insects, and soon became quite accomplished in artistically depicting his finds. He devoured Bowdoin's books on natural history and entered the college at eighteen. After graduating, he began studies with Louis Agassiz, the renowned Harvard zoologist. Packard's affiliation with Agassiz surely sowed the seeds for future conflicts with Riley, for Agassiz was one of the most strident and powerful adversaries of Charles Darwin. Darwin argued that new species arose via natural selection, which operated to favor the survival and reproduction of those forms that were most successful in meeting the challenges of an ever-changing set of conditions. Agassiz found little evidence of such gradual change of life forms in the fossil record, although he admitted that entirely new species often appeared in geological time. As such, he resorted to a hybridization of creationism and science:

> The most advanced Darwinians seem reluctant to acknowledge the intervention of an intellectual power in the diversity which obtains in nature, under the plea that such an admission implies distinct creative acts for every species. What of it, if it were true? Have those who object to repeated acts of creation ever considered that no progress can be made in knowledge without repeated acts of thinking? And what are thoughts but specific acts of the mind? Why should it then be unscientific to infer that the facts of nature are the result of a similar process, since there is no evidence of any other cause? The world has arisen in some way or other. How it originated is the great question, and Darwin's theory, like all other attempts to explain the origin of life, is thus far merely conjectural. I believe he has not even made the best conjecture possible in the present state of our knowledge.

Packard had previously been impressed with the writings of Jean-Baptist Lamarck, whose theory of evolution was based on the notion that environmental factors and biological need caused organisms to change. These changes were then passed to the offspring through what became known as "the inheritance of acquired characteristics." For example, a giraffe's neck became incrementally longer by its reaching high into the trees for food. The elongated neck achieved through a life of stretching was then passed on to the offspring as their starting point in the next generation. Lamarck's theory was perceived as being counter to Darwin's, although Darwin made some use of his adversary's notions because they provided a means for rapid change—and neither the age of the earth nor the mechanism of genetic inheritance was yet known to the scientific community. Given Agassiz's opposition to Darwin, based on an odd amalgamation of religion and paleontology, he found Packard to be a welcome ally. Indeed, Packard would later write a biography entitled "Lamarck, the Founder of Evolution." Riley had derived considerable intellectual status from his association with Darwin, and so evolution became not only a flash point within society but a sore point within the U.S. Entomological Commission.

Packard's personality was also rather contrary to Riley's. The former was variously described as, "fair, modest, retiring, and dignified . . . kind and courteous . . . entirely honorable, and never forgot to give credit for assistance of any kind to younger men, in a day when this was by no means invariably the custom." In short, he had few qualities in common with Riley. Although he was unassuming, Packard also had "a tremendous spirit when roused to anger." And who could provoke this quiet man? Authoritarians. Along with the other assistants in Harvard's museum, Packard revolted against Agassiz's strict discipline and low pay, a situation that came to open rebellion when a new regulation decreed that assistants could not have private collections—all of their material was to be given to the museum. Although Packard left Cambridge over this conflict, he remained on good terms with Agassiz, a testament to the young man's conciliatory ways. But Packard surely bristled under the leadership of Riley, who was even more impolitic than Agassiz.

In 1864, Packard earned his bachelor's degree from the Lawrence Scientific School at Harvard and his M.D. from the Maine Medical

School. He then received a commission as Assistant Surgeon of the First Maine Veteran Volunteers. During his service in the Civil War, Packard saw stiff action in Virginia and won a commendation for bravery. And so not only was he a graduate of the oldest and most elite university in the country, he was something of a war hero. Riley's degrees were honorary distinctions from an embryonic university in the Midwest, and his war service consisted of standing guard duty.

After the war, Packard published an impressive series of works on natural history and traveled to Europe to meet a bevy of famous scientists. By October 1876, when the western governors were meeting in Omaha, Packard had already published the standard textbook of entomology and had just completed work with one of Hayden's surveys. Packard was well on his way to becoming one of the foremost zoologists in the country. And in his role as state entomologist of Massachusetts, he had recently expressed concern that economic entomology in the United States was lagging far behind that in Europe. So, who better to ensure the scientific veracity and intellectual credibility of the country's first Entomological Commission?

Packard might have trumped his chief's academic record, but Riley had an ace in the hole. He had the high ground in terms of authentic connections to rural life: Riley had been a farmer. Having worked the land, Riley had firsthand experience and a devotion to agriculture that Packard could not assert, had he been the sort to make self-serving claims. Although degrees and diplomas were fine, Riley had devoted his career to applied entomology, and he was intimately familiar with the struggles of the farmer. But then there was Cyrus Thomas.

Thomas had led a Lincolnesque life. His earthiness was rooted in rural Tennessee and village schools, far from Riley's gentrified London and art academies. Born in Kingsport, nestled between the Appalachian and Great Smoky Mountains, Thomas never went to college but studied math, science, and law on his own. The gifted young man was admitted to the Illinois bar at the age of twenty-six and practiced law in Murphysboro on the banks of the Big Muddy River. Comfortable in his legal practice, Thomas decided to expand his horizons and sought a branch of science in which to carve a niche for himself. Having come from rural obscurity, he aspired to fame—and entomology was his ticket. Thomas, an exemplar of pragmatism, reckoned that the study of insects was eminently affordable and the objects of interest were invariably close at hand.

Despite the calculated practicality of Thomas's decision, he was soon motivated by an authentic sense of excitement and accomplishment. He loved contributing articles on economic entomology and published his first paper while still practicing law. Thomas soon found chasing insects far more to his liking than pursuing litigants, and he emerged as a potent and respected force in the field of science. With his penchant for legal debate, Thomas entered the fray in various entomological controversies, including the infamous brouhaha over the armyworm's biology (recall the nasty argument between Benjamin Walsh and John Klippart in the nation's agricultural press). However, his real strength was in collaboration rather than argumentation. Thomas is widely acclaimed for having laid the foundation for the Illinois Natural History Survey, serving as its catalyst and first curator. Having flourished for 145 years, this survey constitutes the nation's largest and most successful such venture. With more than 200 scientists and staff, including 22 economic entomologists, Thomas's legacy represents one of the finest ecological research units in the modern world.

Although there is no record of Thomas's role in the Civil War, this was a period of dramatic personal transformation. With the death of his wife in 1864, Thomas quit the practice of law and became an evangelical Lutheran minister. But his "intense independence of thought" did not predispose him for a long career in religion, so he abandoned this profession for his lifelong calling—science. However, his theological training was not so easily deserted and caused him to struggle with the emerging theory of evolution. In recounting a discussion with a minister-naturalist colleague, he quipped, "You can imagine the scene: these two ex-ministers of the Gospel, having the advantage over other members of the cloth in being naturalists, puzzling their brains in the effort to harmonize the facts of nature with the teachings of the church." Later colleagues characterized his position as being theologically nuanced but generally supportive of evolutionary theory. Yet Riley would have none of it. In reviewing the biology of the Rocky Mountain locust, Riley considered the possibility of gradual changes between generations and caustically asserted, "The same possibility has also been suggested by Prof. Thomas—a professed anti-Darwinian—in an elaborate paper published in October, 1875."

Whatever his stand on evolution, Thomas was able to recommence his scientific studies and soon returned to prominence. Like Riley, Thomas's academic credentials were unconventional but served his purpose. He was awarded an honorary Ph.D. by Gettysburg College and was appointed professor of natural sciences at Southern Normal University in Carbondale, Illinois. The following year, Thomas was appointed as the third state entomologist of Illinois (after Benjamin Walsh's death, William LeBaron had served in this capacity until his own untimely and unusual death due to sunstroke). The state, however, was too beggarly to provide him with anything more than a salary, thereby vindicating his choice of entomology as a science that could be productively pursued on a shoestring. Lacking the capacity for practical fieldwork, he devoted his labors to taxonomy. Thomas's accomplishments were noteworthy and landed him a position as entomologist on Hayden's survey in 1873.

The survey's goal was to assess the agricultural resources of the western territories, and this objective offered Thomas the opportunity to demonstrate his intellect and integrity. Despite ardent claims by land speculators, Thomas argued that there was simply too little rain to sustain crop production throughout much of the country west of Iowa and Missouri. But unlike Riley, who loved nothing better than publicly refuting an opponent, Thomas was almost apologetic in his assertion that promoters had been painting a deceptively rosy (or verdant) picture of the Great Plains: "I dislike to make such statements, but I deem it my duty to speak plainly on this point." Such truthfulness put him in good stead with Hayden, who valued scientific objectivity. Consequently, when the opportunity arose to form an Entomological Commission, Thomas was well positioned to take an active role in politicking through the Department of Interior.

So it was that a European artist-turned-farmer/writer-turned-entomologist teamed up with a Harvard zoologist-turned-physician-turned-entomologist and a country-lawyer-turned-minister-turned-entomologist to form the first U.S. Entomological Commission—one of the most formidable teams of scientists to ever tackle a problem of the natural world. But first, they had to tackle their own problem: how to work together. The solution was as practical as the task before them. They'd simply divide the country into sectors and go their separate ways, coming together only when necessary to exchange information or conduct business. Riley would serve as the chief, which meant that he would be the spokesman and play the central role in drafting and editing the commission's reports and recommendations. Not only did he covet the mantle of leadership, but his lack of attention to administrative details and his propensity for financial expediency made the roles of secretary and treasurer highly inappropriate. This arrangement seemed to suit Packard and Thomas just fine, as they were happily occupied with their travels and studies. They viewed the venture as a wonderful scientific expedition and a substantive contribution to the nation. Being neither naive nor altruistic, both would parlay the experience into ascending careers in science. However, neither saw the venture with the political acumen of their extraordinarily ambitious leader. Only Riley had the vision to leverage his position into one of truly impressive power and national influence.

A SCIENTIFIC REVOLUTION

Riley's cardinal principles in guiding the work of the commission were succinctly summarized in the opening paragraph of an early report: "Knowledge is power in protecting our crops against the ravages of a tiny insect, as in all other undertakings; and according as accurate knowledge regarding this locust plague is disseminated among our people, will they be able to vanquish the common foe." Never before had such a systematic and rigorous scientific approach been taken to a complex environmental or agricultural problem. The breadth and depth of the commission's work is difficult to summarize, involving everything from beautifully rendered drawings of the locust's internal anatomy to massive tables of climatological data pertaining to the insect's outbreaks. However, the trio's greatest impact on science and society clearly lay in the dual capacity to debunk erroneous notions about the locust and to reveal new insights into its biology. Of course science had been making discoveries about the world's flora and fauna for many years, but the commission's breakthrough was in converting natural history into practical knowledge—knowledge that could be used to formulate effective strategies for altering ecological processes. In short, the commission's work demonstrated that the field of ecology—a term coined in 1869 by Ernst Haeckel, a German biologist—could provide a powerful foundation for modern agriculture.

Riley and his colleagues made a series of fundamental discoveries that set the stage for developing effective control methods. The commission pioneered the practice of "integrated pest management" (IPM), a strategy in which complementary control methods are used synergistically to prevent or suppress pest outbreaks—and a method that was supposedly "discovered" a century later (when, in fact, the unoriginal practice was merely given a clever name and acronym) as entomologists realized that sole reliance on insecticides was doomed. Some of the commission's revelations are so readily apparent to the modern entomologist as to be overlooked in their importance, until we realize that such facts were far from obvious more than a century ago.

For example, much of the public believed that the Rocky Mountain locust was the same insect that had plagued farmers of the Old World for millennia, therefore presuming that whatever interventions had worked in other times and places were appropriate for the present onslaught. Moreover, it was commonly held that any grasshopper reaching high densities anywhere in the United States was the nefarious locust. After all, if the beast had crossed an ocean to reach the New World, surely its distribution would not be constrained within North America. Riley and his colleagues were able to show that the Rocky Mountain locust was unique to this continent, being taxonomically distinct from the locusts of Africa, Asia, and Europe. Furthermore, they convinced farmers and others that the grasshopper outbreaks in Georgia, South Carolina, and New England were not the work of the Rocky Mountain locust. These infestations had entirely different origins and required fundamentally different responses. Indeed, what we now accept as the common name of the locust was assiduously defended by the commission against other alternatives. Riley felt strongly that the species' name should reflect its biogeography and thereby remind the public of the creature's origin.

Biogeography arose as a scientific venture with the capacity of nine-teenth-century European explorers to travel the globe and catalog the world's flora and fauna. Driven by curiosity and economics, these expeditions—the most famous being Darwin's voyage on the British survey ship the *Beagle*—revealed striking patterns in the distribution of living organisms. The ability of the U.S. Entomological Commission to travel the West by rail and horse provided these entomological explorers with the mobility necessary to map the distribution of the Rocky Mountain locust. And what they found was tremendously important. Riley and his commission were able to document the origin of the locust's outbreaks within the area that they designated as the Permanent Zone. They also traced its migration circuit (from the mountains into the plains and back again over the course of several generations) and its ecological limits. Contrary to impassioned cries that the locust would overrun the country, the entomologists showed that the swarms invariably petered out near the Mississippi River. As Riley noted:

> To the unscientific mind there are few things more difficult of apprehension than that species, whether of plants or animals, should be limited in geographical range to areas not separated from the rest of the country by any very marked barriers, or by visible demarcations. Yet such is the fact, known to every naturalist; and the geographical distribution of species form at once one of the most interesting and one of the most important studies in natural history.

Fundamental discoveries of the locust's population dynamics also repudiated other prevalent misconceptions about causes of the creature's outbreaks. Fallacious reasoning had given rise to the prevalent notion that droughts were caused by prairie fires set by settlers to clear the land for planting. In turn, the dry air allowed the Rocky Mountain locust to fly easily through the atmosphere and extend its depredations into the Great Plains. Based on these notions, legislatures considered laws prohibiting farmers from setting fire to the grasslands. Riley argued that the cause-and-effect sequence was entirely mistaken. Rather than fires causing drought, drought created the conditions that fostered both natural and man-made fires. Furthermore, his studies showed that locust flight was not extended by a parched atmosphere but that the hot conditions during a drought created longer periods during the day in which the cold-blooded creatures could sustain activity. The commission maintained that outlawing the burning of prairie grasses would have little effect on suppressing the locust—indeed, quite the opposite. They advocated burning fields where the locusts had laid eggs to deprive the hatchlings of food.

Even the locusts' behavior was the subject of misunderstandings, which might well have led to absurd management practices if not refuted. The entomologists found that, contrary to popular opinion, the bands of immature nymphs were not led by "kings or queens," nor were their movements governed by large "guide locusts." Had such an insectan command structure existed, then the bands could have been dispersed or sent into chaos by the strategic destruction of their leader—and considerable resources would have been wasted in such a misguided effort. Riley discovered that the nymphal bands were leaderless mobs, orienting to one another and to environmental cues. What farmers presumed to be guide locusts were simply the brightly colored adults of an earlier-hatching species that sometimes exploited the same fields as the locust nymphs.

Understanding the locust's biology also allowed the commission to narrow the time and space into which management practices could be most effectively concentrated. The widely held belief that females could lay only a single pod of eggs had led to understandable confusion as to how so many locusts could hatch from the fields after a swarm had passed through. By proving that females could lay more than a single pod of eggs—thereby potentially increasing the locust population 100-fold from one generation to the next—Riley was able to account for the startling reproductive capacity of the locust. Moreover, knowing when and where eggs were laid, what time of year hatching commenced in various locales, and the distances that the nymphs moved before fledging set the stage for a scientific approach to control.

The commission understood that although the most spectacular phase of the locust was the swarms of adults, the creature was virtually unassailable at this time. No amount of frantic beating, or acrid smoke could avert a descending swarm. The key lay in the locust's least conspicuous and most vulnerable life stage—the egg. The ento-mologists knew that the sedentary eggs could be subjected to system-atic assaults for months on end. Riley conducted extensive and elabo-rate experiments on how moisture, temperature, and soil properties could reduce the survival of eggs. Although these laboratory studies were often flawed in their design, Riley made up for his lack of formal scientific training through keen observations in the field. These real-world assessments were sufficient to demonstrate that plowing, har-rowing, and flooding the locust's egg beds were not simply ways of flailing at the egg beds and giving farmers a sense of "having done something" but were the ecological key to quashing an outbreak. Riley was also a staunch supporter of the bounty system for eggs, arguing from his research that for every bushel of eggs that was destroyed, 100 acres of crops could be saved. The widespread adoption of these ovici-dal tactics and bounties can be largely attributed to the commission's work.

The commission advocated the widespread use of ditches to control the nymphs before they could become swarming adults. Understand-ing the labor involved, the entomologists studied the efficacy of vari-ous configurations and developed what became the standard set of di-mensions for a ditch that would minimize the amount of digging while maximizing the rate of trapping. Even so, the commission real-ized that the scale of trenching was beyond the capacity of many fron-tier communities. Alluding to the use of the army against locusts in Algeria and France, Riley pressed hard for the use of the military in providing labor to suppress the locusts. At the 1875 meeting of the American Association for the Advancement of Science in Detroit, Riley laid out his case for using the army to "carry the war into Africa"—that is, to take the battle into the locust's native land in the Rocky Mountains. Although federal troops were never mobilized, the commission's position supported state legislation allowing conscrip-tion for "locust armies."

The entomologists were rather less enthusiastic about various con-traptions for controlling locusts, as their efficacy and expense were rarely justified. The commission's chief, however, managed to parlay the farmers' entrepreneurial fervor into a bit of notoriety for himself. The "Riley Locust-Catcher" became perhaps the best known of the machines, courtesy of a rave review in an early issue of *Scientific American*: "Professor Riley, of the Entomological Commission, perfected last summer a grasshopper machine, which seems to be just the thing." It was, in fact, a hybrid of components drawn from other devices. He had the further savvy not to patent his machine—assuming that it was sufficiently novel to warrant this protection. Such legal niceties were marginally enforceable and economically worthless on the frontier. Moreover, Riley could gain far more in terms of status and public acclaim by generously offering his device to the besieged farmers, and not exercising his putative right to patent "unless it should be found necessary to prevent others from doing so."

The commission enthusiastically endorsed the use of biological control for suppressing the locust. They clearly understood that the greatest natural mortality was through the action of various unheralded parasites—mites, flies, and beetles—that ravaged the locusts. Although they could not see many opportunities for enhancing or augmenting these tiny allies, their studies of the locust's ecology laid the foundation for our modern methods of biological control that emphasize the use of host-specific parasites and pathogens. Without the technical means of rearing and releasing biological control agents, the commission turned to the conservation of locust predators. In this context, their reports provided a bully pulpit for Aughey's earlier work and the political leverage to impel the passage of legislation protecting native birds. Much to his credit, Riley shied away from calls to intentionally spread exotic species, such as the English sparrow. He maintained that this bird was unlikely to consume many locusts and that if it could thrive in the locust's range, then it would spread there on its own. As an ecologist, Riley seemed to intuit the risks of invasive, nonnative species to natural and agricultural landscapes, a prescience that unfortunately has not been widely shared by economic entomologists even into recent times.

Perhaps the entomologists' most lasting legacy was their advocacy of a strategically diversified agriculture. They realized that although the locust was omnivorous, not all plants were equally susceptible. There was no equivalent of the American grape rootstock's resistance to phylloxera, but Riley knew that evolutionary pressures would surely have caused some plants to be more tolerant of the locust than others. The commission catalogued reports of damage from dozens of farmers to piece together a set of recommendations for which crops to plant. Mixed plantings of peas, beans, sorghum, broom corn, tomatoes, and sweet potatoes were recommended as viable alternatives to other far more susceptible vegetables and cereals. If a farmer insisted on planting wheat, then the entomologists advised using one of the bearded varieties that seemed more resistant. The commission even suggested planting a strip of timothy—one of the locust's most favored foods—around fields of corn or wheat; the grass served as a trap crop that could be treated with a poison once the locusts were concentrated in the strip. Riley also encouraged a program of tree planting across the Midwest, as he believed that the natural barrier of forested lands kept the locusts from moving beyond the Mississippi and that this ecological Maginot Line could be extended to the west. Finally, the possibility of large-scale, strategically located fallows was seriously considered as a means of starving the hatchlings. However, the imposition of such crop-free zones never materialized as no government had the courage to order farmers not to plant after they'd already been decimated by the swarms.

By far, the strangest approach to locust management was Riley's recommendation to simply eat the insects. Nearly five pages of the commission's first report were devoted to an argument for consuming locusts. Although Packard cracked the door to entomophagy in suggesting in his previous writings that humans had delighted in consuming other arthropods (lobster, crab, and shrimp all being considered delicacies), Riley shoved the door open in enthusiastically advocating the culinary uses of locusts. Although his early experiments were not terribly encouraging, he stuck with it:

> I found the chitinous covering and the corneous parts—especially the spines of the tibia—dry and chippy, and somewhat irritating to the throat. This objection would not apply, with the same force, to the mature individuals, especially of the larger species, where the heads,

legs, and wings are carefully separated before cooking. In fact, some
of the mature insects prepared in this way, then boiled and afterward
stewed with a few vegetables, and a little butter, pepper, salt and vine-
gar, made an excellent fricassee.

Not only did he prepare them himself, but he also enticed chefs to
explore the possibilities: "I sent a bushel of the scalded insects to Mr.
John Bonnet, one of the oldest and best known caterers in Saint Louis.
Master of the mysteries of the cuisine, he made a soup which was really delicious, and was so pronounced by dozens of prominent Saint
Louisians who tried it." To affirm that the palatability of locusts was
not the consequence of an uncultured palate, Riley took fried specimens to France and England, where "they were tasted and reported
better than expected." Faint praise, perhaps, but to Riley a ringing en-
dorsement.

As odd as it was to suggest that locusts should be converted into
delicacies, the notion did not seem to undermine Riley's credibility. He
took pains to explain that this venture was neither fancy nor folly, but
a pragmatic approach to human suffering. Acknowledging that his efforts to test the locust for edibility and to develop simple recipes
would provoke "ridicule and mirth, or even disgust," Riley pushed
ahead, contending, "Yet I was governed by weightier reasons than
mere curiosity; for many a family in Kansas and Nebraska was in
1874 brought to the brink of the grave by sheer lack of food, while
the St. Louis papers reported cases of actual death from starvation in
some sections of Missouri, where the insects abounded and ate up
every green thing in the spring of 1875." Knowing the cultural obsta-
cles to eating locusts, Riley still maintained that if his analyses allowed even a few people to avoid suffering and starvation, then "I
shall not have written in vain."

Unfortunately (at least for those hoping to demonstrate the power
of science as a means of altering the course of nature on a continental
scale) the Rocky Mountain locust plague began to subside a year after
the commission started its work. Given Riley's enormous capacity for
self-promotion and the extraordinary contributions that the commission had made to developing scientifically sound management methods, the politicians and the public were delighted to attribute the locust's

demise to the work of the entomologists. Riley might have fiercely rebutted the logical fallacy that attributed droughts to prairie fires, but
he wasn't about to suggest that there was any error in linking the existence of his commission and the adoption of their methods to the
precipitous decline in the locust's populations. To be fair, short-term
regional applications of the commission's recommended methods had
proven enormously effective and remarkably efficient, and had the
outbreak persisted it may well have been defeated by the integrated
tactics the entomologists recommended.

Perhaps most important, even these preliminary results of scientific
pest management were widely seen as being entirely sufficient to establish the efficacy of applied research in solving grave national problems. The country's grand experiment in publicly funded science was
declared a rip-roaring success. And so, with the insects in retreat and
his reputation soaring, Riley made his move.

Riley had laid the foundation for a power grab in Washington in his
reports as the Missouri state entomologist and echoed these sentiments in his role as chief of the commission. Using a carrot-and-stick
approach to political lobbying, Riley first stroked the egos of any
politician who had the foresight to appreciate the coming revolution
in entomology:

> There yet are, and doubtless ever will be, those who—dwelling in
> cities, and familiar only with such lectularious insects as cause them
> bodily inconvenience—have little appreciation of Agriculture or En-
> tomology in its connection with it; and consider the study of "bugs,"
> as they contemptibly call everything that creeps, a fit subject for
> ridicule. . . . Fortunately, such persons are becoming fewer and fewer,
> and the following pages bear witness to the fact that not only in sev-
> eral States in our Union, but in several countries of the "Old
> World"—in monarchies, empires and republics alike—the authorities
> have manifested a remarkable appreciation of economic Entomology.

With governments around the world seeing the light, surely the U.S.
Congress—or at least its wisest members—would understand the incredible value of finally winning the war against one of humanity's

most ancient and formidable enemies. But, a sympathetic senator or representative might argue, "Don't we already have a Department of Agriculture and isn't this agency taking the lead in ensuring that modern practices are being developed?" Riley anticipated such a rejoinder and was loaded for bear:

> We have, it is true, a Department of Agriculture which, if under intelligent and scientific control, might employ the large sums it now fritters away in the gratuitous distribution of seeds, to better advantage; but the people have lost all hope of getting much good out of that institution as at present organized, or so long as the character of its head and management depends on political whim or fancy.

When Townsend Glover, the USDA's inept entomological head, fell ill in 1878, Riley was poised for ascendancy. In June, he was appointed chief entomologist to the USDA, a position that would allow him to alter the course of economic entomology. His fellow entomologists had rather less ambitious goals. With the locusts in recession and the commission's work on the crisis dwindling, the other two entomologists pursued paths as divergent as their personalities.

Packard was appointed professor of zoology at Brown University, where he continued a long and distinguished academic career. He was one of the first entomologists to realize that there were more orders of insects than those described by Linnaeus a century earlier, and Packard substantially improved the taxonomy of insects. He expanded his research to include studies of a wide range of other invertebrates, describing fifty new genera and nearly 600 new species of insects, spiders, crustaceans, and mollusks throughout his career. This immense body of work was recognized by his being named to the National Academy of Sciences. In his later years, he turned his attention to more philosophical and theoretical aspects of zoology. Despite the growing acceptance of Darwin's concepts, Packard remained loyal to the Lamarckian theory of evolution. Following a visit to France, Packard wrote an authoritative biography of Lamarck, a tribute to his lifelong fascination with this French naturalist. This was to be his last substantive work, as he fell ill and died at the age of sixty-six.

Thomas returned to his faculty position in natural history at Southern Normal University and his work as state entomologist. But as he was a classical nineteenth-century natural scientist, Thomas's interests were eclectic and he was increasingly fascinated by anthropology. And so, at the age of fifty-seven, he resigned from his state duties to join the Smithsonian Institution. Working with the Bureau of Ethnology he became a renowned authority on archaeology and an expert on Mayan inscriptions, the mound builders in the Mississippi Valley and Gulf states, and the Cherokee and Shawnee people. Having served as the president of the Bureau of American Ethnology and published such seminal books as *Introduction to the Study of North American Archaeology*, Thomas is now remembered more for his anthropological than for his entomological studies. He died at the age of eighty-five, having enjoyed a rich and varied life practicing law, ministry, and science.

After the triumvirate disbanded, one of Riley's first acts revealed the compassionate side of this otherwise megalomaniacal figure. Although Riley seemed to have nothing but contempt for his predecessor, he took pains to ensure that Glover was fairly compensated by the House Committee for Agriculture for the meticulously rendered copper plates that he had produced on his own. One might posit that Riley's recent marriage had soothed his restless spirit. Or perhaps the serene setting of his new workplace calmed his nerves. The lily pond just inside the entrance to the grounds, rows of elegant ginkgoes bordering the main drive, and the surrounding park of rolling lawns punctuated with groves of trees in neat, botanical groupings should have put him at ease. But Riley had the passionate heart of an artist to go along with the rational mind of a scientist, and it was not long before he was once again mired in controversy.

Riley's assistant and the man who would one day succeed him, Leland O. Howard, described his chief as "a restless, ambitious man, a great schemer, and striving constantly to make his work appear more important." As was the normal practice of the time, Riley's name appeared as the author of many bulletins and reports that were entirely written by his assistants. As Howard noted, "This was considered quite ethical, in fact, the proper thing to do. The assistants accepted the situation, not because it was right, but because there was nothing they could do about it." Howard was close enough to Riley to infer that some of his irascibility might be physiological, as well as psychological. While living in Washington, Riley often suffered from headaches and insomnia. After he discovered that he could sleep in a barber's chair better than a bed, on restless nights he'd go to his barber and pay by the hour to sleep. For all of his pragmatism in the field of entomology, Riley apparently never thought of simply putting such a chair in his house.

Outside of work—a world of intense striving and fierce competition, largely of his own creation—Riley was a different man. He was a loving and tender father to seven children, although his role was limited by poor health and excessive work. In public he could be absolutely charming, "discussing almost any topic with versatility and good humor." In Washington social circles, he was usually a genial guest, full of grace and wit. But even in polite society Riley could be cantankerous when matters of science became even peripherally involved. When he was invited to a seance, a popular diversion in the late 1800s, Riley nearly put an end to the evening by irritably voicing his disbelief in the proceedings. His host warned that such acrimonious skepticism could hinder the appearance of the sensitive spirit, but Riley was undeterred in his expostulation about the evening as senseless tripe.

Whereas flamboyance could be a delightful quality in a dinner guest, the staid Department of Agriculture had little tolerance of showboating. Riley's success in making direct appeals to Congress during the formation of the Entomological Commission convinced him that direct lobbying was a viable tactic, a singularly appalling approach within the chain-of-command structure of the USDA. The department was headed by William G. LeDuc, a Civil War general who was constantly irritated by his insubordinate chief entomologist—and by the shenanigans of his staff. The department head enjoyed giving tours to important visitors and especially liked taking his guests to a box of pinned specimens of the Rocky Mountain locust, the creature of greatest intrigue and interest to high-ranking officials. LeDuc would make a beeline to this one box, whose location he knew, read the Latin name aloud for his visitors, open the box with a flourish, and show the contents with the portentous pride of a learned expert.

Just prior to such a tour, one of Riley's assistants—encouraged by his boss's defiance of authority—altered the position of the boxes as a practical joke, leaving LeDuc confused and embarrassed.

Throughout his seventeen years with the USDA, Riley was constantly in hot water because of his impatience with bureaucratic bungling and his intolerance of inefficiency. He resented administrative constraints on his program, which led to his resigning twice. The first time came after an elaborate scheme to secure his appointment as Assistant Secretary of Agriculture failed and Riley became so embittered that he was "allowed to resign." After a change of administrations Riley was reappointed to his position as Chief Entomologist. However, he resigned in a "fit of temper" some years later over accusations that he had violated travel restrictions and deceived his superiors. Such conflicts surely exacerbated his bouts of "nervous exhaustion," which frustrated him terribly. But despite these difficulties—or one might argue that, in part, because of the rabid intensity that led to them—Riley was able to create a legacy of economic entomology that continues to define this field.

His rapidly growing program made tremendous advances in terms of new insecticides, machinery, and biological control methods. Perhaps his most famous accomplishment was saving the nascent California citrus industry from collapse under the ravages of the cottony-cushion scale. This fecund insect arrived in 1868, and within twenty years it had devastated citrus groves throughout the southern part of the state. The scale had been accidentally introduced from Australia, a key fact that Riley was able to deduce from his understanding of ecology, biogeography, and entomology. He convinced the California Fruit Growers Convention to appeal to Congress for assistance through the USDA. Riley suspected that the solution to the problem lay in the insect's native land, and he also knew that the appropriation bill for his agency had a rider prohibiting foreign travel (aimed specifically at Riley and his junkets). Riley, of course, was undeterred. He used federal funds to have one of his field agents travel as a putative representative of the State Department to the International Exposition in Melbourne, his actual purpose being to find natural enemies of the scale. The man shipped back parasitic flies and predacious ladybird beetles. After successful field-cage experiments, thousands of the small beetles were distributed across southern California. Within months of releasing these voracious predators, Riley knew he had achieved what has been called "the greatest entomological success of all time." This was the world's first case of "classical" biological control (the suppression of an exotic pest by introducing a natural enemy from its homeland), and the method has become one of the most effective and widely used pest management strategies in modern agriculture.

Riley's innovations in terms of the nation's agricultural and scientific infrastructures rivaled his purely scientific advances. To his other duties, he added the office of honorary curator of entomology to the Smithsonian Institution. This position allowed him to found the U.S. National Insect Collection. Today, the museum's 25 million specimens are overseen by ten Smithsonian curators and another eighteen specialists from supporting agencies. Riley advocated the creation of a system of agricultural experiment stations, which were manifested in the Hatch Act establishing these facilities in the Land Grant Colleges of Agriculture across the United States. With the dawn of this immense network of educational and research centers, Riley played a powerfully influential role in defining these organizations via their staffs and mandates. A branch unit in economic ornithology arose because of Riley's insistent demands, and this office became the Bureau of Biological Survey and then metamorphosed into today's U.S. Fish and Wildlife Service.

The USDA's elevation to cabinet status in 1889 may not have been a direct consequence of Riley's work, but his high-profile efforts were vital to the growing credibility of the agency. As for his own unit, Riley set a such trajectory for growth that the Division of Entomology's budget increased 100-fold by the turn of the twentieth century. Whereas in 1876 Congress had anguished for weeks over the appropriation of $18,000 to create the first Entomological Commission, in 1929 it required only a few hours of deliberation to provide $750,000 to fund an eradication program for the Mediterranean fruit fly in Florida. Today, of course, the investment of human and material resources in economic entomology is on the scale of thousands of scientists and tens of millions of dollars.

After Riley's second resignation, he began to fade from public view, devoting his time to curatorial work at the Smithsonian—an ironic decision in light of his antipathy for Townsend Glover's priorities. A year after stepping down, Riley and his fourteen-year-old son were speeding down an incline on Columbia Street in Washington when the front wheel of the father's bicycle struck a stone and he was thrown over the handlebars. Riley's head struck the pavement and he died within hours. At the age of fifty-one, America's greatest entomologist was dead, killed in the prime of his life by a freak accident, just like his mentor, Benjamin Walsh.

The obituaries and memories of Charles Valentine Riley were a carefully blended mixture of deep respect and personal distance. He had been a great scientist, but his passion and ambition did not allow for close friendships. A Canadian entomologist who turned down an invitation to take over Riley's post in the U.S. Department of Agriculture offered perhaps the most tactful and honest appraisal of his obstreperous friend and brilliant colleague: "As an economic entomologist, take him all in all, he was far and away the most eminent that the world has ever seen."

As if in counterpoint to the Lord of the Locusts, the swarms of insects had continued to decline in notoriety during Riley's rise to fame. The insects that had been the springboard of the great scientist and the entire field of entomology were now dormant. Some believed that the management methods tested and recommended by Riley and his fellow commissioners were to be credited for the continuing recession. However, like superstitious gamblers, many agriculturalists held to a "slot machine" view of nature. They were sure that as each passing year yielded few locusts, a "jackpot" outbreak became more likely. And the insects seemed periodically poised for an encore. A swarm descended on Otter Tail County, Minnesota, in 1888; locusts infested farming communities in middle and eastern Nebraska (including the state capital) in 1892; and spotty infestations were seen in Iowa. To many farmers, these small incursions were simply omens of a massive invasion just around the corner. Now, with Riley gone, would the locust return in a grand reprisal?

8

The Locust Disappears

NORMAN CRIDDLE IS BEST KNOWN TO THE WORLD
through his grasshopper antidote, which was widely promulgated throughout the western states and provinces in the early 1900s. What came to be known as the "Criddle mixture" was a rather simple—and absolutely disgusting—concoction.

The recipe began with measuring out a pound of Paris green. Although evoking the romance of springtime in the heart of France, the name for this essential ingredient in Criddle's recipe has a malevolent origin. Copper acetoarsenite was originally used as a bright green pigment in wallpaper, but in the mid-eighteenth century, the French discovered its potent insecticidal properties. Another arsenic-based pesticide was given a similarly enticing name: Calcium arsenite was called London purple. According to Criddle's recipe, a pound of the Parisians' poisonous powder was added to fifty pounds of horse manure, along with a pint of molasses, and mixed thoroughly (one didn't want lumpy batter).

This mess was then shoveled or otherwise pitched from a wagon as it passed through a field infested with grasshoppers. The manure provided a rather palatable—at least, to grasshoppers—carrier for the Paris green, and the molasses appealed to the insects' sweet tooth. An "improved" Criddle mixture was developed in 1917, in which a half dozen lemons or oranges were substituted for the molasses, although it was never entirely clear whether fruit juice represented a better feeding stimulant than molasses.

Entomologists rarely achieve much notoriety. Perhaps having a poisonous blend of horse manure named after you is better than anonymity, but this is surely one of the least celebrated paths to fame. Criddle knew that he had been oddly immortalized via his mixture, but he did not know that he would be associated with a rather more pivotal event in the history of the frontier—and particularly, in the story of the Rocky Mountain locust. But then, Criddle's life was one of very peculiar circumstances and events.

Norman Criddle was born in Addlestone, England, in 1875. His father, Percy, was educated in law, medicine, arts, and languages. His mother, Alice, was a graduate of Cambridge University, with a specialty in Sanskrit. Although Norman was Alice's first child, he was Percy's sixth (eventually, Percy would father thirteen). Evidently, Percy was highly attracted to both good books and intelligent women—the latter weakness extending beyond the propriety of Victorian England. Having courted Alice in London and gained her affections, Percy left to study in Heidelberg. There, he commenced a love affair with Elise Vane, who had received her education in Europe's most prestigious universities. Upon completing his studies in Germany, he returned to England with Elise and their five children—and he reestablished his relationship with Alice. Shortly thereafter, he proposed to her, hiding the existence of his other family until after the wedding. In an understatement, the degree of which is only possible in a British account of family history, we learn that "the discovery came as quite a shock." But Percy was apparently both a fertile and a resourceful man. He managed to keep his two households separate and their simultaneous existence secret in the social circles of London, where he worked as a wine merchant. For his part, Norman spent long hours in the garden, learning the names of dozens of plants and insects by the time he was three years old.

After many years of reasonable success in the world of business, Percy decided to start a new life with his two families in Canada. Norman, whose health was fragile at the best of times, suffered immensely on the voyage, but he managed to survive. The overland trip from New York, north to Winnipeg, and then out to Manitoba also was arduous, but the family arrived safely in Manitoba. The only things they lacked upon their arrival in the Wawanesa area were any skills relevant to pioneer life. They were cultured Victorians, intensely interested in intellectual pursuits, sports, and leisure—hardly the foundation for a prairie farm family.

The family's funds were dwindling, but they had more money than know-how. So they paid the neighbors to construct a log house for the two families. What they lacked in ability, the Criddles and Vanes made up for in gumption and labor, and the farm slowly took shape. In time, Percy replaced the log home with a mansion, and Elise and her children moved to a separate house at the edge of the Criddle homestead. The de facto polygamy was wearing on the emotional state of the adults, although the children got along together quite well. In a truly impressive conspiracy of parental misdirection, the children were blissfully unaware that they were half brothers and sisters—a fact that might never have been revealed to them had there not emerged a budding romance between one of the Criddles and one of the Vanes. Upon learning of their relationship, one can imagine that they were every bit as shocked as Alice had been many years earlier.

With his farming enterprise flourishing after much trial and error, Percy put in tennis courts and a nine-hole golf course on his estate. Along with his family, the surrounding community enjoyed these facilities. The open-air life on the prairie invigorated Norman. The frail boy was growing into a strapping young man.

Percy continued to encourage Norman's interest in the natural sciences. The elder Criddle made systematic observations of the plants and animals in his region, but perhaps his greatest infatuation was with the heavens. He had a telescope shipped to him from England and spent long hours peering into the night sky. Percy dreamed of becoming a famous scientist, and when the world-renowned naturalist and writer Ernest Thompson Seton visited the Criddles, Percy hoped that his guest would facilitate the publication of his observations of the local flora and fauna. His ultimate goal was to thereby gain entry into the prestigious scientific societies in the eastern cities. However, Percy's dream never materialized, and it was his son Norman who would be recognized for his contributions to the world of science.

Rather than skating or playing cricket with his siblings, Norman devoted much of his youth to developing and refining his science and art. He learned both the skills of making incisive observations of the natural world and the methods of creating beautiful renderings of the prairie. Soon, he was held in high regard by zoologists, and his paintings of plants brought him considerable fame. In the course of his naturalistic studies and art, Norman made extensive collections of the plants and insects of Manitoba. And it was one such venture in the summer of 1902 that immortalized him in the history of science.

On July 19th of the fateful year, Criddle collected a male and female *Melanoplus spretus* from his father's estate and labeled the specimens according to the standards of museum preservation. Through an untraceable path, over the course of half a century, these specimens found their way into the insect collection of the Smithsonian Institution. Meanwhile, Norman turned his attention to conservation, and he became one of North America's earliest environmentalists trying to preserve Canadian forests and habitats. So it is ironic that his name is most commonly associated with a poisonous manure-based concoction for killing insects. But because of those two specimens housed in America's greatest museum, we also know that this kindly lover of nature can be more fittingly described as the last man to have seen a living Rocky Mountain locust.

WHY NOBODY NOTICED

After the staggering outbreaks of the 1870s, the Rocky Mountain locust irrupted sporadically until the turn of the century. The realization that the locust was gone dawned very slowly in America's heartland. It seems incredible that the loss of an insect that eclipsed the sun would not be readily apparent and even widely hailed. By way of modern comparison, if in the course of a few years hurricanes stopped pummeling the coastline of the United States, we'd surely catch on to the absence of these natural disasters. There would be congressional investigations, research initiatives, media speculations, and plenty of armchair science going on. So, how could the disappearance of a creature as obvious as the Rocky Mountain locust go unnoticed?

Although one might guess otherwise based on patterns of coastal home building, hurricanes strike the eastern seaboard every year. Sometimes there are significantly more or fewer storms than "normal" (which works out to about six hurricanes between June and November), and sometimes they arrive with unforgettable fury. The names Andrew, Camille, and Hugo stir memories of awesome power and incomprehensible destruction. As sure as the waters of the Atlantic warm in late summer, the tropical storms will develop, and some will grow into full-fledged hurricanes. Locust outbreaks were quite another story. Many years could pass without swarms of these creatures sweeping down from the Rockies. At least some western states reported no locusts for periods of five to ten years. Although there were small swarms most every year, full-fledged plagues were erratic events. So, when the storm clouds of locusts failed to darken the skies over the Great Plains for years, people were not particularly encouraged—or surprised.

We would be less likely to notice a lack of hurricanes if, during the time of their absence, tornadoes, blizzards, droughts, and floods occurred with increasing intensity. An increase in one type of disastrous weather event might well obscure the disappearance of another. While the Rocky Mountain locust was fading into the past, other grasshoppers rushed to fill the empty niche—ready and able to take the locust's place in harassing prairie farmers. Ecologists use the term *competitive exclusion* to describe the phenomenon in which species prevent one another from exploiting the same set of resources. The legendary American ecologist Aldo Leopold wrote in his *Sand County Almanac,* "Just as there is honor among thieves, so there is solidarity and co-operation among plant and animal pests. Where one pest is stopped by natural barriers, another arrives to breach the same wall by a new approach. In the end every region and every resource get their quota of uninvited guests."*

This exploitation of opportunity is a bit like the world of business. For a while there might be both eight-track players and cassettes, or Betamax and VHS formats, but eventually competitive exclusion takes hold. In short order, the niche is filled and fiercely protected by one or the other of the product manufacturers. And if the Rocky Mountain locust of the computer world suddenly disappeared—if Microsoft collapsed—we could be sure that another operating system would quickly fill the gap. Likewise, when the American chestnut— the dominant hardwood tree of the eastern United States—disappeared from the landscape in the early half of the last century because of a blight, our forests filled in with other species. It seems that nature abhors a vacuum in ecology, as well as in physics.

Serious outbreaks of two close relatives of the locust stifled whatever sigh of relief might have come with the demise of the Rocky Mountain locust. The migratory grasshopper, *Melanoplus sanguinipes*, and the redlegged grasshopper, *Melanoplus femurrubrum*, were waiting in the wings. With the curtain falling on the locust, these other grasshopper species rushed onto the stage. Minnesota's Agricultural Experiment Station reported terrific infestations of the migratory grasshopper in the early 1890s, and farmers in western Colorado, Kansas, and Nebraska battled grasshoppers at the turn of the century. In what seemed a weird act of insectan revenge, for the three years after Norman Criddle caught the last known Rocky Mountain locusts, farmers in Manitoba were inundated with grasshoppers.

Farmers in the Plains states barely had time to relish their scattered victories before the grasshoppers resurged in 1908 and persisted until 1912. And as grasshoppers were retreating in the United States, they were advancing again in western Canada, with a major outbreak lasting from 1912 to 1914. The two species that ravaged the farms of the Midwest were joined by others in Canada, including the two-striped grasshopper and the clearwinged grasshopper. Five years later,

---

*In this 1949 classic, Leopold also celebrated the contributions of four amateur naturalists— and one of these was Norman Criddle, whom Leopold saw as an authority "on everything from local botany to wildlife cycles."

Kansans plowed thousands of miles of roadsides and fencerows to destroy grasshopper eggs. And when this campaign failed to control the outbreak, they applied nearly 7 million pounds of poison bait, including the "Criddle mixture," to an area larger than the state of Delaware. Sporadic grasshopper damage was reported across the West throughout the 1920s.

Grasshoppers and drought devastated the Great Plains during the "Dirty Thirties," and what the grasshoppers didn't eat, the dust covered. In Missouri, the grasshopper damage from 1935 to 1938 was termed the "worst since 1874–76," an allusion to the days of the Rocky Mountain locust. From 1938 to 1940 vast areas of the West were crawling with infestations of the migratory grasshopper. Some of these populations matured into locustlike swarms capable of traveling thirty miles or more a day. In the midst of this outbreak, New Mexico and Texas mobilized their National Guards to deliver poison bait to afflicted farmers and ranchers, echoing the role of the military as a means of provisioning agricultural communities sixty-five years earlier. Kansas alone lost $21 million worth of crops to the grasshoppers in a single year.

As damaging as these grasshopper infestations were, they paled in comparison to the psychological, sociological, political, and economic damage wrought by the Rocky Mountain locust. The grasshoppers were largely of local origin, and the swarms of migratory grasshoppers were only a pallid imitation of the cataclysmic inundations by the mighty locust. Because the intensity and scale of destruction by grasshoppers were more limited and the tools for pest management were better known (in large part as a result of the work of the U.S. Entomological Commission, as at least some of their methods were applicable to these insects), grasshopper infestations were less traumatic. Furthermore, agriculture was on a more stable footing, and established farms had a greater economic capacity to battle the grasshoppers and absorb losses than the homesteaders had just a few decades earlier. Finally, state and federal governments had developed rather sophisticated capacities for assessing and mobilizing resources during natural disasters. Although grasshoppers could not equal the locusts when it came to provoking fear and causing damage, there was enough similarity to exploit allusions to the old enemy in securing resources to battle the new foe.

The political motivation for the federal government to subsidize the control programs by providing poison bait harked back to the days of the Rocky Mountain locust. Some of the allusions were reminiscent in their language, crossing into biological hyperbole, such as the impassioned editorial in the *Minneapolis Tribune*:

> The grasshopper, numbered by billions, with an insatiable appetite, is crawling out of the sod of North Dakota, South Dakota, Minnesota, and Montana.
>
> . . . Once he has wings he can mount thousands of feet into the air. He can fly with the winds hundreds of miles in all directions. He can come down in thick clouds on fields and strip them clean of vegetation in a few hours.
>
> He can devour our billion-dollar crop, the first we have had in years. He can leave thousands of farmers without enough food for themselves and their livestock. Last year the Red Cross fed 40,000 farmers in the two Dakotas.
>
> . . . This year the condition of the crops is excellent—either for the grasshoppers or the farmers. If we let the grasshoppers alone there will be no harvest, there will be more appeals to the Red Cross, more money asked from the Government, and stagnation throughout the Northwest.
>
> A million and a half dollars will save our crop. A misinformed Congress neglected to make the necessary appropriation with which to buy poison bait. Congress can still remedy this disastrous mistake. Congress will do so if the Northwest will only speak its mind.
>
> . . . If we do not take this precaution we have every prospect of bare fields, gaunt cattle, and pall of gloom over the land. Deserted farms, vacant stores, closed banks will greet the eye in every direction. And thousands of men and women, the backbone of our Government and the foundation of our institutions, will give way to despair.

Even the Secretary of Agriculture got into the act. Arthur Mastick Hyde was born in the midst of the Rocky Mountain locust's grand finale and had served as the governor of Missouri. So perhaps Hyde can be forgiven for his letter to Congress in 1932 in which he allows his language to slip, referring to the notion that any control campaign should "poison the young locusts as they first emerge from the egg beds and before they have any opportunity to migrate from such areas in the fields." Most of the rest of his letter refers to the insects as "grasshoppers" and suggests that it might be too late to act, but his use of the term *locusts* early in his message was surely a provocative linguistic tactic.

Within Congress, references to the locust plagues of fifty years earlier were even less subtle. Perhaps the most dramatic testimony was offered by Edward Thomas Taylor from Colorado. Serving in the House of Representatives for thirty-two years (no one from his own Democratic Party dared oppose him), Taylor carried great political weight in Congress. He authored the Taylor Grazing Act, which is the law that still governs livestock grazing on public lands. His personal tale, along with his enormous political will, undoubtedly influenced his fellow members of Congress in their decision to provide assistance in battling the grasshopper outbreak: "Mr. Speaker, like the gentleman from Texas, I had a sad personal experience with grasshoppers. When I was a small boy [Taylor was born in 1858] my parents located on the extreme frontier of northwestern Kansas, and for three years everything we planted was eaten by grasshoppers [almost certainly the Rocky Mountain locust]. We were compelled to practically walk out of that country, disheartened and completely bankrupt, so I know what this scourge is."

To obscure matters even more, the migratory and redlegged grasshopper looks a lot like the Rocky Mountain locust. Although they don't form the breathtaking swarms or reach the astounding densities, there can be a hundred or more per square yard, stretching across thousands of acres. In the early decades of the twentieth century, many agriculturalists assumed that the grasshopper infestations that devastated their crops were localized outbreaks of the locust. Even species utterly unlike the Rocky Mountain locust—at least to the eye of an entomologist—were confused with this species. In Minnesota, farmers were convinced that they were being overrun by the locust when the culprit was the Carolina grasshopper—a species that is dusty brown (rather than olive green), has jet-black hindwings (rather than colorless wings), and is twice the size of the Rocky Mountain locust. Utah farmers confused infestations of the clear-winged grasshopper, which does bear a very superficial resemblance to the Rocky Mountain locust, with their old nemesis.

Grasshopper problems—and federal subsidies for their control, rooted in the cultural memory of the locust plagues—have continued sporadically into the present. When I joined the entomology faculty at the University of Wyoming in 1986, grasshoppers were once again devastating western agriculture—and 20 million acres of insecticide treatments did little to stem the tide. A grasshopper outbreak in 1998 encompassed 430 million acres of the West (an expanse ten times larger than New England or about the combined areas of France, Germany, Italy, and Spain) and caused $500 million in damage. And the outbreak unfolding across the West at the turn of the twenty-first century once again released a flood of federal funds. So perhaps it is no wonder that people failed to note the passing of a locust, when its relatives were trying so valiantly, albeit less dramatically, to fill those big, empty shoes.

The social psychology of the news has changed little in the past century. Let's say that this summer no hurricanes strike our shores. We wouldn't expect a headline announcing, "Good News: No Killer Storms Yet." Even if we went into early fall without a hurricane, it seems unlikely that their absence would galvanize the media. If there are no hurricanes with which to draw viewers and thereby sell advertising on the nightly news, surely there is an epidemic, a war, or a political scandal. Thus, it is hardly surprising that when locusts didn't return to the farmlands of the Great Plains, the newspapers failed to proclaim the good news. The absence of locust swarms was noted in passing within a few agricultural reports. But even technical publications are reluctant to report what scientists refer to as *negative results*. Scientific journals don't tend to publish papers that list a whole bunch of chemicals that won't cause cancer, species that aren't becoming extinct, or pests that aren't outbreaking.

Even when the grasshoppers were newsworthy in their depredations, they had the cards stacked against them in terms of publicity. When the insects were booming, as in the early 1900s, rebellions, earthquakes, monopolies, and World War I became the crises du jour. In fact, grasshopper and locust outbreaks often correspond with other natural and economic disasters. These insects flourish during droughts. And crop failures may have precipitated, or at least exacerbated, economic depressions, especially during more agricultural times. Thus, reports of these insects were often moved aside for more compelling accounts of human suffering.

If hurricanes were to decline in frequency and severity, our National Weather Service would surely note the change. After all, we have a National Hurricane Center that employs a cadre of scientists to keep track of these storms, and they'd start getting nervous if we ran out of hurricanes. But with the collapse of the Rocky Mountain locust outbreak in the late 1870s, the coordinated national survey of the U.S. Entomological Commission dissolved as USDA entomologists turned their attention to other pests and the state entomologists returned to local problems. In short, it wasn't anyone's job to notice that the locusts weren't still around. But this isn't to say that various folks didn't eventually catch on.

A Montana entomologist might have been the first to sound a note of suspicion in 1904, in reporting that he'd failed to collect a specimen in five years. In 1913, the Nebraska state entomologist added, "So far as our information goes, the true Rocky Mountain grasshopper did not occur anywhere in the state during the abnormal abundance of grasshoppers in the past four years." At the same time, Melvin P. Somes, a rather peripatetic entomologist then working in Minnesota, became the first person to broach the possibility of extinction. He suggested that the Rocky Mountain locust, "is today apparently extinct, or practically so."

The author of a 1917 bulletin from the Utah Agricultural Experiment Station took a rather more cautious stand, noting, "The Rocky Mountain locust, with its long wings and wonderful power of flight, is a thing of the past. Like the buffalo, another inhabitant of the same region, his millions have dwindled almost to extinction. We still see the buffalo in our parks and museums, but a Rocky Mountain locust would be a greater curiosity today than a buffalo." The writer maintained that he'd kept a sharp lookout for this species in all his travels in the West since 1900 and had not seen a single one.

In the same year, Norman Criddle—unaware that he was likely the last human to see the Rocky Mountain locust—was also struggling to comprehend the locust's vanishing act. He'd received a government appointment and funds for a laboratory a few years earlier, and he was quickly making his mark in the field of entomology. He wrote:

> There is somewhat of a mystery surrounding this insect at the present time which may, indeed, never be solved. We know that its breeding grounds once extended over a very wide area, much of this having been classed as permanent by Riley and others who investigated the plague at that time.

By now, Criddle hadn't seen a locust for fifteen years, and it was starting to look as if Riley's Permanent Zone was incredibly ephemeral.

Cognitive dissonance—the utter disbelief that a creature so abundant, so absolutely dominant on a continental scale could actually be gone—became the prevailing mind-set. The USDA reflected this uncertainty in its noncommittal position in 1927. The agency simply stated that the Rocky Mountain locust had "ceased to be a pest of any great importance." In our hypothetical scenario involving hurricanes, the National Weather Service might similarly hedge its statements: "Tropical storms of hurricane intensity have, for some time, ceased to be significant weather events." But government scientists were not the only ones reluctant to declare that events of such staggering proportions as locust plagues were safely relegated to history. Even in 1931, more than forty years after the last encounter with a locust swarm in his state, William W. Henderson, an entomologist from Utah, couldn't bring himself to believe that this species was gone. He maintained that the disappearance was more a matter of muddled science than an ecological reality: "What has become of the old-time Rocky Mountain locust causing clouds in the sky several miles wide, 10 or 12 miles long, and thick enough to hide the sun? It is probably extant, if it were possible to solve the confusion associated with it."

Norman Criddle died in 1933, still uncertain as to the fate of the Rocky Mountain locust. However, his inability to come to terms with the disappearance of this creature was echoed in expressions of ambivalence that prevailed into the 1950s. USDA scientists cautiously noted that there had been "no recurrence of the tremendous, devastating flights of the last century." The foremost experts felt compelled to leave open the possibility that the Rocky Mountain locust was still lurking in a remote corner of the West. And such became the standard view in science.

From the turn of the last century to the turn of the present one, entomologists gradually accepted that the Rocky Mountain locust was not coming back. Today, they now openly and flatly assert that locust swarms are a thing of the past. If pushed, some might concede that a few individuals of the Rocky Mountain locust could be hiding out somewhere like an aging gang of bandits. But as a force of nature this species is a washed-up has-been with no possibility of returning to its former glory.

The history of the last 120 years leaves no doubt that the Rocky Mountain locust—at least, the ecological manifestation of this creature—is gone. The caveat here reveals a profound intuition about what is "real" in the natural world. It is as if the swarm or even the process of swarming, rather than the individual locusts within the swarm, constituted this remarkable species. This insight is counter to the material terms in which we usually conceive of the world. For example, we typically define a species as a bunch of individuals with the capacity to successfully interbreed. But this definition presumes the metaphysical truth of materialism. It equates being real with being made of matter, and the Rocky Mountain locust challenges this perception.

Ecology is beginning to slowly shift focus with tentative explorations of what the world would look like if process, rather than matter, were the basis for reality. What if we defined a species in terms of its life processes? We might seriously doubt whether the California condor or the tallgrass prairie can be "saved" or even "restored." Perhaps we can re-create some local conditions that foster a few nests of condors or a few acres of prairie. But the life process of the condor ended with the urbanization of the California foothills, and the living ebb and flow of the tallgrass prairies died with the plowing of the Great Plains. What if we suggested that a thing *is* what it *does*? In this light, the Rocky Mountain locust was an immense, aperiodic energy flow that linked life processes on a continental scale.

If we choose to describe the locust as a process, there is no doubt that this species was extinct in the late 1800s. That is, its ecological role and biological activities ceased well before its last corporeal manifestation disappeared. This notion of life-as-process might seem unusual in a society in which material existence is primary. But such a perception informs our deepest understanding of life. Indeed, life-as-process underlies our notion of euthanasia. When loved ones are simply bodies, devoid of the capacity to care, respond, or relate ever again in a way that we can recognize as being "them," we understand that they are gone even before they are dead.

There is no question that the Rocky Mountain locust as a dynamic phenomenon disappeared a century ago. But biological existence is far more often transformed than destroyed. How many of us could see a gorgeous flitting butterfly and then identify the drab caterpillar from which it metamorphosed, or pass by the sandstone formations of the desert Southwest and recognize them as the resurrected seafloor of the Cretaceous? Although swarms of locusts no longer descend on our towns and farms, could the Rocky Mountain locust itself—the material entity—still exist, but in a form that we don't readily recognize?

When Charles Riley witnessed clouds of locusts and Norman Criddle held the last known specimens, these eminent scientists did not imagine that the locust had a great secret. They knew that some insects could metamorphose from larva, to pupa, to adult. The other insects, including the grasshoppers, become gradually larger without any radical changes in form. A newly hatched grasshopper looks very much like a miniature version of the adult. It lacks wings, but most people would, with a bit of magnification, immediately recognize it as a "baby grasshopper." Locusts, however, represent an entirely different capacity to change their form. This ability to transform their identity confused biologists for nearly 200 years—and cast our understanding of the Rocky Mountain locust's identity and fate into disarray for much of the twentieth century.

A Wolf in Sheep's Clothing?

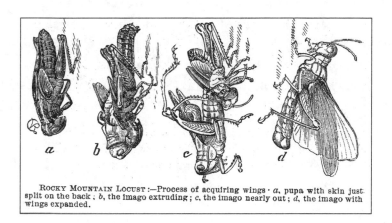

ROCKY MOUNTAIN LOCUST :—Process of acquiring wings · *a*, pupa with skin just split on the back ; *b*, the imago extruding ; *c*, the imago nearly out ; *d*, the imago with wings expanded.

IN 1889, THE CRIDDLES' ESTATE BECAME THE FOCUS of attention for the district. People were coming from all over the countryside to observe the total solar eclipse through Percy's exquisite telescope. At the same time, 6,000 miles due east, Alexandra Uvarov was giving birth to her third son. Boris Petrovich Uvarov had the great good fortune of being born into a family that loved to spend time in the countryside, and of being born into a countryside with a remarkable diversity of grasshoppers, crickets, and katydids. Although the steppe surrounding his hometown was arid and uninviting, Uralsk lay along the Ural River—an oasis teeming with life just inside the border of modern-day Kazakhstan. The Uvarovs went on family outings, filling their horse-drawn wagon with tents, pots, fishing gear, and the family cat. Perhaps this affinity for nature was particularly important for his father, Petr, who worked as a state bank employee and could not have found much of the "tonic of wilderness" within the gray walls of a financial institution. The family spent week-ends camping and hiking, and it was not long before young Boris began collecting insects as a hobby. His drawers of meticulously prepared specimens yielded several prizes, and the teachers at the Agricultural School encouraged him with high praise.

At the age of fifteen, Uvarov began his higher education at the School of Mining in Ekaterinoslav but soon transferred to the University of St. Petersburg. Although this university later developed a premier program in entomology, in earlier days it did not provide an optimal setting for the study of insects. And so, Uvarov settled into a less conventional but decidedly effective "school" while attending the university. He discovered the wonders of the Russian Entomological Society, which held informal meetings every Monday and hosted the reading of scientific papers once a month. The budding scientist was entranced with the opportunity to mingle with the most eminent entomologists in all of Russia.

Through the society, Uvarov was allowed to visit the entomological section of the Zoological Museum in the Academy of Sciences, and he became infatuated with insect taxonomy as surely as a moth is drawn to a flame. In the midst of this love affair, a seminal book on the Orthoptera (the order of insects that includes the grasshoppers, locusts, crickets, and katydids) of the Russian Empire was published in St. Petersburg, and Uvarov's passion became keenly focused. He wrote his diploma paper on the Orthoptera of his beloved homeland, the Uralsk province, basing the manuscript on the collections he had made during summer holidays. Little did he realize that this was the first step toward publishing nearly 500 scientific papers on various aspects of grasshoppers and locusts.

Upon his graduation, Uvarov's life turned from the quiet and intense studies of a university student to the whirlwind of marriage and work. He was appointed as the entomologist to Murgab Crown Cotton Estate in Transcarpia, but a year later he returned to St. Petersburg to join the Department of Agriculture. Romance became a centerpiece of his life. The young scientist had the "white nights" of summer in Russia's most cultured and elegant city to share with his wife, Anna. And he was seduced by opportunities to foster his intellectual passion through travel to the Northern Caucasus for his other great love—locusts.

At twenty-three, he became the first director of the Entomological Bureau at Stavropol, a hotbed of locust outbreaks northeast of the Black Sea. He worked on developing control methods for the Migratory and Moroccan locusts, two of the most devastating insects of Russian agriculture. It was here that Uvarov witnessed a bizarre and initially puzzling spectacle. During his fieldwork, he saw mixed populations of a benign grasshopper and a devastating locust—along with some odd intermediate forms. These observations would serve as the foundation for a theory that would revolutionize entomology, but the idea was so radical that he would not feel confident enough to develop and reveal it for nearly another ten years. While pondering this heretical notion he continued to advance in his career. Uvarov organized plant protection stations and labored to help farmers battle locusts, as their counterparts had done with the help of Riley a generation earlier on the steppes of North America.

Life in Russia deteriorated for Uvarov following Vladimir Lenin's ascendancy to power. The young scientist had been educated during the reign of the czars, and intellectuals were highly suspect in the new Soviet order. In 1919, Uvarov was sent to Georgia, essentially exiled to a distant outpost. He became the Keeper of Entomology and Zoology in the State Museum of Georgia and reader at the State University in Tiflis, reasonably prestigious positions but rife with tension. As a Russian, he was treated poorly by his colleagues. Georgian nationalism was intense, and the people had little toleration for Russians on their soil. To make matters worse, the instability of the early years following the revolution made the new Soviet Union prone to political and military incursions. The same year that Uvarov arrived so did the British army, occupying Tiflis as part of the Allied Intervention that was intended to support Georgian autonomy while sustaining British access to the oil-rich Transcaucasus. The presence of foreign troops irritated the Soviets but proved a blessing to the Russian entomologist.

Uvarov was in increasingly dire straits. He went long periods without pay and often resorted to selling homemade pies in the market square before heading to the museum or university. He was despised by the Georgians as a Russian invader, he was being scrutinized by the Soviets as a member of the elite of the Russian Empire—and he was the husband of an anxious wife and the father of a young son. Uvarov's salvation came through his befriending Patrick A. Buxton, a British officer who was just two years his junior. They must have made an interesting pair—the slight, almost frail, entomologist and the strapping English officer. To Uvarov's great fortune, Buxton was not only an intriguing companion but also well-connected to movers and shakers within the British government. Just a year later, Uvarov received an appointment to the Imperial Bureau of Entomology in London. He would not return to Russia for nearly fifty years.

Freed from the economic and social constraints of Soviet tyranny, the Uvarovs flourished in London. Boris and Anna allowed only the speaking of Russian at home, but they embraced their new life and were warmly accepted into British social circles. At the bureau, however, Uvarov walked a thin line. He was adept at using his supposed awkwardness with English to his advantage, choosing phrases that were painfully direct to the cultured sensibilities of the British. His convenient failure to find the suitably obtuse terms that sustained a genteel air meant that he could be stunningly direct and remarkably effective while skirting the edge of decorum. After a particularly grueling session with an advisory committee, Sir Geoffrey Evans sighed deeply and said, "Uvarov will never learn to understand our English ways!" In fact, Uvarov had become quite familiar with British obfuscation, but he'd found a clever means of avoiding the tedium and formality. Perhaps his approach would not have been as tolerated, or become as oddly endearing, if Uvarov had not also quickly become known as a scientist of tremendous intelligence and vitality. In addition, his small stature and dry sense of humor made his overwhelmingly powerful mind rather less threatening to those around him.

Uvarov's new sense of opportunity and release infused him with the courage to put his ideas regarding the nature of locusts into print. His willingness to present his revolutionary theory to the world after a decade of incubation may also have been prompted by communications with a South African colleague, Jacobus C. Faure. Just as Charles Darwin's publication of his theory of evolution was catalyzed by his realization that Alfred Wallace was close to arriving at—and publishing—the same ideas, Uvarov knew that Faure's work with locusts in Africa was leading him to the same radical notion that

Uvarov had first glimpsed in the Northern Caucuses. And so, in the *Bulletin of Entomological Research*, now one of the oldest and most distinguished journals in entomology, Uvarov published "A Revision of the Genus *Locusta* with a New Theory as to the Periodicity and Migrations of Locusts."

A NEW KIND OF METAMORPHOSIS

In his twenty-nine-page paper, Uvarov undertook what is called a *taxonomic revision*. In biology, the naming of species and their proper assignment to a particular genus are matters of continual investigation. Often we discover specimens or anatomical features that make us rethink whether a species has been properly described, named, and grouped. The goal is to have our taxonomy reflect the underlying biology that defines a species—the sharing of genetic material. Because we rarely have the time or opportunity (the seeming impropriety of biological voyeurism being of less concern) to follow creatures around and see if they are mating and then track the females to see if their offspring are viable, taxonomists use the bodies of organisms as surrogates for genetic similarity. Creatures that look the same presumably have a common gene pool. This approach has recently been challenged by our ability to more directly assess genetic similarity with molecular techniques. Zoologists are finding that sometimes animals that are physically indistinguishable do not share a genetic heritage. However, in 1921 Uvarov was struggling with the opposite problem. He was convinced that what earlier taxonomists had described as two species were really one.

Uvarov introduced his study by noting, "The literature on the economics, biology and especially on the means of control of these locusts is enormously extensive, but at the same time their systematic arrangement is in considerable confusion, and extremely contradictory opinions as to the mutual relationship of the different so-called species exist among specialists." His particular concern was related to two species that to most people were so clearly different that no confusion should have been possible: *Locusta danica* and *Locusta migratoria*. The former species was a grasshopper leading a rather solitary existence and creating no fuss on the part of farmers. But the latter species congregated in staggering numbers, maturing into the devastating swarms of migratory locusts that had caused famines for centuries in Central Asia. The ecologies of the two species were completely divergent. *Danica* was found in many habitat types, including dry grasslands, but *migratoria* was largely restricted to the basins of the Caspian and Aral Seas and Lake Balkash. The locust bred in the reeds of the river deltas, from where the immense swarms would emanate and sweep across the fertile irrigated farmlands of the region.

Based on anatomical appearances, the two species seemed to have very little in common. *Danica* was a bright green creature, whereas *migratoria* was quite variable but often black and orange red. The females of *danica* were much larger than the males, while in *migratoria* the sexes were nearly the same size. Uvarov also noted that the body of *migratoria* was very well suited for flight, with impressively elongated wings and a body filled with air sacs, which he noted were "described long ago by American entomologists in the Rocky Mountain locust, and occurring doubtless in all other migrating species of locusts."

So, if the two species lived in different habitats, behaved in dissimilar ways, and looked markedly distinct, what was the problem? The problem was that Uvarov had witnessed the transformation of *danica*, the insectan Dr. Jekyll, into *migratoria*, the hexapodian Mr. Hyde.

In 1912, Uvarov had arrived in Stavropol, a town on the bridge of land between the Caspian and Black Seas, in time to see swarms of *migratoria* descending on the countryside. Such events were not at all unusual, but it was uncommon for a scientist to thoroughly sample the infestation and follow these locusts through the course of their subsequent generation. When the locusts hatched the next year, Uvarov found a mixed population of *migratoria* and *danica*, a most remarkable discovery given that there were absolutely no *danica* present in 1912. It seemed that *migratoria* was transforming into *danica*. To make matters even more intriguing, he soon learned that the reverse process was also possible.

In correspondence with his friend Vassily Plotnikov, who was working in Uzbekistan, Uvarov learned of experiments in which his colleague had reared *danica* in crowded cages. According to these studies conducted in the summer of 1913, Plotnikov told his friend that "a number of them [nymphs] had the typical colouring of *migratoria*." Uvarov, already a respected taxonomist, was sent some of these insects, and he confirmed that the parents were indeed *danica* and the offspring were well-defined *migratoria*. Plotnikov thought that perhaps they were seeing evolution unfolding before their eyes, and he suggested, "It is possible to suppose that this species is now in the process of splitting off from the primitive species." But Uvarov had an even more intriguing explanation, one that would forever change our views of locust biology, ecology, and control.

Uvarov's revolutionary paper included a three-page section, "The Theory of Phases," in which he laid out his concept for *Locusta danica*, *migratoria*, and *migratoriodes*. This third creature was an African species that was indistinguishable from the Asian *migratoria*, but the two species had been named in the early days of entomology, when communications among taxonomists were erratic at best. Uvarov knew that a single widely distributed species was sometimes independently assigned different names by scientists working in different lands or languages. That took care of merging *migratoria* and *migratoriodes*, but what of *danica*? He made the radical argument that, "as a starting point, I take it as positively proved that the three forms cannot be separated specifically and that they represent taxonomic units of lower grade than the species, which must be called, according to the law of priority, *L. migratoria*."

The law to which he was referring is the International Code for Zoological Nomenclature, which is a set of rules and standards originally developed by a commission of scientists in 1895. This code is one of the few international laws that seems to be both widely recognized and consistently enforced, perhaps because its provisions don't really matter to the big issues of the modern world and the worst penalty for breaking the law is that everyone ignores you. Under this code, when a species has been mistakenly assigned two (or three or more) different names, the earliest given name is retained. Carolus Linnaeus, the Swedish-born Father of Taxonomy, had first named this creature *migratoria* in 1758. Thus, Uvarov used this name to unite the three, formerly distinct, species.

Uvarov then argued that the forms were not simply individual aberrations (such as genetic mutations), subspecies (a term used for different geographical races of a species), or seasonal forms (like the summer and winter coats of snowshoe hares or arctic foxes). He settled on a new term, *phases*, and stated that these phases—the solitary *danica* and the gregarious *migratoria/migratoriodes*—are manifestations of a single species that can be transformed from one to the other and back again. Although he wasn't entirely sure of the factors causing the phase transformations, he knew that they were somehow associated with external conditions and strongly suspected that population density played a role. In this sense, the phase theory was much like Darwin's evolutionary theory: In both cases the process of biological transformation was correctly identified, but the underlying mechanisms were not understood. The mechanisms of genetics and the structure of DNA eventually revealed the workings of evolutionary change. And we have now pieced together the ecological triggers and physiological mechanisms of phase transformations.

Different organisms have adapted in various ways to the boom-and-bust cycles of productivity that typify continental climates, and the locusts evolved phase change as a means of tracking ephemeral resources. During normal years, the locusts persist in their solitary phase, generally avoiding one another to more evenly exploit the available resources. In moist years, their populations begin to increase within their breeding areas. This increase may be sufficient to cause crowding in some habitats such as deserts, where food is normally scarce. In habitats with more reliable food, such as grasslands and meadows, crowding occurs when productive periods are followed by droughts that force the abundant insects into close contact while competing for declining food. In either case, the gregarious phase is triggered by the insects' endocrine system, which is cued both by chemicals released from the crowded insects via their accumulating excrement and by the frequent disturbance of tiny hairs on the hind legs of the creatures.

Although outwardly unchanged themselves, the crowded females lay eggs that are biochemically predisposed to develop into nymphs with a predilection for aggregating rather than scattering. This tendency is reinforced as the growing nymphs are compelled to congregate in the shrinking patches of lush grasses, caused by overpopulation, the onset of drought, or both. The constant jostling and odor of feces continue to induce endocrine changes that complete the locusts' transformation into the migratory phase. The changes in the insect's morphology (such as lengthened wings), behavior (such as the propensity to aggregate), and physiology (such as the delayed maturation of eggs) are all in preparation for migration. For locusts, crowding means an impending famine, and migration into the unknown is preferable to sure starvation.

Of course, this process of transformation is entirely reversible. As the population density declines due to a swarm's being dispersed or suffering high mortality, the cues that elicit development of the gregarious phase diminish. The eggs laid by scattered adults tend to develop into rather unsociable nymphs. With low densities and solitary behavior, the nymphs rarely encounter one another (or other locusts' feces). And so, the locusts transform back into their solitary phase until such time as environmental conditions induce a surge of reproduction, a period of crowding, the possibility of famine, and the compulsion to migrate.

If the phase transformation process of locusts were applied to humans, we would find that an economic downturn had caused our neighborhoods to smell like a sewer and our fellow commuters were constantly pushing and shoving us on the way to work. These sensory insults would trigger hormonal changes turning us into a mob of anxious, red-faced neurotics with a reduced libido and an intense desire to charter a fleet of planes. As the planes unloaded us along the way (or perhaps our ranks thinned by plane crashes), our population density would decline. The stench and jostling would diminish, and we would revert to reclusive, pale-faced homebodies. Perhaps locusts and humans have more in common than we suppose.

Although Uvarov did not understand the biochemical mechanisms, he correctly predicted that the capacity of locusts to radically change their form and function was not restricted to the species that he had investigated. He made explicit mention of Faure's work on the Brown locust of South Africa, noting, "These valuable observations of Mr. Faure's leave no doubt that *L. pardalina* has, like *L. migratoria*, two different phases, which differ in morphology and coloration, but more profoundly in the biology." So whereas Darwin was reluctant to share the limelight of evolutionary theory with Wallace, Uvarov took pains to credit his colleague: "The above-quoted conclusions of Mr. Jacobus C. Faure concerning the transformation of the solitary phase into the swarming one, at which he arrived quite independently of my work on *migratoria*, give a very strong support to the theory of phases as a direct cause of the periodicity."

Uvarov was not a taxonomist of the sort so stridently despised by Riley forty-five years earlier. Not only was Uvarov happiest when working in the field, but he also cared deeply about the use of his studies in alleviating human suffering from the ravages of locust plagues. His insights into the proper identification of *L. migratoria* were eventually recognized as "the greatest contribution ever made by a taxonomist in the solution of a major economic problem." Uvarov immediately understood that his theory would lead to new and powerful means of controlling locusts. Rather than having to wait until they were swarming over the countryside, it would be possible to find and suppress the harmless "grasshopper" (solitary phase) and thereby prevent outbreaks of the rapacious "locust" (gregarious phase). This strategy of preventive control, rather like the suppression of forest fires by finding and quenching lightning strikes before they transform into conflagrations, has come to serve as the foundation for modern locust management programs around the world.

Uvarov was a scientist far ahead of his time with regard to conceptualizing the natural world. The modern science of complexity with all of its attendant forms (chaos, catastrophe theory, self-organized criticality, etc.) constitutes a beautiful and compelling mathematical formalization of the concept that Uvarov articulated for biology and Karl Marx expressed for political economy: "Quantitative differences beyond a certain point pass into qualitative changes." Or, as so concisely expressed by the physicist P. W. Anderson, "More is different." The principle is that in many complex, natural systems, as we increase pressure, size, density, or time, what often emerges is a sudden shift in form or function. With gradually mounting loads, girders instantly snap; with continuously looming intruders, dogs switch from submission to attack; and with slowly decreasing temperature, liquids suddenly solidify. The field of complexity has made exciting progress toward working out the mathematics pertaining to these discontinuities in the natural world. However, it seems somehow arrogant to be declaring that we are creating a "new science," when the fundamental concept of emergence—the appearance of entirely new forms and processes that were not predictable from, and are not reducible to, smaller and simpler scales—was so elegantly and explicitly stated by our predecessors. In 1921 Boris Uvarov comprehended that beyond a certain point, population density triggered a qualitative change in locusts. Perhaps the notion was pervasive among intellectuals in the 1920s, as a pithy dialogue from Paris suggests. F. Scott Fitzgerald commented, "The rich are different from you and me," to which a young Ernest Hemingway replied, "Yes, they have more money."

The phase theory of locusts would prove to be a phase transition in the life of Boris Uvarov. He rapidly transformed into one of the most powerful, effective, and important figures in twentieth-century entomology. Uvarov developed the Anti-Locust Research Centre and virtually created the locust management unit within the Food and Agriculture Organization of the United Nations, which to this day provides global leadership. His philosophy of locust control echoed the sentiments of C. V. Riley—both men argued in favor of ecologically based pest management, eschewing insecticides. And his personality was reminiscent of Riley's in some ways. He did not suffer fools gladly but was far more approachable and personable than his predecessor. Uvarov was eminently practical while being well grounded in the principles of the biological sciences. Like Riley, he was intolerant of bumbling bureaucracy—even to the point of biting the hand that fed him, but not to the point of professional self-destruction. As evidence that his up-to-the-edge diplomatic skills were finely honed, the British honored this brilliant scientist with knighthood in 1961. Sir Boris Uvarov left a brilliant two-volume compendium on grasshoppers and locusts, in which he synthesized more than 7,000 scientific papers published between 1950 and 1970. These books still serve as the definitive synthesis for acridology—a term that he coined for the study of grasshoppers and locusts (family Acrididae). And for those who were trying to explain the Rocky Mountain locust's disappearance, Uvarov's phase theory would provide one of the most trouble-

some false leads in the case—and, eventually, one of the most important clues in solving the mystery.

THE SEARCH FOR THE DR. JEKYLL OF
NORTH AMERICAN LOCUSTS

Even before Uvarov's work, entomologists in the United States had a
vague impression that perhaps the Rocky Mountain locust was an insect
changeling. A report on the grasshoppers of Minnesota in 1913 noted
that to "the student who wishes an idea as to the appearance of the
Rocky Mountain locust, we may say that, with a rather large and somewhat light-colored specimen of [the migratory grasshopper] in hand, by
extending the tegmina and wings somewhat in imagination, he may
have a very good idea of the pest of the early days." Such suspicions
took on new life with Uvarov's phase theory. Perhaps the Rocky Mountain locust was not extinct, only quiescent. Could it be that this locust
was the migratory phase of a species still living right under our noses?

If *Melanoplus spretus* was a migratory Mr. Hyde, there were two
candidates for Dr. Jekyll. These suspects were the grasshoppers that
had apparently filled the niche vacated by the Rocky Mountain locust
at the turn of the century. The long-shot candidate for the role of Dr.
Jekyll was the redlegged grasshopper, which had become a nuisance in
the years following the decline of the Rocky Mountain locust. This
species, *M. femurrubrum* (*femur* referring to the creature's legs and
rubrum alluding to the reddish coloration of the tibiae—the long,
thin, spiny shanks of a grasshopper), was similar in size and shape to
the locust. *Femurrubrum* was identified and named in 1773 by a
French entomologist, Charles De Geer. This poor fellow's name was
so often butchered in scientific papers that a ten-page scientific paper
was published in 1956 entitled "On the Rendering of Charles De
Geer's Surname."

Such details of spelling matter to taxonomists, who are both fastidious in their attention to minutiae and possessed with what, to the rest
of the world, might seem to be a misplaced sense of self-importance.
That is, when scientists first use the name of a species in technical writing, the creature's Latin name is usually followed by that of the person
who first named it—and in some cases the year of naming is added. So

the full and proper name of the redlegged grasshopper is *Melanoplus femurrubrum* De Geer 1773. If the person who named a species placed it within a genus and the species is later moved to a different genus, then the person's name is retained but put in parentheses. Thus, when one is the first to name a species there is a historical legacy, a kind of immortality that forever links the scientist to the creature. The only impermanence in this system comes if a taxonomist discovers that a species has been given two or more different names, in which case only the oldest name is retained and the other—along with the associated name of the errant human—is abandoned. For example, *L. danica* was erased from the catalog of earth's creatures by Uvarov's revision.

The naming of things is a powerful act, given the fundamental importance of language to humanity. Most taxonomists might give some sort of rational explanation for their exactitude, but within Western culture, the Judeo-Christian emphasis placed on the Word plays into the sense that theirs is important, even sacred, work. Taxonomists half-jokingly refer to themselves as the only scientists with a divine mandate. God's first assignment to Adam was to name the creatures, a task that is probably no more than 10 percent completed today.

And so, getting the name of the species—and the person who named it—right takes on an importance that runs deeper than a simple aversion to typographical error. Charles De Geer named a whole mess of species, so his name was rendered in many creative ways. It seems that there were no less than seven versions of his name, including de Geer, DeGeer, Degeer, and Geer. In an exhaustive historical critique that included analyses of the Frenchman's signature, it was concluded that *De Geer* (with a space between *De* and *Geer*) was the correct form. Ironically, the rendering today is almost universally *DeGeer* (no space), suggesting either that entomologists are just plain contrary or that not many folks read the *Bulletin of the Brooklyn Entomological Society,* where the definitive paper was published. Alas, both the spelling of the Frenchman's name and the grasshopper he named failed to sustain great scientific interest in resolving the identity of the Rocky Mountain locust. Although *femurrubrum* bore a certain resemblance to *spretus,* this modern-day grasshopper faded as a suspected alter ego. The attention of entomologists became riveted on a more compelling species.

The prime Jekyllian candidate was the migratory grasshopper, *M. sanguinipes*. This was also one of the species that seemingly replaced the Rocky Mountain locust, into the present day. But at the time in which the phase theory was being applied to the Rocky Mountain locust, the migratory grasshopper had an entirely different name. This species was originally named by Riley as *atlanis,* in reference to its being first found along the Atlantic seaboard. It takes only a moment to notice that a *t* is apparently missing from the species' name. In a weird twist of the rules of zoological nomenclature, the species' name as first printed serves as the immutable spelling, with provisions for egregious errors. It turns out that Riley had intended the name to be *atlantis,* a name that a few people understandably, but inappropriately, adopted in later years. However, the perfectionist Riley blundered into an irreversible error by inadvertently omitting the letter *t* in his original description, thereby creating a name that was a typographical error within a geographic allusion.

Such oddities are rare, and they can create even weirder problems of interpretation and pronunciation than *atlanis*. Yponomeutidae is the family name for the ermine moths, a very diverse group with many beautiful and pestiferous species. The name apparently was intended to be Hyponomeutidae. The prefix *hypo* makes sense. It means "under" or "beneath," as in *hypothermia,* which is a subnormal body temperature. But it seems that the prefix *ypo* has no meaning other than as a testimony to the importance of proofreading.

In 1917, a taxonomic revision revealed an earlier name for the migratory grasshopper and the species became known as *mexicanus,* and a subsequent analysis arrived at the name *bilituratus*. Not until 1962 was the complete history of this creature's name fully revealed. The earliest—and hence "correct" according to the rules laid down in the International Code of Zoological Nomenclature—name was *sanguinipes*. This name was derived from the Latin word meaning "blood," and perhaps referring to the red tibia of this species, a feature often shared with *femurrubrum,* as if the situation was not otherwise sufficiently confusing. Johann Christian Fabricius, a student of Linnaeus and founder of insect taxonomy, named this species in 1798. This original name came to light after a taxonomist reported that he had seen an old specimen with an identifying label during a visit to Copenhagen, where Fabricius had worked. The pinned insect had been collected by Julius Philip Benjamin von Rohr, an adventurer and collector for Fabricius. Oddly though, there was no record of Rohr's having spent time in North America. However, he traveled from London to Central America and the West Indies, and it is likely that this journey took him first to the east coast of the United States, where he made the fateful collection during the layover. He was lost at sea in 1792, but not before having transferred possession of his collected material to Sehestedt and Tønder Lund, pupils of Fabricius, who then presumably passed the specimen on to their mentor and into history.

And so, the three creatures—*spretus, femurrubrum,* and *sanguinipes*—were discovered, named, and renamed over the course of two centuries. In the 1930s, Uvarov's theory had become widely recognized and generally accepted, and American entomologists began to wonder whether *spretus* might be masquerading as one of the two similar species. An entomologist from the U.S. Department of Agriculture, Robert L. Shotwell, reviewed the taxonomic history and available evidence and concluded that the three were distinct species. A year later, Norman Criddle arrived at precisely the opposite conclusion, maintaining that *spretus* was "merely a long winged phase of *mexicanus* [now known as *sanguinipes*]." This position was also held by Morgan Hebard, an eminent taxonomist specializing in grasshoppers. Sides were chosen, lines were drawn in the sand of taxonomy, and the battle was on. However erudite the various arguments based on dead, pinned specimens might have been, a resolution needed living proof. And the phase transformation camp hoped that the definitive evidence would be a simple matter of inducing the phase transformation in living grasshoppers. If Criddle and Hebard were right, it ought to be possible to resurrect *spretus* from the grave. This challenge fell to Faure, the South African entomologist who had very nearly beaten Uvarov to the discovery of locust phase transformations.

Jacobus Faure was entranced by phase variation, and he was convinced that this phenomenon could solve the identity, and hence the disappearance, of the Rocky Mountain locust. He came to St. Paul, Minnesota, in 1932 to conduct the experiments necessary to re-create *spretus*. Using methods that had successfully induced phase transformations of the brown locust in South Africa, he reared *sanguinipes* under crowded conditions hoping that *spretus* would appear. It didn't. However, Faure managed to hedge his interpretations and qualify his conclusions to such an extent that with a bit of scientific sleight-of-hand he was able to argue that, despite his own data, the two organisms were really the same species.

For a period of fifteen years, entomologists tacitly accepted Faure's conclusions, although most writings used phrases such as "believed to be the migratory phase" to describe *spretus,* or "thought to be similar or perhaps identical to the Rocky Mountain locust" to portray *sanguinipes*. But Faure's evidence supporting the explanation of the locust's disappearance via a phase transformation was insufficient to convince Charles H. Brett, a professor of entomology at Oklahoma State University.

In 1947, Brett reported the results of his own experiments to definitively transform *sanguinipes* into *spretus*. Rather than just using crowding as the stimulus, Brett manipulated food, temperature, and humidity, hoping that the ghost of an extinct locust would be conjured up through these manipulations. It wasn't. In fact, many of the environmental conditions in Brett's experiments yielded creatures smaller than the original stock of *sanguinipes*. Undeterred, he concluded that *sanguinipes* would have consistently changed into the larger *spretus* if not for the interference of complicating factors.

In trying to salvage his hypothesis of phase transformation in the case of the Rocky Mountain locust, Brett creatively interpreted his data as revealing a possible cause of *spretus'* disappearance. In particular, he noted that *sanguinipes* adored alfalfa, a food source that produced stunted and malformed grasshoppers in his studies. From this observation of grasshoppers, Brett hypothesized that the introduction of alfalfa into the West had been deleterious to *sanguinipes* (and hence, *spretus*), leading to the demise of the locust.

Soon, entomologists were beginning to drop the extensive and delicate qualifiers from their language that tend to be so aggravating to the rest of the world. Without any further evidence, they were now stating, "Except for its brighter colors, longer wings, and greater flying ability, the Rocky Mountain grasshopper closely resembled the migratory grasshopper. . . . It was an extreme migratory 'phase' of the migratory grasshopper and not a different species." Although the phase transformation of *sangunipes* into *spretus* had not been demonstrated by experiment or observation, it was becoming established by dint of repetitive assertion.

The various and elaborate measurements of specimens by Faure and Brett may have convinced some entomologists, but taxonomists were not fooled by this numerical necromancy. After all, if we take various measurements of a tuna, a dolphin, and a mouse, we're almost certain to conclude that the fish and the dolphin are much more closely related than the dolphin and the rodent. Numbers simply fail to reveal the characteristics that are meaningful evidence of a shared lineage—the presence of lungs or gills, scales or hair, milk glands or air bladders. These are the qualities that allow us to properly reflect evolutionary history and determine the degree of relatedness. In entomology in general, and acridology in particular, we often resort to qualitative differences in structures that most people would find peculiar at best, and perverse at worst. We spend a lot of time peering at grasshopper penises.

The genitals of a male grasshopper are elaborate structures, comprising a number of elegantly working parts. The external features include a couple of hinged plates or "doors" at the tip of the abdomen that are the grasshopper's equivalent of a foreskin, protecting the more delicate internal structures. Also on the exterior of the creature's abdomen are a pair of small, variously shaped protuberances called *cerci*. Some look like clubs, others like hooks, and some like tiny cowboy boots. The internal or concealed genitalia are a bit more amorphous. We refer to these structures as the *phallic complex,* which is not a psychological condition but a mass of variously membranous, leathery, and hardened features. In grasshoppers, the phallic complex is tucked away inside the tip of the abdomen, being prudently encased by the external plates and extruded only when mating is imminent. The phallic complex includes the penis, or more technically speaking the aedeagus, which is the organ that enters the female and through which sperm pass. Actually, I suspect that there is a bit of prudishness and squeamishness in using the term *penis* in entomology—it sounds more clinical and technical to rename a structure that appears so flamboyant compared to our own. Lying above the aedeagus is the epiphallus, a hardened structure that probably plays a role in ensuring a proper fit of the male and female genitals during copulation.

The explanation of why the male genitals of grasshoppers are so intriguing to taxonomists is fairly simple. To begin, these structures exhibit remarkable consistency within species but spectacular variation among species, even in cases where two kinds of grasshoppers seem to be otherwise similar in size, form, and color. The basis for these differences is probably, at least in part, a function of reproductive isolation. For a species to evolve and sustain genetic integrity, its members shouldn't be trying to mate with other species. Species often have distinct body forms and colors that allow prospective mates to readily identify their own kind. Some grasshoppers use elaborate courtship rituals to ensure that the prospective mate is the "right one." Not so for the spurthroated grasshoppers—a subfamily named for the conical protuberance that arises from between their front legs, giving the impression of an enlarged Adam's apple or "spur throat." Species in this taxonomic group (of which *spretus* was a member) are similar in appearance and undiscriminating in their foreplay.

For the spurthroated grasshoppers, sex is a lover's leap. Males often hop onto almost any moving object of approximately the right size and color of a prospective mate, including females of other species and sometimes even other males. In the latter case, consummating the sudden relationship is, of course, hopeless. But in the former case, mistaken matings would seem possible. However, with his weirdly contorted genitals, the male is not able to insert his aedeagus into just any female. When a mismatched male is not summarily kicked off by the female, he spends long minutes tediously probing with his genitalia. But the elaborately sculpted tip of his penis simply doesn't align properly with her genital tract. The result is that the tube that is extruded from the aedeagus in order to transfer the sperm doesn't thread properly into the duct of the female that opens into her pouch that receives and stores the sperm. The system is a bit like a key-and-lock and without the male's "key" finding a matching "lock" in the female, the effort ends in frustration. And so, one might ask, why don't taxonomists use the female genitalia, the "lock" rather than the "key"? The explanation might reflect male chauvinism in science, but there is a more simple answer. Consider your front door—it is much easier to examine and describe the structure of your key than it is the inner form of your lock.

The value of the male genitalia for discriminating among species of grasshoppers was pioneered by Theodore Huntington Hubbell. Having earned his bachelor's degree at the University of Michigan, he pursued graduate studies at Harvard. However, Hubbell left before earning his degree at the behest of a friend to teach at the University of Florida. While teaching, Hubbell managed to earn his doctorate at the University of Michigan and returned to his alma mater as the Curator of Insects in the Museum of Zoology in 1946. Hubbell became the museum director in 1955 and built a collection of Orthoptera (grasshoppers, crickets, and katydids) that now requires hundreds of drawers stacked into towering cabinets filling more than 5,000 square feet of floor space. Within this bonanza of biodiversity, Hubbell discovered the taxonomic Rosetta Stone of these creatures—the size and shape of the various knobs, spines, and twists of male genitals.

To be precise, Hubbell's innovation was based on a rather simple insight, that different species had remarkably unique internal genitalia. Of course, the existence of the aedeagus was well known prior to his work. Plenty of morphologists had illustrated these graceful—and sometimes wickedly armed—structures, but nobody had thought of systematically comparing them among different species. It was here that Hubbell made his contribution by providing spectacular evidence of the diagnostic value of the concealed genitalia of grasshoppers. Soon, the entomological world came to accept this bizarre but effective approach to deciphering the identity of grasshoppers. And when the "gold standard" of taxonomy was applied to settling the identity of the Rocky Mountain locust, the answer was unequivocal. The phase theory had very nearly made the Rocky Mountain locust disappear as a species, but it was to be brought back into existence through its reproductive organ, a fitting means for perpetuating the life of a species.

In 1959, armed with Hubbell's insights regarding the informative power of the male genitalia, the federal government's foremost expert on orthopteran taxonomy declared in utterly unambiguous terms that the Rocky Mountain locust was not simply the migratory phase of *sanguinipes* (then *mexicanus*) but a separate species altogether. Not many scientists have the standing to settle such long-standing debates by fiat, but Ashley Gurney had earned the authority through a lifetime of deep devotion to entomology. He had served as a malariologist in

World War II, and friends recounted his annoyance at having the Japanese interrupt his mosquito collecting through their incessant shooting. Having earned a doctorate in entomology at the University of Massachusetts, he was hired by the USDA and became affiliated with the Smithsonian Institution. The Smithsonian is in the big leagues of taxonomy and by the 1950s, Ashley Gurney had ascended to a position that allowed him to carry on with the job that God had given Adam—naming the creatures.

In one short sentence—backed by pages of diagrams and analyses—Gurney and his colleague, Arthur Brooks from Canada's Department of Agriculture, established the taxonomic standing of the Rocky Mountain locust that has held for nearly half a century: "Our study of the aedeagus indicates that *spretus* is a distinct species." They invited continued tests of their conclusion, but the genitalic evidence was unambiguous. Although similar in size, the genitals of *mexicanus* resembled a soft cotton mitten whereas those of *spretus* were more like a tough leather sheath. They examined the specimens that Brett claimed to have transformed into a *spretus*-like creature a decade earlier, and they found that there was "no approach to the aedeagus of *spretus*."

This work by Gurney and Brooks became the new standard. They clearly understood the implications of their findings: The disappearance of *spretus* was not simply a matter of a biological variant of an existing species having been somehow suppressed. Rather, the disappearance was the extinction of the most abundant form of life ever to sweep across the continent. It could not be "re-created" in the laboratory by the rearing of an extant species under particular conditions. The Rocky Mountain locust was gone forever.

But with the taxonomic status of the Rocky Mountain locust being as resolved as such matters get in classical taxonomy (molecular analyses were yet to come), entomologists were left to face an even more compelling problem. If extinction is like an ecological murder, then we had finally identified the victim. There was no multiple personality, no switched identities, none of the oh-so-clever feints used in detective stories—just a body. So, how did a species that once blackened the skies, sweeping across a continent in swarms larger than any known biological phenomenon on earth, disappear forever in less than twenty-five years?

Beautiful Theories and Ugly Facts

EVEN THOUGH CHARLES BRETT HAD FAILED TO resurrect *spretus* from *sanguinipes* through alterations in temperature, humidity, and food, his experiments left no doubt that a steady diet of alfalfa produced wimpy grasshoppers. And in light of these findings he proposed the first clear hypothesis for the demise of the Rocky Mountain locust. According to Brett:

The disappearance of the Rocky Mountain locust seems to be in part explained by the greatly increased acreage of alfalfa west of the Mississippi River since 1900. *M. mexicanus* [now *sanguinipes*] is strongly attracted to alfalfa, but the studies reported in this bulletin show that alfalfa is unsuited for the best development of this pest. Grasshoppers grown on alfalfa are comparatively small, and sometimes malformed.

Historically, the disappearance of the Rocky Mountain locust appears
to have coincided with the spread of alfalfa throughout its breeding
grounds.

Brett's logic was simple: If *spretus* were the robust phase of *sanguinipes*, then a widespread plant that caused a sickly form could account for the disappearance of *spretus*. If *spretus* had been the Super-
man of grasshoppers, maybe we'd planted a botanical kryptonite
across its landscape. Brett's proposal stimulated some of the first systematic thinking about the causes of the Rocky Mountain locust's
demise. Although it turned out that *spretus* was not the gregarious
phase of *sanguinipes*, alfalfa remained a viable suspect. Could it be
that both species fared poorly on alfalfa and thereby began to decline
in the West?

The importance of alfalfa in the story of the Rocky Mountain locust
became a matter of contention almost as soon as the theory was proposed. As Brett's work was being published, Robert Pfadt was coming
onto the grasshopper scene. Born in Erie, Pennsylvania, in 1915, the
thirty-four-year-old assistant professor had recently arrived at the University of Wyoming. He had developed an interest in grasshoppers
while a student in Wyoming, continued these studies during his doctoral program at the University of Minnesota, and carried this interest
back to the faculty position at his alma mater. Pfadt continued his work
on grasshoppers for half a century, establishing a record of practical research that convinced the university administration to replace him with
another acridologist after he retired in 1984—which is how my position
came to be. His work in grasshopper ecology was not focused on the
Rocky Mountain locust, but he was drawn into the tale of this creature
through his eminently practical work on its kin.

In 1949, Bob published a lengthy work on his experiments concerning the role of food plants as factors in the ecology of *sanguinipes*. The relation of alfalfa to the health of grasshoppers was not
quite so straightforward as Brett has suggested. It was true that this
plant was a very poor food on which to rear nymphs of *sanguinipes*.
If provided only with alfalfa, barely one in five nymphs survived to

adulthood, and they weighed about half as much as grasshoppers fed on dandelion, their most healthful food.*

But Bob was one of the most careful and meticulous researchers of his day. He invariably valued quality over quantity, such that a single comprehensive paper was preferred to a dozen pieces of fragmented science. So, Bob conducted a separate series of experiments to discover whether alfalfa was indeed detrimental to adult grasshoppers. Much to his surprise, when healthy adults were fed alfalfa, versus other food sources, they had superior longevity and egg production. Alfalfa, it seems, was the grasshopper equivalent of a glass of Merlot with dinner: a fine dietary component for grown-ups but not for children. And this finding provided the key to a paradox. Despite Brett's assertion that alfalfa was deleterious, entomologists had often observed that *sanguinipes* flourished in alfalfa fields. Bob attributed the infestations of this species in alfalfa to their consumption of weeds that infest the crop. Even a modest amount of dandelion or bromegrass in the diet of developing nymphs could offset the deleterious effects of alfalfa.

Bob not only cast doubt on whether alfalfa was invariably detrimental to *sanguinipes* (and, by inference, to *spretus*) but also questioned, on two other grounds, the validity of Brett's claim that the planting of this crop could account for the disappearance of *spretus*. First, he noted that we knew very little about the plants on which *spretus* originally depended, so nothing could really be said about whether alfalfa had actually replaced anything of importance to the locust. Even if alfalfa was harmful to the insect—and this was not unambiguously the case—the effect would be marginal unless the crop had replaced a vital food source.

And this argument led to his second concern, which both reflected the contemporary thinking and shaped much of the subsequent discussion regarding the locust's disappearance. Bob pointed out that no matter what the effect of alfalfa, it simply did not exist on a sufficient scale to have impacted *spretus* throughout its range. Even a deadly

---

*Bob's findings have found their way into today's methods of rearing *sanguinipes*—the "white rat" of grasshopper biology—as we continue to include dried dandelion in their diet, and the insects flourish as a result.

poison—and alfalfa fell rather short of this—would need to have been spread over an area much larger than the nooks and crannies of the landscape filled with alfalfa. This crop requires a great deal of water, and although it was abundant in irrigated valleys, the range of the locust was immense and included vast areas of dry uplands where prairie grasses could not be replaced by thirsty alfalfa fields. A decade later, Gurney fully endorsed Bob's contention, noting that he'd also found no evidence of "any pronounced range-plant changes in Montana during the 1860s, 1870s, or 1880s, so far as the general disappearance or replacement of plant species is concerned." It appeared that poor Charles Brett had it wrong again. Not only was *sanguinipes* incapable of giving rise to *spretus,* but alfalfa fields seemed to have nothing whatsoever to do with the disappearance of the locust.

With the dismissal of the "alfalfa theory," a consensus began to form on the fate of the Rocky Mountain locust. In the 1950s, the environmental movement was dawning, and ecologists were thinking in terms of large-scale anthropogenic effects—continental, even global, changes—on other species and ecosystems. And this way of perceiving the growing conflicts between humans and nature fostered the conceptual agreement among entomologists that the disappearance of the locust, a species that stretched across millions of square miles, must have been caused by an environmental change of commensurate scale. Although the precise mechanism causing the decline of the species was not apparent—just as nineteenth-century evolutionists did not understand genetics—the fundamental nature of the process was obvious. The challenge was to find a sweeping change that was concurrent with the locust's disappearing act.

THE ROLE OF BISON

When one thinks of a life form sweeping across the West, locusts are not likely to be the first creatures that come to mind. Rather, the iconic image of the bison fills this legendary place in the lore of the prairies. Although we associate bison with western grasslands, the range of these animals included almost every state, as well as northern Mexico and western Canada. In 1839, Thomas Farnham traveled through a herd of bison along the Santa Fe Trail—for three days. Farnham could see bison stretching fifteen miles in either direction along his forty-five-mile passage, so he estimated that the herd covered more than a thousand square miles. Some thirty years later, Major Richard I. Dodge, traveling along the Arkansas River, encountered the largest reliably measured bison herd. This outpouring of hide and hoof was fifty miles long and twenty-five miles across, and later calculations estimated a population of 4 million animals. These animals were the furry counterparts of the waxy locusts on the continent. Attempts to estimate the total population size of either creature are fraught with speculative assumptions, but the efforts are revealing.

The peak number of bison has been calculated in various ways. Early estimates were based on extrapolations from hunting records. Modern approximations of carrying capacity—a measure of the number of creatures that can be sustained by a particular resource base—set the average sustained population density at 26 bison per square mile throughout their range. Ecologists have also tried to apply historical observations in refining crude guesses from nineteenth-century hunters. Given that the population estimates come from such a diversity of sources, it is somewhat remarkable that they all fall within the same range. Our best guess is that there were 30 to 60 million bison in North America, prior to European settlement.

Estimating the peak number of Rocky Mountain locusts is an equally dicey affair. But let's take the outbreak of the 1870s and presume that half of the reportedly infested area actually had locusts present at any given time. If so, then these insects were present across an area of 500,000 square miles (about twice the area of Texas). The carrying capacity of rangeland for modern-day grasshoppers is around 10 individuals per square yard. Using this figure—which is probably quite conservative, as we're considering the locust during an outbreak—we'd end up with 15 trillion insects, or a couple thousand locusts for every person currently on the earth.

Now then, to put the bison and locust on equal footing, we need some common units. Ecologists tend to prefer biomass—the number of kilograms, pounds, or tons of living tissue. Let's assume that the average bison weighed in at five hundred pounds, using the figure for a juvenile as a reasonable compromise between a mature male weighing a ton and a newborn calf weighing thirty-five pounds. If there were 45 million bison, then there were somewhere around 11 million tons of critters scattered over the continent. As for the locusts, let's assume a weight of half a gram per locust, which is the size of *sanguinipes*. Given 15 trillion insects, their collective biomass would have been about 8.5 million tons. So, bison and locusts had similar, and rather phenomenal, masses of herbivorous tissue. And both were very nearly gone by the turn of the nineteenth century.

Bison were quickly extirpated in regions where they were not particularly plentiful in the first place and humans were relatively numerous. By 1819, there were virtually no bison east of the Mississippi River, and by 1840 these creatures had been wiped out to the west of the Rocky Mountains. However, massive herds still roamed the plains, where people were thinly distributed. These millions of creatures were ultimately doomed by a tragic conspiracy of sociology, economics, and politics. The beginning of the end of the bison came with the end of beaver. That is, by the 1830s, unfettered trapping had decimated the beaver populations, and the American Fur Company and the Hudson Bay Company switched from purchasing beaver pelts to bison hides. With the emergence of this market came the professionalization of hunting. However, bison carcasses are absurdly cumbersome to handle, and the coastal markets were far from the Great Plains. So the demand for bison flesh was restricted to tongues, the prized cut of meat, and millions were shipped to market—with the rest of the carcasses left to rot on the prairie.

With the building of the transcontinental railroad came the means of shipping immense quantities of people into the West and staggering quantities of bison out to the East. Although bison meat was popular in the East after the Civil War, the death knell for these animals came with the development of new tanning methods in the early 1870s. Rather than using plant-derived tannins or minerals such as alum to tan a hide over the course of weeks or months, tanners found that chromium salts could work in a matter of hours. This faster, cheaper process made the hunting of bison for hides extremely lucrative. The slaughter that had begun in the 1850s became a massacre of unprecedented dimensions.

Calculating the scale of the butchery is considerably easier than determining the size of the original population. From various records, we know that at least 31 million bison were killed between 1868 and 1881. In 1872, 2 million bison were killed just for their hides. Take for example, Dodge City, a fledgling community that tried to call itself Buffalo City, only to be rebuffed by the postmaster general in Washington, who decided that confusion would reign given that Kansas already had towns named Buffalo and Buffalo Station. Despite the potential mix-ups in the postal service, the rejected name would have been far more apropos for a hamlet that shipped more than 40,000 hides along with seven hundred tons of bison meat in its first three months.

Professional hunters also kept careful tallies to boost their egos and ensure their fair payment. Consider Orlando A. Bond, whose records indicated that he once killed 300 bison in a single day and racked up 5,855 in a two-month period. He was presumably well compensated for his work, although no amount of money could buy back what he lost in the process. After firing tens of thousands of rounds, Mr. Bond was permanently deafened by the sound of his own rifle.

Economic profits often come at an aesthetic cost. The commander of Fort Dodge lamented, "Where there were myriads of buffalo the year before, there were now myriads of carcasses. The air was foul with a sickening stench, and the vast plain, which only a short twelve-month before teemed with animal life, was a dead, solitary, putrid desert." But for the savvy entrepreneur, even a corpse-strewn landscape was a source of income. The killing grounds were gleaned by "bone collectors" after the slaughters, and their grisly booty was sold for eight dollars a ton for conversion into fertilizer, fine bone china, and a refining agent used in processing sugar. On the hoof, bison were not worth counting, but as skin and bone they were commodities that represented profits—and thus generated reliable records.

The frenzied massacre had political benefits for a region in which settlers were in fierce conflict with the indigenous people. Although some Indians joined in the commercial slaughter to supply the buffalo-robe trade, more saw their cultures collapsing along with the bison.

Many of the native tribes heavily depended on bison to feed their bodies and spirits. The bison were vital to the physical well-being of the Indians in the form of food and shelter, but they were also a source of social and religious inspiration. In the words of Old Lady Horse, "Everything the Kiowas had came from buffalo. Their tipis were made of buffalo hides, so were their clothes and moccasins. They ate buffalo meat. Their containers were made of hide, or of bladders or stomachs. . . . Most of all the buffalo was part of the Kiowa religion. . . . The buffalo were the life of the Kiowas."

This dependence of native people on these creatures was not lost on those attempting to solve the "Indian problem." General Sheridan praised the bison hunters, noting, "These men have done in the last two years, and will do in the next year, more to settle the vexed Indian question than the entire regular army has done in the last thirty years." Although the extermination of bison as a strategy for suppressing the Indians was never explicitly stated as an objective of the government, there can be no doubt that this aspect of the industry was well understood and heartily endorsed.

In less than a century, the bison population in North America had been reduced to just 0.2 percent of its original size. By 1889, there were fewer than a thousand of these creatures left on the continent. The effects were far-reaching. With the bison no longer selectively grazing the grasses of the prairies, broad-leaved plants lost their competitive edge. Those grass species that had evolved to flourish under the erratic but intense grazing pressure of bison were also at a disadvantage. And rather than nutrients being rapidly passed through the process of a herd's feeding and defecation (the dung being ground into the soil by the action of millions of hooves), the cycles of carbon and nitrogen became much more diffuse. Trees invaded the prairie margins as bison no longer rubbed them to death as scratching posts. The bison wallows filled in like so many neglected ponds. In a myriad of subtle but pervasive ways, the ecology of the prairie was changed forever.

A century after the massive slaughter of bison on the Great Plains had begun, the fate of these animals was circumstantially linked to that of the Rocky Mountain locust. The cause-and-effect relationship was rather counterintuitive, but the modus operandi was not entirely absurd. In 1954, Irving Cantrall and Frank Young proposed that the extirpation of bison had been the cause of the locust's outbreaks. They reasoned that when the bison were removed from the land a change took place in the vegetation that was favorable for the Rocky Mountain locust. This alteration of the prairie accounted for the locust's massive outbreaks in the 1860s and '70s. Thus, Cantrall and Young maintained, the population explosion of the locusts was the consequence of a profoundly disturbed and out-of-kilter ecosystem. In rather short order, ecological succession restored the balance of nature, and the habitat recovered. They argued that with this reordering of nature, the conditions again became unfavorable for *spretus* and it disappeared.

The core of Cantrall and Young's notion involved the overlap of bison and locusts in three ways: space (both species existed on immense scales extending from the Rocky Mountains to the Mississippi River), time (the extermination of bison preceded the irruption of locusts), and ecology (locust plagues being evidence of a perturbed and dysfunctional ecosystem arising in the absence of bison). In terms of spatial overlap, their argument was compelling. Brett's alfalfa hypothesis might have been dismissed for being absurdly patchy and localized, but eliminating tens of millions of bison surely had sweeping effects across the grassland ecosystem where the locusts had flourished. However, the temporal sequence of events was problematic. In criticizing the "bison hypothesis," Ashley Gurney pointed out that outbreaks of *spretus* had preceded the great bison hunts. Records of phenomenal swarms reached back into the 1830s, when bison were still abundant across the Great Plains. Thus, he argued, the outbreaks of the Rocky Mountain locust could not have been stimulated by changes in the landscape resulting from the elimination of bison.

The ecological foundation of the "bison hypothesis" also relied on the notion that insect outbreaks were the consequence of a disturbed system. Indeed, this idea continues to pervade our understanding of ecology. We seem to believe that, as with a well-behaved child or a good worker, species should refrain from extreme outbursts. The concept of a Golden Mean or "everything in moderation" is rooted in the ancient Greeks, the progenitors of Western culture. This idealization of the world has been variously manifested throughout history, and it formed a pillar of Charles Darwin's evolutionary theory. Darwinian gradualism as an explanation for continuous modification of species was derived from geological uniformitarianism—the notion that the physical forces in the world were constant. This position emerged both from empirical evidence and as a reaction to the Church's reliance on catastrophes to explain the history of the earth. The Victorian interpretation of moderation in the natural world reflected the ideal emotional state—a balance of tranquil stability. The same concept was embodied in the ecological principle of succession, in which disturbed ecosystems return in an orderly manner to their original condition. And the ideal of equilibrium has lived on in our perception that an outbreak or crash of a population is an unnatural aberration, an indication of a troubled species.

But the leitmotif of the Rocky Mountain locust was its phenomenal flights of reproductive fancy. Manic swarms swept over the plains only to subsequently collapse into pockets of exhausted survivors. Evidence that this pattern was natural and normal came from Indian accounts, which revealed that locust outbreaks had happened well before European alterations of the western landscape. The Indians had witnessed what scientists were at pains to deny.

In recent years, the emerging field of complexity is finding that sudden catastrophic changes may be inherent in some systems, including populations. My own work in the field of catastrophe theory suggests that modern grasshopper outbreaks may be precisely such systems. Their erratic dynamics are entirely normal, although we can exacerbate the outbreaks by mismanagement of the rangeland. We've even found evidence that grasshopper populations exhibit a phenomenon called *self-organized criticality,* in which they naturally develop to the point where outbreaks and crashes are triggered by their own biology. And so, impetuous, even explosive, population dynamics do not require anthropogenic disturbance, nor do they reflect dysfunctionality.

Of course, people, species, and ecosystems can manifest extreme dynamics during times of trouble. But we are alarmed by nonconformity because of our self-interest in having a predictable world, our social intolerance of radicalism, our economic objective of slow but steady growth, and our Protestant ideal of moderation. Sometimes the outburst of joy from a child, the cry of anguish from a neighbor, or the outpouring of life by a species does not need to be "fixed," controlled, or managed but understood, accepted, and honored. And so, Cantrall and Young's attempt to explain locust outbreaks in terms of a degraded ecosystem was ultimately founded on a false premise deeply ingrained in our society—the presumption that sudden change is unnatural.

The next theory explaining the locust's disappearance would avoid this pitfall by embracing the notion of natural, even rather sudden, change. In an attempt to link the most widely known dramatic and large-scale alterations of nature with the decline of the locust, a new suspect was found.

THE ROLE OF CLIMATE

Amid the current debate regarding the rate and causes of global warming is a central point of consensus: Dramatic changes in the climate can occur naturally. Although there is no doubt that human activities can alter the weather on various scales, we also recognize that droughts, hurricanes, and ice ages unfold without our prompting. The Little Ice Age between 1450 and 1890 saw temperatures one to two degrees colder than those of modern times. Such a change might not seem very dramatic, but consider the alarm associated with a similar rise in temperature being forecast in the course of the next century.

The Little Ice Age was felt around the world, although more keenly in the Northern Hemisphere. In Europe, glaciers began to advance menacingly from the Alps, slowly swallowing entire villages and farms. The people of Chamonix, at the base of Mount Blanc, were terrified that their town would be engulfed, and so they appealed to the Church. The bishop of Geneva—perhaps aware that locusts had been repulsed by holy edicts—performed a rite of exorcism at the toe of the glacier. And the ice retreated, but only for a few years. Fishermen in Iceland battled against sea ice that choked the North Atlantic, and the famished island dwindled to half its previous population. By 1370 not a single human survived on Greenland, which was cut off

from seagoing travel for more than a century. In southern China, citrus groves that had flourished for hundreds of years were decimated
by cold. In the United States, New Yorkers walked across the frozen
harbor between Manhattan and Staten Island during the winter. The
Little Ice Age nearly turned the course of American history, as the horrific winter at Valley Forge almost fatally crippled George Washington's forces. The coolest periods of the Little Ice Age were during the
seventeenth and nineteenth centuries—1816 was called "the year
without a summer."

Modern-day entomologists are predicting that the ongoing warming
trend will cause both the expansion of subtropical disease vectors into
our otherwise healthy temperate zones and the loss of alpine species
that can't migrate northward for lack of movement corridors. The
possibility—to some, a near certainty—that climate change will cause
the loss of species suggests that such a lethal process might account for
past extinctions. Could climate changes at the end of the Little Ice Age
explain the disappearance of the Rocky Mountain locust?

In the 1950s, Ashley Gurney rejected the alfalfa and bison theories of
the Rocky Mountain locust's demise as lacking the necessary scale and
the requisite timing, respectively. By the process of elimination he
could find only one factor that had the ecological potential and spatial scope to do in the locust. Although not entirely satisfied, Gurney
was left favoring climate as the key suspect. In hindsight we can see
that there were two problems—one in practice, the other in principle—with the "weather theory."

The practical limitation to establishing a link between the decline of
the locust and potentially abnormal weather events in the late 1800s
was the paucity of data concerning temperature and precipitation during this period. However, circumstantial evidence was most intriguing
in some instances. The outbreak in the 1870s was certainly quashed in
many midwestern locales by an unusually wet spring in 1877. However, the locusts never persisted for very long in the Midwest, so this
decline could hardly have portended the extinction of the species
across its entire range. Fortunately, Riley's reports during the locust's
decline included some local records from within the Permanent Zone

of the locust. But the available information, although somewhat limited in the number of sites, provides no support for there having been a remarkable change in temperature or precipitation. For example, the spring weather in Havre and Missoula, Montana, during the outbreak years of the 1870s was quite similar to the annual mean temperature and total precipitation between 1880 and 1900. There were tremendous blizzards in the late 1880s in Montana, but there were also deadly winters in the western states in the early 1870s. So if the locusts survived the winter storms of 1871 and 1872 to reach plague proportions just five years later, then surely the harsh winters of the 1880s should not have been lethal. And this reasoning leads to the greater problem with blaming the weather for the locust's demise.

For a climate change to drive a species to extinction, the scale and severity of the conditions must be extreme, functionally unprecedented within the history of the species. The Little Ice Age reached one of its peaks in the nineteenth century, and there were certainly some severe winters and cool summers during this time. However, the same can be said of the seventeenth century—and the locusts obviously survived these conditions. It may well be the case that the woolly mammoths and cave bears of the Pleistocene declined with the end of the Ice Age some 12,000 years ago, but such dramatic events unfolded across millennia or centuries, not in a matter of two or three decades. Although climate change had the spatial scale that entomologists sought for a viable suspect in the death of the Rocky Mountain locust, the severity and duration of weather changes in the waning years of the Little Ice Age were simply insufficient to have extinguished the life of this species.

If anything, the generally warmer and drier conditions that began to prevail at the end of the 1800s should have favored the locust. Riley had noted that the population explosions of *spretus* were due to "the fact that the western climate is more subject to excessive droughts, which cut off the supply of nourishment at a time when the insects are acquiring wings, and thus oblige them to migrate." Like locusts from other temperate climes, the Rocky Mountain locust entered the migratory phase when dry conditions forced the nymphs to crowd into a shrinking habitat. Suitable vegetation in the Permanent Zone would have been found along watercourses and drainages. Like bone-chilled campers huddled around a dying fire, these locusts were crammed into the bottom lands that provided edible food. In mid-August, I've seen rangeland where there are perhaps 5 or 10 grasshoppers per square yard on the hilltops and more than a hundred per square yard seething in the vales, where a bit of green vegetation lingers. For the locusts a bit of localized adversity engendered continental opportunity. By swarming into new habitats, the Rocky Mountain locust would have survived the worst that the weather had to offer in the late 1800s.

Perhaps these shortcomings in the weather theory should have been apparent to Gurney, but entomologists were clinging to a model dictating that some large-scale factor could account for the locust's extinction. In his groundbreaking book, *The Structure of Scientific Revolutions*, Thomas Kuhn sagely pointed out that scientists are loathe to abandon a paradigm, even given apparently fatal flaws, until a viable alternative can be identified. Balancing on a teetering bridge is preferable to falling into a yawning canyon. For Gurney and others, even a weak argument within the accepted context of the science was preferable to admitting defeat. And so, the search for a more robust large-scale ecological factor became imperative.

What entomological detectives needed was an ecological suspect with a more direct link to the victim, something that was intimately connected to the time and place of the murder. The most obvious suspect in light of their well-documented effects on the western landscape and prairie ecology—bison hunters—had an alibi. They were not on the scene when the locust was flourishing, so they could not be implicated in its subsequent demise. But by the late 1960s ecologists were becoming cognizant of the intimate yet often inconspicuous connections among species—even organisms that appeared to have little in common. So, what if we were missing some critical ecological link in our reconstruction of the events leading up the locust's demise? Could there yet be a way of tying the mass killing of bison to the end of the locusts?

THE ROLE OF BISON REVISITED

Fifteen years after Cantrall and Young published their theory linking the bison's demise to locust outbreaks, Paul Riegert, a brilliant Canadian entomologist, inverted the bison-locust equation and arrived at a most enticing theory. If, as Gurney had pointed out, the locusts and bison were busy swarming and stampeding over the continent in earlier times, then perhaps the decline of the two creatures was linked after all. But rather than the loss of the bison being favorable, albeit temporarily, for the locust—as Cantrall and Young hypothesized— Riegert advocated precisely the opposite consequence. He suggested that the changes in the landscape following the extirpation of bison were detrimental, over the long term, for the locust.

Riegert proposed, "The breaking up of the sod and the overgrazing that followed hard on the heels of the bison migrations changed the grassland habitat for many species of grasshoppers." There is no doubt that the herds churned the soil into a pulverized mixture of manure, dust, and roots. Riegert asserted that members of the genus *Melanoplus* found the disturbed soil to their liking, and perhaps this was true in some species. We often find *M. bivittatus*, the two-striped grasshopper, laying its eggs along roadsides and crop borders where the soil is pulverized. However, there was no evidence that *spretus* favored such soil conditions. Indeed, Riley's work strongly suggested that the locusts preferred to lay their eggs in compact, rather than loose, soils. The locust generally avoided laying eggs in newly plowed land. It seems that the locusts were entirely capable of producing viable pods of eggs in habitats that would not have been transformed by bison.

Riegert also proposed that overgrazing favored the locust. He contended that the locally intensive grazing of bison, especially in drought years, would have created conditions conducive to the breeding of locusts. Although it is true that *spretus* laid eggs in heavily grazed pastures, grassy and weedy fields also were quite acceptable. Indeed, almost any dry, reasonably compact, sandy site would do in the midst of an outbreak. The only habitats that appeared to be consistently rejected were those with rank vegetation in saturated conditions. Both overly loose or heavily compacted soils were often avoided as well. Moreover, the hatching locusts needed food—which is why Riley advocated burning the prairies in the spring to starve out the nymphs. So, an immense swath of overgrazed land in the midst of a drought would hardly have offered the ideal conditions to foster a buildup of locust populations. Perhaps as a last gasp for this aspect of the theory, Riegert even suggested that the locust nymphs might have made use of bison dung for food, presumably allowing the insects to dine in recently denuded grasslands. Although *spretus* was observed to feed on dung, this was surely a minor and suboptimal food source. After all, Riley reported that hungry locusts would also consume dead mammals and sheep's wool, both of which were abundantly available in the years of the bison's decline, when the range was stocked with domestic animals.

Nobody exploits a good logical fallacy as well as the advertising industry, and the most egregious snake-oil salesmen almost invariably evoke *post hoc, ergo propter hoc*, which translates as "after this, therefore because of this." On television, a woman applies a bit of Carnal perfume in the opening scene, and the next moment we see men drooling as she flits by. In magazines, the first picture has the bald guy's head, the next one has a bottle of Scalp Fertilizer, and the final one shows the fellow with Sampsonesque locks (and sometimes with entirely different features, although we're supposed to believe that the tonic grows hair rather than altering eye color or the shape of one's nose). To avoid litigation, the clever advertiser never actually states that the perfume elicits lust or the tonic produces hair—these leaps of illogic are left to the viewer. But we are enchanted by the power of cause and effect, and so we presume that sequential events are causally related. The decrease of the bison right before the decline of the locusts was just too neat and obvious for the former not to be the cause of the latter. But Riegert's ecological linkages were weak, and it seemed to some at the time that his version of the "bison theory" failed in the context of a final consideration.

While bison were being wiped out across the Great Plains, cattle and sheep were being shipped in. Wyoming had fewer than 10,000 cattle in 1870; just fifteen years later there were more than a million. And this trend was seen across the West. The population of livestock in the eleven western states grew from perhaps 9 million animals to more than 25 million between 1870 and 1890. So, while 30 or 40 million bison were being gunned down, millions of cattle were being bred up.

In terms of feeding and movement, cattle are not the exact ecological equivalents of bison. Cattle are much more dependent on water sources, and their herds are smaller and less mobile than bison herds. But there are some substantial overlaps in the effects that these two grazers have on the rangeland. For example, both have a strong preference for grasses and churn the soil with their hooves. And so, 20 or 30 million cattle certainly sustained many of the conditions, at least in some locales, that the locusts may have exploited.

Overstocking the range became the norm in the early 1880s. Texan and eastern cattle were added to herds already feeding on the northern plains. By the fall of 1883, about 600,000 head of cattle filled the Montana range, along with an equal number of sheep. Although the range was at its capacity, the natural increase of the herds and the importation of more animals from Texas in 1884 led to deteriorating conditions. A rancher noted, "It takes 20 acres on a new range to feed one cow, after the range has been grazed two years it will take almost 25 acres, and after six years all of 40 acres." Overgrazing and trampling were inevitable, even if these effects were more continuous and evenly distributed than with bison.

And so, alfalfa, weather, and bison all had unimpeachable alibis. The list of suspects that had the means of victimizing the locust was dwindling fast. There was, however, one last factor with the spatial scale to end a life as sweeping and glorious as that of the Rocky Mountain locust.

THE ROLE OF FIRE

Although bison stretched across the Great Plains, there was an even more ubiquitous life form with far greater effects on the environment of the Rocky Mountain locust: the American Indian. Indeed, the elimination of the bison was an ecological means to a political end—the suppression of the Indians in the western United States. The native people and native insects were viewed as serious impediments to realizing America's destiny. Allusions to their one-two punch were exploited in the free-for-all competition for settlers in which neighboring states referred to one another as a "barren, grasshopper-ridden,

Indian-infested desert where no farmer was likely to succeed." During the late 1800s, the population of Indians in the western states was reduced by as much as 50 percent by disease, war, and starvation. But this numerical decline does not begin to reflect the scope of the changes wrought on the native people and their land.

The establishment of the reservation system and the consequent displacement of virtually all Indians from their homelands by 1885 resulted in drastic changes across the West. With this uprooting and resettlement in strange and unfamiliar places, the people were unable to conduct their lives as they had for thousands of years. Along with the brutal and sudden suppression of the Indians themselves, their activities—hunting, gathering, fishing, planting, and harvesting—vanished from the landscape. The Native Americans were intimately dependent on a host of plants and animals for food, clothing, and shelter. Could such relationships have been reciprocal, with locusts having adapted to conditions or resources made available by the Indians? Could a strange and perverse twist of history have led to a sequence of events in which the decline of the native people somehow precipitated the extinction of the Rocky Mountain locust?

In the 1970s and '80s, anthropologists were coming to realize that the Indians didn't simply live in passive harmony with nature. Rather, they extensively and intentionally altered the landscape. The "noble savage" conceptualization of these people gave way to a much more sophisticated understanding of Native Americans as savvy environmental engineers. In 1982, Stephen Pyne, an ecological historian at Arizona State University, made this radical assertion: "So extensive were the cumulative effects of these [ecological] modifications that it may be said that the general consequence of the Indian occupation of the New World was to replace forested land with grassland or savannah." Although there is still ardent debate as to the role that the earliest Americans played in the extinction of the mammoths and other giant (and presumably tasty) mammals of the Pleistocene, there is no argument concerning their role in shaping the quality and quantity of the prairies. As Pyne so effectively documented and clearly expressed, the greatest ecological change imposed by the Indians was the use of fire to vastly expand the grasslands upon which the bison—and ultimately the people—depended. By burning the land, the Indians shifted the competitive balance in favor of grasses. Fire killed sprouting shrubs and trees, whereas the grasses quickly regrew from seeds or root crowns. And although Pyne did not make the ecological connection explicit, the entomological implications were compelling: Locusts, like bison, favored grasslands over forests.

Among Riley's various recommendations for preventing outbreaks of the Rocky Mountain locust, he had advocated an aggressive program of tree planting. He recognized that forested areas were never used for egg laying and that heavily treed lands were barriers to the advance of the locusts. Riley even hypothesized that forests were the factor limiting the eastward spread of the locust. By his estimates, forests covered about 6 percent of the land from the Mississippi River to the Rocky Mountains and 30 percent of the land to the east of the Mississippi—a sharp change in the landscape that served as the Maginot Line for locusts.

Riley repudiated the idea that grass fires caused the droughts that triggered the locust migrations. He did, however, admit a possible connection among Indians, fires, prairies, and locusts. This conspiracy involved a far more ancient ecological association:

> These fires, encouraged by drought, and either kindled by accident or *intention* [emphasis added], have swept over the country for ages, and while they leave the roots of the grass uninjured, they destroy the germs of most other plants, including trees; and Mr. Lapham [an early ecologist from Wisconsin] pictures to himself a long-past struggle between forest and prairie, in which the latter, by the assistance of the Fire King, has gained and held the vantage ground.

If Indians did sustain the ecological conditions suitable for locusts by burning back encroaching shrublands and forests, then they may have been even more clever than we suppose. Locusts are a serious problem for farmers, but they are a valuable food for hunter-gatherers. An anthropological study at Lakeside Cave at the western edge of the Great Salt Lake revealed human feces consisting mostly of grasshopper parts with a matrix of sand. The scientists witnessed grasshoppers being blown into the lake and forming rows of up to ten thousand bodies per foot, with a light coating of sand. As such, one can easily imagine the Indians scooping up this salted, sun-dried feast. We now know that grasshoppers were a regular food for Indians in the Great Basin and on the Colorado Plateau, including the Ute and Southern Paiute. John Wesley Powell, the famed geologist-ethnologist of the late 1800s, noted that:

> Grasshoppers and crickets form a very important part of the food of these people. Soon after they are fledged and before their wings are sufficiently developed for them to fly, or later in the season when they are chilled with cold, great quantities are collected by sweeping them up with brush brooms, or they are driven into pits, by beating the ground with sticks. When thus collected they are roasted in trays like seeds and ground into meal and eaten as mush or cakes. Another method of preparing them is to roast great quantities of them in pits filled with embers and hot ashes. . . . When these insects are abundant, the season is one of many festivities.

Compared to the danger and labor of hunting bison or other wily mammals, locusts were a fantastic bounty. These little morsels are 60 percent protein and chock-full of calories. According to anthropologists, one person could collect 200 pounds of sun-dried grasshoppers in an hour. With no processing time, this crunchy load would yield 273,000 calories, the equivalent of 500 supreme pizzas. A person gathering seeds or nuts would be lucky to provide 1,000 calories in the same time. A deer or antelope would likely net only a tenth of this energetic sustenance. As for taste, the Goshute Indians of western Utah, after first tasting shrimp, called them "sea crickets." Riley would have been pleased.

All of this makes a wonderful ecological and ethnological circle linking Indians to fire, fire to prairies, prairies to locusts, and locusts back to Indians. But does breaking this cycle by eliminating the Indians provide a plausible basis for the extinction of the Rocky Mountain locust? Probably not. Although there is evidence of forests encroaching on grasslands after the Indians were extirpated, the scope and rate were far less than necessary to reasonably account for the disappearance of the locust. After all, we're talking about forests, and trees don't invade large areas in a matter of twenty-five years. And, of course, Indians were not the only source of fire in the West. Lightning certainly sparked conflagrations on a regular basis, toasting trees and scorching shrubs. Fire-dependent plants did not disappear along with the Indians, so it seems most unlikely that the locust would have suffered an even more drastic fate than these plants. Furthermore, even in the complete absence of fire not all grasslands would convert into forests or shrublands. Precipitation and other factors limit the distribution of woody plants on the Great Plains. In the final analysis, the ecological links were simply too weak, and the case against the accused was dismissed.

On Sir Boris Uvarov's last visit abroad, he returned to his native land. Uvarov attended the International Congress of Entomology in St. Petersburg in 1968, where he was welcomed as a hero and honored as a long-lost son. Although a lesser man might have been cast as a defector, Uvarov had been instrumental in helping Russian science rise to a justly deserved status by ensuring that his countrymen were well placed in the world and that their work was published in widely read journals. In his address to a packed auditorium, he maintained that the study of locusts "would make possible a gradual replacement of direct control by methods of ecological regulation of populations." He considered insecticides "mere palliatives." What we needed was the capacity to change ecological processes on the scale of whole landscapes, undermining the very resources that locusts needed to develop into swarms and devastate agriculture. What we needed in Asia and Africa was whatever had happened in North America to snuff out the Rocky Mountain locust.

But twenty years after Uvarov's vision of the future, we were still floundering for an explanation. Entomologists typically offered some obtuse arguments about a complex set of large-scale ecological changes involving bison, weather, and fire. Paul Riegert's contention was fairly typical: "With the relatively fast removal of the bison from the plains, came the quick extermination of *M. spretus*. The cause and effect relationship may not have been absolute but it certainly was contributory." That was the best we had, a diffuse assurance that some sweeping environmental alterations had somehow conspired not to just prevent locust swarms but to entirely decimate the last vestiges of the species.

One of my favorite television shows while growing up was *Columbo*. I liked *Mannix* and *The Rockford Files,* too. For that matter, I'll even confess to having a soft spot for Mickey Spillane stories. My favorite part of *Columbo* was when Peter Falk would seem to have finished interrogating someone and be headed out of the room. He'd suddenly stop, cock his head, turn back to the suspect, and say, "Just one more thing. I was wondering . . ." And he'd proceed to completely undercut the neat-and-tidy alibi of the poor sap. That's a bit how I felt coming onto the scene in 1986.

I was aware of the various theories regarding the murder of the Rocky Mountain locust. For the scientific community, these explanations were collectively sufficient to consider the case closed. It wasn't a tidy story, but it was good enough for the inherent uncertainties of a death that had occurred before any of the active investigators had been born. But being the new kid at the scientific stationhouse, I sensed that there were too many loose ends and holes, too much logical leaping and scientific supposing. I didn't buy the vague story that had been assembled. My own sense was that each of the suspects had a convincing alibi. There was no murderous factor—either natural or human—across the West. You can't derive the whole truth from an assemblage of half-truths. In my estimation, the case of the Rocky Mountain locust's disappearance needed to be reopened. But nearly a century had passed since the last individual was seen, there were no living witnesses to provide insights, and two generations of entomological detectives had puzzled over the available information. It's easy to dismantle someone else's case—it's not so simple to build a new one.

Secrets in the Ice

ACENTURY AFTER THE HEYDAY OF THE ROCKY MOUNTAIN locust, the trail of clues leading to the demise of the species had grown cold. No new evidence had surfaced since Ashley Gurney provided the insight that had elevated this creature to a valid, but extinct, species. I had nothing more to work with than the previous generation of entomologists, but the mystery was simply too compelling, the existing "explanations" were just too full of holes, and my desire to build a reputation in my newfound field of study was too intense to let the case go. Of course, as a new assistant professor at the University of Wyoming in 1986, I didn't bet all of my chips on this one longshot gamble. I pursued studies of grasshopper feeding, biological control with pathogens, and modeling of population dynamics. But with a sense of adventure and a bit of funding, it seemed that I could pursue at least one line of investigation concerning the Rocky Mountain locust that hadn't been exhausted—and for a very good reason: The evidence was locked away in ice, two miles above sea level.

A proper—and fundable—grant proposal provides a compelling scientific rationale for the planned research. My proposal to the National Geographic Society included what seemed to be some rather convincing arguments for funding an expedition to what early geologists had come to call Grasshopper Glacier, a magnificent and mysterious body of ice just north of Yellowstone National Park that had attracted western travelers for decades. The most obvious justification for my project was that no entomologist had been to the site in forty years. It also seemed that the condition of a natural phenomenon and national treasure of this sort ought to be monitored. After all, recession had been ongoing since at least 1931, when observers reported a gagging stench emanating from the foot of the glacier, where a four-foot pile of rotting locusts had melted out of the ice. With similar reports in 1952—the last time a scientific expedition had been to the glacier—one had to imagine that this remarkable resource could be in serious trouble and that the chances of collecting the uniquely preserved insects were dwindling.

The frozen creatures were probably ill-fated swarms of the Rocky Mountain locust, but remarkably—almost unbelievably—none of the specimens collected between 1914 and 1952 had made it back to a museum. The only entomologist to examine the icebound insects had been Ashley Gurney, but he had made his observations before he was aware of the differences between the genitalia of *sanguinipes* and *spretus*. So, his identifications indicated that these were the migratory phase of *sanguinipes,* which may well have been *spretus*. If it was the Rocky Mountain locust embedded within the ice, it could represent a bonanza of biological material and sufficient evidence to reopen the case of the creature's disappearance. Furthermore, there were other Rocky Mountain glaciers purportedly containing frozen grasshoppers, although none had ever been studied by an entomologist. There were specimens of *spretus* preserved in various museums throughout North America, but all of these had been collected in the last few years of the locust's existence, so they did not represent the species in its vibrant, healthy condition. Perhaps more important, not many specimens existed. A species that once blackened the skies was now a rare scientific commodity.

There are dozens of insect collections in the United States, housed in universities and natural history museums. The largest collection is Riley's legacy: The National Museum of Natural History contains 30 million specimens, a couple million more than London's Museum of Natural History. Harvard's Museum of Comparative Zoology is the largest of the university collections, with 7 million insects tucked away. At the University of Wyoming, we have a modest collection of 250,000 specimens housed in tall, steel cabinets. Looking among our drawers of neatly pinned and labeled insects, you're likely to find that the largest numbers of specimens represent the most common species.

The closest specimen of the Rocky Mountain locust is seventy-five miles to our south, in the Colorado State University insect collection. Deep in the bowels of this collection, five dried locusts are impaled on pins. Across the continent there are another 482 specimens scattered among half a dozen collections, the majority of these being at the National Museum. For an insect that once numbered in the trillions, this is a infinitesimal record. And to make matters worse, many of these specimens were identified before the definitive anatomical features were known, so a portion of these collections actually could be the migratory form of *sanguinipes*.

As such, we had a rather limited pool of specimens to expend on various tests. Any specimen lost to analysis was an irreplaceable relic of American history and ecology. But there were now powerful—and destructive—analytical methods with the potential to shed light on the nature of the Rocky Mountain locust and the events leading up to its extinction. For example, we had methods of characterizing subtle differences in the proteins of organisms. By passing an electrical charge through a gelatinous film on which proteins of an organism had been placed, it was possible to separate these "building blocks of life" based on subtle differences in their electrochemical charges. Because proteins are made of amino acids, which are the direct products of genes, they can serve as sensitive indicators of genetic differences in populations and species. The problem was that the museum material had been preserved in the standard manner: They were dried specimens mounted on pins. Proteins are like chemical origami, elegantly folded and layered molecules. When these complex chemicals dry, the bonds holding the folds in place are broken and the integrity of the molecule is lost. This process, called *denaturation,* occurs in the cooking of an egg. The proteins are heated, which causes the original bonds to break and new ones to form, thereby transforming a gooey fluid into a rubbery lump. And it is impossible to reverse the process: Scrambled eggs cannot be turned back into their slimy progenitors. However, tissues frozen for centuries in ice just might be well enough preserved that we could analyze the proteins. And if so, then molecular analysis could be taken a step deeper into the very foundation of life.

I maintained in my proposal that the rapidly developing field of molecular genetics could well provide even more telling clues. If the ice had preserved the insects' DNA, the chemical blueprint of life, then important questions could be directly answered. We could determine whether the species had been in a long-term decline, with extinction being the culmination of a process that had begun long before human disturbance. Molecular analyses could reveal whether the locust had suffered from inbreeding, causing a genetic "bottleneck." If we could examine frozen specimens of various ages—and photographs of the glacier clearly showed that there had been layers of locusts at various depths within the ice—it would be possible to detect a constriction in genetic variation. This evidence would strongly indicate that *spretus* had been reduced to abnormally small and isolated populations before dying out. Furthermore, these analyses of the genetic material, rather than bodily structures (including penile oddities), could directly address the fundamental basis for declaring that a life form constituted a true species—the century-old question of *spretus*'s taxonomic status could be definitively answered. And in the 1980s, such investigations required types of evidence that couldn't be found in museums.

So, to make progress on these fronts, we had to have biological material with three qualities. First, we needed numerous specimens from which to derive representative values. Next, the specimens had to be in a well-preserved state for chemical analyses. Finally, and most important, we needed material that represented the natural state of the locust. To understand what may have happened in the final years of *spretus*'s existence required us to compare its normal, healthy condition to the biology of the creature in its last dying days. Ideally, we could view both time frames by using well-preserved specimens extracted from the ice, but even if only centuries-old material were frozen in the glaciers, the museum specimens would provide at least some context for assessing the species' condition at the end of its life.

In addition to providing tissues with these qualities, the glaciers potentially offered a direct window into the locust's history. If the layers of locusts reported by earlier investigators represented separate depositions over time, then radiocarbon dating could be used to determine when the swarms had lived. In this way, we could know whether outbreaks of the Rocky Mountain locust had been a natural feature of the North American landscape for centuries. Even with Native American accounts, our perspective only extended to the early 1800s. We also hoped to discover whether outbreaks became more frequent with European settlement. Although the theory had been largely dismissed by force of rhetoric, there might have been something to Cantrall and Young's contention that the irruptions were aggravated, maybe even caused, by human disturbances. Clever arguments and rebuttals are fine, but hard data were needed to refute various theories—and perhaps to develop a viable alternative case.

The grant review panel concurred that Grasshopper Glacier was a fast-disappearing resource. So fast, in fact, that the panel judged my proposal to be a long shot (Gurney's reports were, after all, forty years old). Disappointed, but undeterred, I scraped together funding from a faculty development grant and the Office of Research at the University of Wyoming. They were no more convinced of my finding frozen treasure, but through later conversations I learned that the decision makers had been drawn into a vicarious sense of intrigue and adventure concerning the mystery of the Rocky Mountain locust and the secrets of Grasshopper Glacier. Such a subjective basis for allocating research funds might seem unscientific and oddly emotional. But then, science is, at its core, a profoundly personal enterprise, irrationally motivated and driven by passion.

Perhaps the most wonderfully wicked irony in science is the notion that the clearest vision into the world is provided by a "double-blind" experiment. In this method, neither the individual measuring the effects of a treatment nor the subject of the experiment is informed of which, if any, treatment has been administered. I was well aware of the ideals of experimental design, as this approach to science was the primary focus of my research program. Although I'd become fascinated with unraveling the story of the Rocky Mountain locust, I had been hired by the University of Wyoming's College of Agriculture to pursue far more practical matters, such as developing new treatments for rangeland grasshopper outbreaks. In this development research, we sometimes approximate the double-blind design by default. We don't intentionally keep secret what insecticide was applied to which plot. Rather, as we position thirty or so plots, each the size of forty football fields, on a grassland with few landmarks, it is easy to lose track of what went where. We use plot maps and coded stakes, but it would take a cryptographer or someone with a phenomenal memory to match these with our inevitably arcane coding system. The plot numbers always make sense at the beginning of the summer, but their logic tends to fade with the patina of the prairie as the season unfolds. And as for the subjects of our experiments, the grasshoppers are not informed of which treatment they have received. I sometimes suspect, however, that the condition of their comrades and the declining frequency with which they are encountered leave the insects with a decent picture that something is amiss.

The double-blind approach to evaluating the effect of a drug or an insecticide is intended to remove the biases from the outcome of the experiment. As a student, I was taught that the power of science lies in its commitment to the ideal of objectivity. The goal was to design, conduct, analyze, and interpret experiments with absolutely dispassionate, uncontaminated reason. In light of the standard "experiments" conducted in the requisite college biology, chemistry, and physics laboratories, this approach was philosophically correct—but demonstrably bad—advice. The student who managed to create matter (a common outcome of syntheses in organic chemistry—most probably the fruit of mismeasured reactants, incidental side products, and worn-out scales) was not rewarded for objective reporting. No praise was offered to the budding geneticist who refuted Mendelian

inheritance (a frequent result with fruit flies—most likely the consequence of the winged ones escaping and the wingless ones becoming
mired in their gooey food, thereby skewing the proportions of these
forms). However, we understood that in the course of "real" science,
one had to adhere to the ideal of objectivity with uncompromising
devotion.

The problem with this pedagogical approach was that once I became a professional scientist, nobody was handing me a lab manual
full of preconceived experiments. I was hired as an insect ecologist at
the University of Wyoming to explore the world of grasshoppers, with
a particular eye to managing populations of these creatures when they
became unruly. In graduate school at Louisiana State University, my
research had been quasi-independent, guided by a gentle mentor and
a thoughtful committee. As a new faculty member, I relished the lack
of oversight—but freedom is scary stuff. I discovered that the most
important and difficult phase of science is asking a good question.
Our ignorance of the natural world is such a boundless resource that
one must attempt to navigate through a mindscape of tangled paths,
blind alleys, twisted streets, and unsigned roads. I had learned the
principles of objectively designing experiments, impartially collecting
data, rigorously analyzing the results, and neutrally interpreting their
meaning. I knew how to answer questions via science, but standing in
the midst of a few million grasshoppers milling about on the mixed-
grass prairie or a few thousand scientific journals crammed onto the
shelves of the university library, I realized that generating results was
the easy part of science. The hard part was figuring out what to ask.

In this defining phase of inquiry, the ideal of objectivity not only
fails to provide guidance; it becomes an absurd—if not utterly impossible—standard. I've sometimes wondered what it would be like
for a scientist to select questions in a purely dispassionate, utterly dis-
connected manner. Many scientists approximate this condition in
pursuing topics that are deemed important by the collective consciousness of their peers in a socially sanctioned, positive-feedback
system that provides comfort and security. But this effort to become
the lead sheep in the flock, a biologically problematical but concep-
tually apt metaphor, lacks an objective rationale. Some scientists use

the standard of "publishability" and choose the questions that are most likely to yield manuscripts, and still others select the measure of "fundability" and focus on those matters most likely to yield grants. But selecting the putatively objective criterion—peer approval, publication, or funding—is an act loaded with subjectivity. Perhaps the only possible tactic would be to construct a database of all possible scientific questions and then to randomly select one for examination. Such silliness simply reflects the absurdity of the claim that science is a purely objective venture.

I could not possibly have devoted seventeen years of my life to the study of grasshopper biology and ecology without a passion for these creatures and the lessons they offer. Even taking out time for teaching, meetings, and other duties of academia, I've spent a bit more than 2,000 working days—nine years of full-time labor—trying to understand grasshoppers. No sane person would devote such labor, let alone so much of one's life, to the pursuit of questions that did not touch the heart and soul while stimulating the mind. To have invested that much of life is either a tragic waste of human potential or an expression of faith that there are mysteries and lessons worthy of this expenditure. If each passing day represents an irretrievable gift, then to squander this blessing on the heartless, soulless interrogation of nature would be to offer oneself as a martyr to the cult of objectivity.

Although my expedition to Grasshopper Glacier was founded on rational thinking and reasoned argument, my desire to explore the frozen remains of the Rocky Mountain locust was personal and subjective. I wanted to stand in the presence of such a strange and wonderful natural phenomenon. There is a grandeur of scale that draws humans into the natural world. For me, outbreaks of grasshoppers and swarms of locusts are a portal into a joyful terror that has long been an inexplicable part of my being. Like being drawn to the edge of a towering cliff or into the deep water beyond the crashing surf, I find myself pulled toward these irruptions of life.

In the summer before my first trip to Grasshopper Glacier, I remember standing at the edge of the dirt road as the dust from my truck hung over the road for a quarter mile along Whalen Canyon. There, I came to understand how a hundred grasshoppers per square yard transforms the world. They blanketed the skeletons of the sage-brush, gripped the shreds of yucca, and lined the shady sides of the fence posts to avoid the searing heat. In the draws, where the only hint of green vegetation remained, the grasshoppers formed a virtual carpet. They ricocheted off my face and chest, clung to my legs, and boiled in every direction. At this density, the grasshoppers melded into a single, seething ecological tissue into which I was absorbed. One never fully returns from these dream-places where mental, spiritual, and physical experience are inseparable, where we glimpse the vastness of the heavens and the depths of the earth.

Whether for better or worse, whether driven by objective knowledge or subjective experience, whether seeking the tangible or the inconceivable, I was compelled to see for myself the frozen forms of the creatures that had eclipsed the sun. I was drawn to witness the immensity of life captured in the ice long ago. To touch the jumbled masses of locusts, to lift a corpse from its glacial grave, would be to make these fantastic life forms—the individuals, but even more powerfully the superorganisms that emerged as swarms—real in a way that historical accounts and woodcuts never could. Maybe such intimate contact with the creature in its final resting place would trigger a connection, an intuition, a missing link in the chain of events that had ended with the dawn of the twentieth century. Or perhaps it would simply feed my irrational fascination with immensity, my craving for the infinite.

ROTTEN RESULTS

The most famous Grasshopper Glacier lies at 11,800 feet in the Beartooth Mountains, just ten miles northeast of Yellowstone National Park. At least three other bodies of ice in the Rockies bear the name, but this is the only one that has achieved notoriety. Although the glacier was omitted from U.S. Forest Service maps before the 1940s, it was known to the miners of the region, who came across the site while seeking gold, silver, and copper. When Riley and his commission were looking for locusts, grizzled prospectors were surveying the West for riches.

The first scientific expedition to the glacier was in 1914, when it was proposed that the Rocky Mountain locust was the creature embedded in layers within the ice. Specimens were collected on four subsequent expeditions between 1919 and 1952, but none were preserved. For a while there was even a flourishing tourism industry, with jeep tours taking people to the glacier from Cooke City, Montana (sardonically nicknamed "Cooked City" when the 1988 Yellowstone fires swept to the edge of the town).

Perhaps the greatest source of speculation concerned the age of the locusts. Since the 1930s respectable publications had reported that the swarms had been entombed "since prehistoric times," and a credible entomologist, Arthur G. Ruggles, maintained that the insects were hundreds of thousands of years old. In 1953, Ashley Gurney conducted the first and only scientific study of grasshoppers preserved in glacial ice prior to our work. He asserted that the Rocky Mountain locust comprised the layered deposits, but he noted that a few years earlier a colleague had collected live specimens of another migrant species, *Melanoplus rugglesi*. Ironically, this species had been named for Arthur Ruggles, the man whose wildly speculative estimate of the age of the locusts in the glacier was about to be refuted. Gurney used radiocarbon dating to estimate the age of specimens from the glacier. Unfortunately, the analytical methods of the time were quite imprecise, and the resulting age of the insects was reported as 45 ±650 years. This was a very difficult value to interpret and may have arisen from relatively old specimens, although far less than 100,000 years, having been contaminated with recently deposited material.

When we arrived in 1987, a weathered sign—painted on a dilapidated cabin, announcing "Jeep Tours to Grasshopper Glacier"—was Cooke City's last remnant of the glacier's heyday as a tourist attraction. By the time of our expedition, a wilderness border had been declared between Star Lake and Goose Lake, four miles short of the glacier. We were, however, heavily equipped with camping, climbing, and traveling gear—along with a U.S. Forest Service map that included a tentative, broken line that purportedly traced the trail from just outside Cooke City into Grasshopper Glacier. I'd long since learned that such markings on Forest Service maps represent an odd combination of rumor, folk wisdom, and seat-of-the-pants cartography. The former jeep route had deteriorated to a meandering ghost trail.

Fortunately, my team had a sense of adventure. Dick Nunamaker, a research scientist with the USDA laboratory on campus, lived in a tiny log cabin on the windswept plains outside Laramie, so he was well adapted to adversity. Larry DeBrey, my research associate, had been a construction worker, a logger, and a firefighter, so the expedition was well within his comfort zone. Tim Christianson, my doctoral student, had been working on a demanding field project studying insect communities in a sagebrush shrubland at 9,000 feet, so he was conditioned for the trek.

Within the first five miles, we had lost the trail twice and changed a flat tire. The road was so bad that the other three fellows decided to walk in front of the four-wheel-drive truck that was hauling our gear. Their logic was that they could hike faster than I could drive, so they could scout ahead for passable routes. And walking involved far less physical abuse than banging around in the cab or bed of the truck— not unlike the logic used by pioneers who chose to walk alongside the prairie schooners. At times, my crew took to rolling small boulders from the badly eroded track in an attempt to preserve the oil pan and avoid using our last spare tire. In the course of seven hours, we traversed the fourteen miles to Star Lake. This serene site was surrounded by craggy outcrops and a few courageous pines—a perfect location for a camp. Angry gray clouds soon rolled over the distant peaks, and a fierce wind buffeted our tents all night.

The next morning dawned crystal clear, with a heavy dusting of snow on the higher peaks—not an unusual condition for August in the high country. With light packs, we headed out from camp and around Goose Lake, which stretches from the wilderness border to the pass that would take us up to Grasshopper Glacier. The thin patches of stunted trees above camp quickly gave way to patches of alpine meadows and by the time we reached the pass, the only signs of life were palettes of orange, green, and gray lichen splattered on granite boulders, some scattered tufts of grass sprouting from the windblown soil between the rocks, and a few mountain goats across the way. As we reached the top of the pass and crested the ridgeline, the glacier came into view. The great crescent of ice rested in a classic cirque, an immense bowl of rock at the head of a boulder-strewn valley. The saddle was flanked by Sawtooth Mountain's Iceberg Peak and Mount Wilse's Glacier Peak. Winds funneled up the granitic gorge and across the ice—a perfect trap for any airborne insects attempting to cross the Beartooth range.

Our thrill at having successfully reached the glacier was quickly dispelled, as we realized that the frosty spectacle was courtesy of the previous night's storm. Two inches of fresh snow covered the ice—and buried any chance of seeing grasshoppers at or near the surface. A couple hours of scraping and searching convinced us of the futility of attempting to locate specimens under these conditions. We were seeking needles in an immense, frigid haystack. But mountain weather is notoriously fickle, and what the clouds bring the sun soon takes away. Although it was evident that the day would yield nothing more than a couple of reddish tibia collected from a patch of exposed ice beneath a boulder, we also realized that the snow was rapidly melting.

Over the next three days, the glacier was stripped of its snowy mantle, and the pitted gray ice was revealed. The warm days sent torrents of water down the face of the glacier, making the work wet and treacherous. The constant hazard was falling, as the resulting slide could quickly deposit a careless climber over the low shelf at the toe of the glacier. The short drop would end with a plunge into the sapphire blue meltwater lake that fed West Rosebud Creek far down the valley. With ice axes and crampons, such a spectacular descent was unlikely, but slips and stumbles were not uncommon. Such mishaps yielded painful reminders of the virtues of keeping one's gloves on, even as the temperatures climbed into the high forties. The surface of a glacier does not resemble a frozen lake but is strikingly similar to a cheese grater, being formed of thousands of tiny, sharp-edged pits that efficiently rasp the skin from unprotected hands.

A much greater, but highly sporadic, threat arose from the boulders that would break free of their icy moorings and plummet down the face of the glacier. All afternoon we heard the rumbles and crashes of rocks that the sun had worked loose. A large section of the glacier was entirely covered in a shifting jumble of boulders, and others were eager to join their brethren. During lunch on our second day, I found a sunny spot alongside a stable boulder, which provided an effective barrier to the wind. From a couple hundred yards away, I heard a faint cry and saw Larry waving. I figured that he was coming to join me, so I waved back and shouted an invitation to lunch.

A few minutes later he came trudging up, shaking his head. "You never saw it, did you?" he asked.

My pithy reply, "Saw what?" answered his question.

"I wasn't waving at you, I was warning you that a rock had broken loose."

He had watched in horror as the stone, the size of a cooler, careened down the slope toward me but out of my line of sight. Having yelled my reply to him, I'd never heard it coming, and it had passed behind me before I knew it was there. "It couldn't have missed you by more than ten feet," he said. This was probably our closest brush with death in what was to be five years of expeditions.

After a lunch of dried apples, beef jerky, crackers, and M&Ms we went back to work, mucking rotten grasshoppers from the surface of the ice. We could find no whole bodies, but there were clumps of jumbled, decomposing corpses. In mats a couple inches thick and several square yards in area, the remains were like soggy peat moss—black, tangled masses of organic material. Amid the soft matrix, we could readily discern scraps of wings and broken legs. The most numerous parts were tiny jet-black mandibles, the hardest body parts of a grasshopper but no larger than a typewritten *v*. There was another part in abundance, but for all our combined entomological expertise, we didn't positively identify these until we returned to the laboratory. About the same size and shape as a typewritten *H*, these were fragments of the *tentorium*. Relying on a hardened shell-like cuticle for protection and support, insects don't have an internal skeleton. However, the pressures that are generated by the powerful muscles controlling the grasshopper's mandibles would collapse their heads without internal support. And so, the exoskeleton is involuted and forms bracing within the head; this support structure is called the tentorium.

Most of the thin cuticle covering the body had been reduced to indistinguishable bits, littered throughout the soft, rotting tissues.

On our last day at the glacier, we scraped up as much soggy grasshopper gunk as we could from the patches that had surfaced. Then, Dick took charge of digging a series of three-foot-deep pits in search of embedded layers, for which he was rewarded with an exceptionally aerobic workout but no specimens. On the way back to camp, we hauled out nearly a hundred pounds of slushy organic debris. Larry, the workhorse of the team, carried half the load. Dick and I split the remaining Ziplock bags, as Tim's energy was clearly ebbing. A diet of rehydrated foods, long hikes over shifting rock, cold nights on a lumpy meadow, and hard labor at more than two miles above sea level had taken their toll. After dinner that evening, Dick cleared his throat, pulled out a sample bottle of meltwater that he'd hauled down from the glacier, and with a grand flourish poured the contents into a flask that he extracted from one of the food boxes.

"To us!" he declared passing the concoction to me, "Twenty-year-old scotch and thousand-year old water—a fitting close to a successful expedition."

Back in Cooke City, I was stretched out on a hotel bed after a luxuriously hot shower when Dick pounded on my door. "Check this out," he said, handing me a black-and-white photograph. He'd met up with a local couple, Frank and Roberta Williams, who had lent him their family treasure—a photograph of the face of Grasshopper Glacier from 1900. This image was fully forty years earlier than any previous record of the glacier's condition, and the implications were staggering. It was no wonder we'd found only decomposing remains of the locusts; in just a hundred years the glacier had dwindled to less than a twentieth of its past expanse. Where we had encountered a twenty-five-acre lake lapping at the toe of the glacier, there had once been an eighty-foot wall of ice towering over a small pond.

After returning to the laboratory, we dried the masses of debris and discovered that more than 90 percent of the sample was water, leaving us with less than a pound of material. And of this, a scant 2 percent was readily identifiable grasshopper remains—the rest being windblown dust, pebbles, and pulverized soft tissues of the insects. In a single glass flask we had some of the most valuable material ever mined from nature. With this jumble of dried grasshopper parts weighing in at about a quarter of an ounce, the cost of the flask's contents worked out to nearly $30,000 a pound. But we had enough pieces to conduct radiocarbon dating, which placed the time of the locusts' deposition at 800 years before the present. When medieval knights were jousting in Europe, a swarm of locusts had been swept up the valley and blown onto the ice. But could we be certain that these were the remains of the infamous Rocky Mountain locust?

Embedded within the contorted genitals of male grasshoppers are some hardened structures. When a grasshopper decays, the soft tissues rot and leave behind these oddly shaped pieces, a bit like the disarticulated skeletal remains that persist after a corpse decomposes. From these diagnostic structures, we knew that the remains belonged to the genus *Melanoplus*—and most likely to either *sanguinipes* or *spretus*. Based on a few hundred measurements of legs, wings, and other identifiable remains, the statistical balance tipped in favor of *spretus*. But without whole bodies from which intact genitalia could be studied, the identification could not be definitive. Moreover, the condition of the remains was such that there was little biological evidence that could be gleaned in terms of genetic or other molecular analyses.

Perhaps our scotch-and-water toast to "success" had been a bit premature. I had, however, learned a great deal about glacial prospecting for locusts. First, it was clear that, as we had suspected, this resource was rapidly disappearing. Indeed, we guessed that the exposed debris was the last of the preserved swarms. Our conjecture was based on having found no deeper layers of locusts and the fact that our radiocarbon dates were at the outer limits of those that Ashley Gurney had reported for the deep layers exposed at the foot of the glacier in 1952. If we were going to find well-preserved specimens of the Rocky Mountain locust, the clock was ticking and every passing summer meant that valuable material was rotting from the melting glaciers of the West.

Next, I had figured out what pieces of equipment and which supplies were actually needed for such ventures. Future trips would require far more lean and efficient logistics. Other sites were even less accessible, and the luxury of hauling gear in a truck was not likely to be repeated. Rather, we'd be backpacking a week's worth of scientific and camp supplies into a remote site.

I also realized that a tremendous investment of resources and time could be negated by the vagaries of weather. We'd been lucky to have only a light snow, which melted within a day or two. But if a foot of snow had fallen, then we'd never have had a chance to see the surface of the glacier or find deposits of preserved insects. In these mountains, the time between the final melt of one spring's snow and the first coating of the next autumn can be a matter of days. In some years the window is entirely closed. It was also clear that hauling a hundred pounds of slush to extract a few grams of locust parts was brutally inefficient. We had to find a method of extracting the needle without carrying the haystack back to the laboratory.

In light of the first expedition's qualified success—we had, after all, managed to recover remains of what appeared to be the Rocky Mountain locust—I immediately sought funding for the next expedition. My contention was that we had to act quickly because an irreplaceable natural resource was melting from under us. A Cooke City resident told us of having seen whole bodies of locusts on the glacier just six years before our work. A review of various geological reports revealed that there were other glaciers in the Rocky Mountains that contained the remains of grasshoppers (or locusts), and because of their high elevations and northern exposures they had a good chance of still containing well-preserved specimens.

I gambled that this sense of urgency would parlay into funding. I lost the bet. Reviewers latched onto the rotten state of affairs at Grasshopper Glacier instead of the possibility that other sites would be in better condition. Rather than interpreting our findings as cause for an emergency intervention to preserve a dwindling resource, my colleagues took the proposal as an obituary. Once again, I had to beg for some meager funding from my own institution, rather than partake of the riches of the National Science Foundation. However, my harshest lesson came when we attempted to publish our findings from this first expedition.

In 1988, we submitted a paper describing what we had found, including the condition of the glacier, the location of deposits, the types of insect parts we had extracted, the radiocarbon dating, and the analyses that had led us to believe we had recovered the remains of the Rocky Mountain locust. As it was the first report of such a study in nearly fifty years, we hoped that the manuscript would be well received. It was rejected. The editor of *Environmental Entomology* at that time explained that the study did not constitute a controlled experiment. I wondered where we were supposed to find a "control glacier" and what experiment could have been done if we had located such a resource. My written appeal to the editorial board—the only time I have ever been brazen enough to take such a step—was denied with the incisive summary, "You have mistaken natural history for science." It seems that replication, statistical design, and controlled experimentation defined science, at least at that time, for the entomological community. This view suggested that initiatives such as the Human Genome Project (decidedly lacking a clear hypothesis), the entire field of cosmology (there is, after all, only one universe), and entire projects devoted to unreplicated discovery (NASA's deep space probes) were not science. It was as if nothing of value was left to describe in the natural world—a remarkable position for entomology, a field in which no more than a tenth of the fundamental units of study (insect species) are even known.

Still more disturbing was the notion that science required manipulation of the natural world, rather than patient observation or thoughtful description. The Rocky Mountain locust was gone, and no experiment will ever show the course of events that led to its demise, explain the role it played in western ecosystems, or reveal what other species may have perished along with it. Its tale would be told, if at all, to those willing to listen rather than to those demanding answers. In the end, the paper was published in *American Entomologist*—a semipopular journal without the technical rigor and prestigious status of *Environmental Entomology*—and I received more reprint requests for it than I have for any paper that involved a controlled experiment. Maybe this response was because I do not develop very interesting experiments, or perhaps because even scientists find value in stories and marvel at the tale of the Rocky Mountain locust.

Most important, this conflict solidified in me a personal passion to find unimpeachable evidence of glacially preserved Rocky Mountain locusts, to bring back a whole body of this magnificent creature to prove that my idea of their having been preserved somewhere among the peaks of their homeland was not a quixotic flight of fancy. I bridled at my colleagues' suggestions that the search for the last bodies of *spretus* was in vain. I was thirty years old and still had the belligerent defiance of my youth—a quality that was both a wellspring of internal drive and an occasional source of unnecessary conflict. I could appreciate Riley's passion and for me, nothing was so motivating as to be doubted, even mocked (as would happen in later reviews of my work). The gauntlet had been thrown down, and my expeditions to the glaciers of the Rocky Mountains became a search for a lost locust—and for professional pride.

A quarter mile into the hike and I was dying. "This is going to hurt," I gasped. "A whole lot," Dick wheezed. Even Larry had dropped to his knees. The new guy on the team, Jeff Burne, a wiry faculty colleague in entomology, had the look of a man who had been duped. "If we have another five or six miles of this, it's going to be a long day," he offered. The map hadn't shown such a brutal ascent. The prospect of carrying seventy-pound packs up the Cottonwood Creek drainage leading to this Grasshopper Glacier was increasingly daunting. I reflected on the irony of this glacier's being situated in Montana's Crazy Mountains. We had to be insane to attempt this hike fully loaded with a week's provisions and all of our collecting and climbing equipment.

According to a twenty-five-year-old geological report, this glacier was supposed to contain plenty of grasshoppers. No entomologist had seen this site, and the geologists who had filed the report were clearly more interested in bringing back rocks than insects. So the identity of the grasshoppers was anyone's guess. Although the elevation was lower than that of our first glacier, the topographic maps showed that this body of ice had a strong northward aspect. I hoped that this protection from the sun's rays had delayed recession, leaving some grasshoppers—perhaps the Rocky Mountain locust—well preserved. My plan had all the makings of success, or so it seemed to me: The glacier was well situated and known to contain grasshoppers; the weather in August of 1988 was warm and dry; and the planning and packing had proceeded flawlessly. The only glitch was that the map had indicated a climb of perhaps a thousand feet spread over several miles, not a thigh-burning struggle up a wicked slope.

We shouldered our packs and headed up the hillside, hoping to find that hypnotic hiking rhythm that allows a certain detachment of mind and body during long, hard treks. Much to our delight, within another few hundred yards the trail leveled off to a relatively mild grade, following the creek bottom. For the rest of the morning, we walked easily and managed to joke about our personal misgivings at the start of the day's hike. By noon we had arrived at Cottonwood Lake, fed by the clear glacial runoff from Grasshopper Glacier. From camp we could look across an alpine meadow to an immense terminal moraine, a pile of rock a half mile wide and 200 feet high that the glacier had pushed down the valley, marking its furthest advance. Somewhere behind this bulwark of stone lay the glacier and its frozen contents.

The climb up to the glacier was tedious and treacherous. Clambering over car-sized boulders was tiring, but when they shifted and settled with stony groans, the adrenaline rush provided a surge of energy that kept us moving upward at a brisk pace. Cresting the moraine at 9,700 feet, we sighted the glacier. It lay at the base of a gargantuan amphitheater, the sheer cliffs rising a hundred feet above the graying ice. The glacier was cradled between the rock walls, and we discovered that even during these long summer days the sunlight managed to creep into this recess for only a few hours. Even so, the amount of exposed ice had shrunk to about eleven acres. There was a much larger expanse of ice beneath the rock slides that had littered the sides of the glacier as it receded, but finding anything beneath this jumble of scree and stone would be impossible. Our 1972 map showed an area of ice ten times larger than the one we had encountered, meaning that the glacier had receded by 90 percent in just sixteen years.

The first, beautifully preserved grasshopper that Larry found in a shallow pit in the ice generated tremendous excitement. I gently lifted the specimen from its icy grave using the blade of my ice ax to avoid contaminating it with oils from my hand. It was in remarkable condition, and I could immediately see that it was in the genus *Melanoplus*. But the tiny cerci were in the distinct shape of a cowboy boot, completely unlike those of *spretus*. In fact, the creature appeared to be *M. infantilis*, a prairie species not known to form swarms or fly for long distances. This was a most surprising discovery, hardly what I was hoping to find, but intriguing in its own right. Within minutes, Jeff called out that he'd found a body, and then Dick shouted from above us that he'd come across two more. Each specimen was put in a small vial for later examination, as our time was better invested in collecting as much as possible rather than stopping to identify each grasshopper. And *grasshopper* seemed to be the right term—all of the specimens appeared to have been deposited in recent weeks; their colors were intact and their legs and wings were all attached. Radiocarbon dating later confirmed the recent origin of our specimens. Dick's ice pits turned up empty, although he delighted in the shower of shards that flew during his excavations. And the *bergshrund*—the crevasse that forms at the top of a glacier as it pulls away from the rock face—provided a view into the glacier but gave no evidence of deeper layers of insects.

In the evenings, I worked by lantern light to identify the day's collection. After three days of searching, we had managed to gather 134 grasshoppers. Among these were twenty different species, most of which we also found in the meadows above camp. Clearly, the majority of grasshoppers in the glacier were alpine species, recently blown up the valley and onto the ice. The relatively low elevation of the glacier and the lush meadows probably accounted for this chronic deposition of insects and the name of the glacier. However, there were a half dozen surprises—rangeland species not previously known to engage in long-distance flights. A couple of species had been previously considered flightless, having only tiny stubs for wings. In both cases, fully winged individuals were considered quite rare, and the fact that they could disperse for miles was not even imagined. Perhaps the most intriguing finding was a set of 40 specimens of *Aulocara elliotti*, the bigheaded grasshopper. This is a serious pest of grasslands, which had never been reported at high elevations. Moreover, these specimens had wings that were a third longer than normal. The rather abundant, long-winged individuals provided the first, circumstantial evidence of a migratory phase, perhaps even swarming, in this grasshopper.

Although Grasshopper Glacier had not yielded any ancient specimens or long-lost locusts, the weather was balmy and the creek was yielding trout to supplement our fare. So we stretched our expedition to encompass another, unnamed glacier. Our first view of this site had been profoundly unnerving and very nearly disastrous. On our last day at Grasshopper Glacier we climbed to the apex of the ice and onto a steep and crumbling slope. This 150-foot chute led to a notch in the rock wall behind the glacier, through which, if our maps were accurate, we figured that it should be possible to view a glacier on the other side of the ridge. The plan was to see if we could access this other body of ice by climbing up and over the wall surrounding Grasshopper Glacier. Larry, Jeff, and I started the ascent, but it was soon apparent that between the narrow chute and the loose rock, someone would end up getting clobbered in a shower of shale. To make matters worse, the slope became perilously steep within a couple dozen yards of the notch.

Larry was the strongest climber, so I sent him ahead and then ducked behind a boulder with Jeff to avoid the hail of rocks knocked free during the ascent. The sporadic avalanches assured us that he was making progress, but our hopes of a suitable access route to the other glacier were fading. When the scree stopped sliding down the chute, we assumed he'd made it to the notch, which was just out of sight of our precarious position. After ten minutes of quiet, we began to worry. Coming down from the notch should have been faster than going up, and Larry was only supposed to be making a quick reconnaissance, not exploring the other side. After nearly twenty minutes, we heard the clatter of sliding rocks and knew that he was on his way down. As he came around the boulder, he looked uncharacteristically shaken.

"We thought you'd stopped for lunch," I joked.

"Nearly lost my lunch is more like it," he replied.

"What happened?" I asked, as the color slowly returned to his face.

"I got to the notch and reached up to pull myself onto the ledge so I could see through it and over the other side," he began, "and as I pulled my head and shoulders into the gap and looked over, the world fell a thousand feet."

"It fell? What do you mean?" I asked.

"The other side of the ridge drops straight down to a valley. So, as you cling to the foot-wide ledge of the notch, behind you is a slope of loose rock and in front of you the world drops into oblivion." He paused while we tried to picture the dizzying perspective. "I've never had vertigo like that," Larry said. "It was all I could do to hang onto the ledge. That's why I was up there for so long."

Here was a guy who had spent his days logging, hunting, and fishing. He'd hiked, climbed, and wandered for hundreds of miles. If Larry had been intimidated by this route, there was no way the rest of us were going up and over.

"Did you see the other glacier?" I asked, hoping at least that he'd found the object of our climb.

"Yeah. It's plastered onto the side of a slope, well to our northeast. This shortcut over the ridge is insane. But I think the ridge drops off to a pass further to the east. Maybe that would get us there," he replied.

"Let's work our way back down and check out the maps," I said, hoping that we might find a way onto the other glacier that would be less traumatic.

As it turned out, the expanse of meadows above our camp led to the pass that Larry had suggested. It was a tiring climb up the soggy, frost-heaved meadows, but those two hummocky miles were far easier than the ascent to the ridge above Grasshopper Glacier. The glacier that we found covered an area twice that of its better-known sister, but we collected only a couple of grasshoppers. It was clear that being big was not all it took for an ice field to serve as an effective insect trap. The critical factor was whether the glacier was oriented within a valley where the prevailing winds would carry grasshoppers onto the ice.

With this factor in mind, we focused on a third Grasshopper Glacier in 1989. Appropriately named, but never investigated by an entomologist, this body of ice lay at a slightly higher elevation than the first Grasshopper Glacier. And in the late 1950s, it had been at least twice as large as its somewhat distant and much more famous neighbor. Flanked by 12,000-foot peaks, the high elevation deep-freeze should have kept its contents in good shape for the last few centuries. The glacier looked reasonably accessible if we followed its long, gradual drainage, and establishing a horse-supplied campsite near its base appeared to be feasible. Although fastidiously avoiding any public allusion to numerology, we had to wonder whether three would be our lucky number.

Inside the timbered lodge of the Squaw Creek Ranch just outside Cody, Wyoming, we unfurled the topographic maps that revealed the lair of Grasshopper Glacier. The outfitter that we'd hired to pack us into the site evinced complete confidence, assuring us that he could get us at least to the edge of Black Canyon Lake, the mile-long body of meltwater fed by the glacier.

"No problem," he declared.

"And if you can't get us beyond the near end of the lake, then which shore should we take to get up the canyon?" I asked.

"Stick to the west side of the lake," he replied. "It's not nearly as steep."

From the far end of the lake, it was a mile to the glacier—or at least to where the toe had been in 1956. With recession, the glacier had almost surely retreated up the canyon. Confident that our plan was as well conceived as possible, I took up Jim's challenge of a cribbage game. Jim Wangberg was my department head and had wanted to join the expeditions for some time. This year, he'd managed to set aside the time—and with his penchant for swimming, he certainly had the lean build of a man who would be able to make the haul up the canyon. Larry, my Man Friday, was along again, and by now we were nearly telepathic in the field, each anticipating the other's position and needs. His brother, Bill, was the other newbie on the team. If there was ever a need to demonstrate the fickleness of genetics, Larry and Bill were my living examples. Tall and lanky, with dark wavy locks, Bill bore almost no resemblance to Larry's sturdy, broad-shouldered build and straight sandy hair.

The gear and horses were loaded into the trucks and trailers the next morning, and we drove over the Chief Joseph highway—one of the most scenic roads in the country. From the crest of the highway we could see a sharp promontory among the rugged mountains in the distance. At over 12,000 feet, Beartooth Peak jutted from the northern flank of Grasshopper Glacier, which was tucked safely into the recessions of Black Canyon. We dropped into Montana, parked at the trailhead, and prepared the pack mules and riding horses for the thirteen-mile trek into Black Canyon Lake. The mid-August morning was bright and sunny, until the trail turned southward into the canyon. Within a few hundred yards of entering the wide mouth of the canyon, the forest became a dark maze of fallen trees. A windstorm had created a giant's game of pickup sticks, and there was no possibility of getting the horses through the tangle of trunks. We turned back and made camp at the edge of a sunny meadow, well below the canyon. The next day would be the most trying we had faced in our search for the Rocky Mountain locust.

We began our trek to Grasshopper Glacier early. The three miles up to Black Canyon Lake required a couple of tedious hours picking our way through forest. Whatever trail might once have wound its way up the mouth of the canyon, it was lost among the snarl of fallen trees. We did not realize until we finished the last hundred yards of our climb over a jumble of rock that we were ascending the immense—and now largely overgrown—terminal moraine of the glacier. Like an Ice Age bulldozer, the glacier had shoved a huge earthen dam into the mouth of Black Canyon. Behind this mound, marking the furthest advance of the ice, lay Black Canyon Lake, a two-mile-long jade-green stretch of frigid water. From the terminal moraine, there was no sign of the glacier. But our maps indicated that the canyon curved to the west, forming a deep alcove into which, we presumed, the ice had retreated in the last few decades. Heeding the advice of the outfitter, we headed along the west side of the lake, which, in the distance, appeared to be a lush alpine meadow. Appearances can be deceiving.

The "meadow" turned out to be krumholz—thickets of gnarled trees, stunted by brutal cold and twisted by constant wind. Pushing, stumbling, and occasionally climbing our way through two miles of this Lilliputian forest took more than two hours. We stopped for lunch at the far end of the lake, still unable to see any ice above us. Searching for a flat, dry place to eat, Jim came across a skull resting alongside one of the rivulets feeding the lake. "This is where the mountain goats come to die," he joked, holding up his prize. Between our weariness from the morning's trek and the ominous clouds gathering at the rim of the canyon, the skull seemed an ill omen.

We began to ascend the narrowing canyon, climbing over an interminable series of moraines, marking the one-step-forward-and-two-steps-back retreat of the glacier. These thirty-foot battlements of loose rock and crumbling soil seemed to be the dying glacier's way of keeping intruders from reaching its sanctuary at the end of the canyon. As we worked our way up, the clouds dropped into the canyon and a light mist began to fall. By mid-afternoon, we had reached remnant patches of rotting ice tucked between the moraines at 10,000 feet. Cold, wet, and tired, we searched these patches and recovered a dozen fragments of grasshoppers, mostly legs and mandibles. With one final push up the canyon, we worked our way to the top of a particularly impressive moraine, and Grasshopper Glacier came into view, still a mile in the distance. We could see that the glacier, shrouded by clouds and mist, was now reduced to a sheer slab of deeply crevassed ice clinging to the deepest wall of the cirque. Like a slashed corpse, the pale body of the glacier had shrunk to barely a third of the area that it was in 1956, as a result of a continued warming trend in the West. Not wanting to be caught in the canyon for the night, we headed down.

On the return journey, we passed around the east side of Black Canyon Lake. This route meant two miles of scrambling over scree-covered slopes, but at least we didn't have to bushwhack through the krumholz. We all would have made it back to camp by sunset, except Jim suffered a painful groin pull while clambering over the shifting rock. Larry and I moved ahead to prepare a hot dinner, while Bill helped Jim make his way out of the canyon. A steaming pot of chili and a lip-blistering cup of coffee were waiting as they dragged into camp with the last slate-gray hints of dusk.

The next morning, Bill was limping with a twisted ankle that he'd suffered shortly after Larry and I left him with Jim—whose groin pull had stiffened like a frozen cable overnight. We were battered and humbled, but at least the sun was out, so a warm, dry day of rest seemed an ideal remedy. After a morning of fishing for grayling at a nearby lake, we met over lunch to discuss our options. We had another three days before the packers would come for us, and it was evident that if we were going to make another assault on the glacier it would be best to wait until the last day. If injuries had healed sufficiently, then by heading up the east side of the lake we thought it might be possible to make it onto the glacier. We estimated that most of the ice was at a precipitous thirty-degree slant, but the flanks of the glacier looked to be a bit more accessible. In the next two days, Larry and I made a reconnaissance hike to the valley that held Hopper Glacier. Although this body of ice could be seen from the trail, getting there would require a grueling climb, perhaps even nastier than the route into Grasshopper Glacier.

After two days of glorious weather, the dark clouds returned with a vengeance. The afternoon before our planned return to the glacier, a soft rain began to fall. By the time we were huddled under a tarp making dinner, the rain had changed into a heavy snow. As night fell, so did our hopes. It was clear that the window of opportunity had closed. Under these conditions, an attempt to reach the glacier would be foolhardy, and even if we made it, the ice would be blanketed in snow—just as we'd found on our arrival at the first Grasshopper Glacier two years earlier. I sat damp and dejected in my tent. A few grasshopper parts tucked away into a small vial were all we had to show for our expedition. The horses would haul out four hundred pounds of equipment and about four milligrams of specimens. Sometimes, however, adversity is the mother of invention.

After returning to my lab in Laramie, I laid out the five mandibles, like chips of polished ebony. "That's it?" asked Scott Schell, one of my graduate students at the time. He had a keen sense of the time and expense that had gone into getting these tiny structures.

"Yeah," I replied, "not much to work with, is it?" I didn't want to figure out the cost per ounce of the material from this expedition.

"Well, I don't know," he answered, "Wasn't there a paper back in the 1940s where some guy associated mandibles with feeding preferences in grasshoppers?"

"That's right," I replied, the wheels starting to spin. But Scott was ahead of me.

"If mandibles differ enough to distinguish what types of food a grasshopper eats, then maybe they could also tell us what species they came from," he offered.

Zoologists often rely on teeth to differentiate species of mammals, and dental records are a standard method for identifying human remains. Nobody had ever tried to use insect mandibles in this manner, probably because it would be crazy to extract these structures for taxonomic purposes when the insects had such wonderfully varied and readily accessible legs, wings, antennae, and other features. The grasshopper's mandible is very much like a tiny molar, used for grinding its food. We had also found a lacinia, a hardened, scythe-like mouthpart used like our incisors to cut pieces of leaves from a plant. However, we'd found only one of these, and the lacinia is not as elaborately sculpted as the mandible. Scott made a series of fine measurements of the mandibles from a range of grasshopper species, including four specimens of *spretus* that the curator at the University of Nebraska was kind enough to allow us to extract from his precious charges. With the statistical assistance of another of my graduate students, Chuck Bomar, it was soon evident that forensic dentistry was a bizarre but effective approach to sorting out grasshopper species. The mandibles from Grasshopper Glacier matched those of *spretus*, whereas all of the other species were clearly separate and distinct. Excited by both the discovery of *spretus* (as far as we could determine) and the development of a unique method for identifying grasshopper remains, we submitted a manuscript for publication.

Although the paper was accepted, my colleagues were clearly unimpressed. With this third paper on glacial remains claiming that the ghost of *spretus* was seen in decomposed remains dug from icy graves, the reviewers made acerbic reference to my lab having yet again "found" the long-lost locust. The sense was that our objectivity was compromised by our devotion to the search—that we were

looking so hard that we were destined to see the Rocky Mountain locust whether it was really there or not. The reviewers begrudgingly
accepted the use of mandibles as a means of identifying the grasshopper remains, insisting that we restrict our conclusions to the narrow-
est possible interpretation—that we had found mandibles more consistent with those of *spretus* than with those of the other species
examined in our analysis.

We'd gained a small victory by having our latest work published,
but it was evident that the scientific community was not going to tol-
erate any more discoveries of rotting and fragmented insects from
glaciers. As one reviewer tersely noted, "This paper only warrants a
very short note. . . . The authors already have five articles on these
grasshoppers." If we wanted to claim that glaciers of the West harbored a hidden biological treasure, then a few flecks of gold were not
going to cut it. We had better find the mother lode—intact and unambiguous specimens of the Rocky Mountain locust—or drop this crazy
treasure hunt.

The Mother Lode

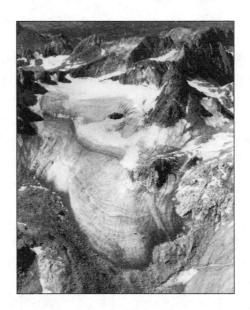

WHILE WE WERE SCOURING THE GLACIERS FOR biological treasure, other scientists were documenting their disappearance. The largest concentration of glaciers in the American Rocky Mountains is found in the Wind River Range of western Wyoming, and seven of the ten largest glaciers in the Rockies are nestled among these rugged peaks. These storehouses of frozen water are the aquatic savings accounts for thirsty agricultural enterprises downstream. Although the precise contribution of these ice fields to the region's water supply has not been fully determined, we know that runoff from just two of the sixty-three glaciers accounts for nearly a tenth of the flow into the Wind and Green rivers. These watercourses are the lifeblood of hundreds of farmers with irrigated fields of sugar beets and alfalfa. In recent years the annual snowfall in the mountains has been inadequate to fill the rivers, so glacial meltwater has become increasingly important, especially in late summer and early fall, when the previous winter's snowpack has disappeared.

Consuming these ancient stores of water is the equivalent of a business constantly drawing on its capital. There will come a time when the water bank—the high mountain glaciers—runs dry, and irrigated agriculture will evaporate. These glaciers are receding at a rate of 10 to 40 percent each year, and no fund can long withstand such a rate of depletion. Dinwoody Glacier is the second largest glacier in the Wind River Mountains, and the account of its recession is profoundly sobering. The amount of water remaining in this glacier is equal to that which was lost between 1958 and 1983. If this rate of retreat continues, the glacier will disappear in about twenty-five years.

Such worrisome figures have generated intensive studies of the glaciers, as scientists attempt to forecast the loss of these vital resources. A geologist and a hydrologist from the Water Quality Laboratory at Western Wyoming Community College in Rock Springs have spent years monitoring Knife Point Glacier, a sweeping expanse of ice that is part of a string of ice fields stretching for ten miles along the continental divide. This complex comprises the largest store of frozen water in the United States, including the two largest glaciers in the American Rockies. Craig Thompson, the laboratory's director, is a vibrant fellow with an irrepressible sense of curiosity. He is a consummate organizer and made the logistical nightmare of the twenty-five-mile treks into the glacier possible. His partner, Charlie Love, is the son of Wyoming's most famous geologist, David Love, immortalized in John McPhee's *Rising from the Plains*. Charlie is a weathered and irascible fellow who looks as if he's probably been "nearly sixty" for a good many years. He is an accomplished geologist, but he is best known for his anthropological work on Easter Island. In 1987, when we were on our first trip to Grasshopper Glacier outside Cooke City, Craig and Charlie had chipped loose a couple of softball-sized hunks of ice from Knife Point Glacier. They were intrigued by the composition—the samples were encrusted with insect parts.

Wyoming has been described as a "small town with very long streets," a reference to the fact that with only 490,000 people there is a statewide sense of being a community—and news manages to find its way throughout the populace. So it was not surprising when I received a call from Craig shortly after our return from the glacier in 1989. He said that he'd read my papers about the search for the Rocky Mountain locust and that Charlie could give me their frozen blocks of insect remains on his way through Laramie in a couple of weeks. I knew from the moment Charlie lifted the first frozen block from the cooler that this had the potential to be the mother lode we'd been seeking. The ice looked like something that had been chipped from a filthy roadside days after a snowstorm. But rather than pebbles, twigs, and trash, the ice was blackened with grasshopper—or locust—parts. Legs and wings were packed into the most wonderful crusty mass of frozen detritus that I'd ever seen. I thanked him profusely (never had such gratitude been offered for such an ugly gift) and promised to call him with the results of our extraction.

After thawing, the smaller block of ice yielded just two ounces of dried matter. But from this scant material we managed to harvest more than a thousand grasshopper mandibles. This was easily the richest deposit that we'd encountered since beginning our research. However, within the larger chunk we found a biological gem—the intact bodies of two grasshoppers or locusts. Although the bodies were horribly crushed and twisted, they were undeniably in the genus *Melanoplus*. Upon ever so gently teasing away the accretions of grime and silt adhering to the abdomens, we found that both were females. We had found what was likely to be the treasure chest, but the key was missing! The various measurements were all consistent with these being Rocky Mountain locusts, but without the male genitalia we could not be absolutely certain. There was only one course of action. We began to make plans to join Craig and Charlie the next summer on their trek to Knife Point Glacier.

In the intervening months, we obtained radiocarbon dates for the specimens. The deeper deposit yielded an age of 400 to 500 years, and the shallower collection site provided material that was 150 to 250 years old. We now knew that the mutilated females had become embedded in the ice when the Rocky Mountain locust was alive, so the motivation to reach the glacier became all-consuming and the winter dragged on interminably. To make matters worse, plenty of snow was falling. The possibility that the summer melt would not uncover the ice at 12,500 feet was a miserable prospect.

Spring comes late in Laramie, snow flurries being a tradition during the university's commencement exercises in mid-May. Given the cost and effort needed to trek from the outfitter's lodge to the glacier, Craig and Charlie had learned that investing in a reconnaissance flight by small plane was a wise strategy. But there was no point in even looking for a window of opportunity until August. So, through the summer, we conducted our research on rangeland grasshopper outbreaks in the balmy conditions of the Platte River valley, just a couple hours east—and 3,000 feet lower than—Laramie. Roasting in the 100-degree heat near Wheatland, Wyoming, in July, we could look forward to the possibility of frosty nights that loomed just one month later and nearly two miles higher. In early August we got the call from Charlie: "Our flyover yesterday came off without a hitch. Patches of ice are showing through, so we should plan to be on the glacier within a couple of weeks. You guys ready to go?" We'd never been more ready for an expedition.

Gary and Sue Weiss were tremendously hospitable outfitters, feeding us huge slabs of prime rib the night we arrived at the lodge and regaling us with stories of harrowing trips and wild adventures. In the morning, they supervised the packing and saddling of the horses. Our wrangler, a rather sullen but seemingly competent fellow, mounted his horse and led us from the lodge before the sun had peeked over the ridge. The day was clear and we made good time for the first twenty miles. Then the trail deteriorated as we climbed through alpine meadows. The wet rocks and muddy quagmires fed by the last of the melting snowbanks made for treacherous riding conditions. After nearly seven hours on a horse, hiking the last five miles was a relief and gave my legs a chance to stretch in more accustomed ways.

We camped on lush, spongy tundra about a thousand feet below Indian Pass—the gap in the continental divide that would take us to the top of Knife Point Glacier. On the rocky slopes near camp we marveled at the tiny haystacks drying in the sun. Hearing panicky peeps and catching fleeting glimpse of gray, we knew that these were the work of pikas. Resembling giant hamsters, but most closely related to hares, these creatures are taxonomic oddities, having been placed in a family that has a single genus. Above our camp, Harrower Glacier clung to the side of the valley and looked reasonably accessible, but there had never been reports of grasshoppers embedded in this ice. Various geological reports from the 1930s made mention of five glaciers in the Wind Rivers as having grasshopper deposits. However, surveys in the 1950s did not report the presence of grasshoppers within these bodies of ice, so their contents had presumably been lost to recession and melting. It seemed that Knife Point Glacier was to be our last great cause for hope.

When we reached Indian Pass the next morning, Knife Point Glacier lay below us, stretching more than a mile down the windswept valley. The top of the glacier was still covered in a thin crust of snow. Knowing the upper reaches of the glacier were deeply crevassed and that fragile snow bridges may have formed over these gaps, we roped up to descend to where the ice had shed its snowy blanket. Working systematically, Larry and I scoured the upper reaches of the glacier while Charlie and Craig went about their business of collecting water and ice samples and surveying the glacier for comparison to earlier measurements. They had told us that the best places to find insects on their previous trips had been lower on the glacier, but we wanted to carefully inspect as much of the ice as possible. Starting at the top made sense logistically, but not emotionally. The day was a complete bust, except for finding a few scattered moths and wasps that had obviously arrived in recent times.

The next day we worked our way down to an area where the glacier leveled out, just below an immense rock buttress that emerged from the middle of the ice field. It was easy to imagine this outcropping extending under the ice, creating a dam that caused the glacier to cascade in slow motion over the submerged ridge. Within minutes I heard Larry shout. The glacial ice crunched under my crampons as I hurried from the edge of the moraine, where I'd been jotting notes.

As I reached him, I dropped to my hands and knees. The surface of the rotting ice was pockmarked with small pits. In the cavity that he'd marked with the tip of his ice ax lay a crumpled form about an inch long, soaked in meltwater. Its legs were missing but the bulbous head, powerful thorax, tapered abdomen, and straight wings left no doubt that this was the body of a grasshopper—or a locust. In the intense sunlight that cuts through the thin air of 12,000 feet, the soggy black remains had warmed faster than the surrounding ice and the body formed a meltwater pool. The area was littered with bodies. Like a Lilliputian version of the *Night of the Living Dead,* the insect corpses were emerging from their graves.

Larry's ruddy face split into a grin. He had indeed found the "mother lode," as we came to call this section of the glacier. He'd stuck with me through August snowstorms, lung-searing climbs, and horrifically bad advice from local guides. The afternoon passed in quiet exuberance as we gently placed the limp and sodden bodies in numbered vials.

The exquisite preservation of so many individuals was a direct result of the mechanism by which this and other glaciers trapped insects. Swarms originating on the western slopes of the Rockies were funneled up the mountain valleys by winds and carried over the passes. A few of these valleys, because of their orientation relative to prevailing winds and their proximity to the habitats where the locusts emerged and aggregated, functioned as thoroughfares during the insectan rush hour (actually a matter of a few days or weeks each year). Some of these montane routes had been carved by glaciers and the rivers associated with their runoff, and in a few cases the ice still persisted at the head of the valley. As the locusts were carried upward, the falling temperature chilled a portion of the swarm, which dropped to the ice, where it was soon immobilized by the cold. In some cases, as the air was funneled through the frigid gaps in the mountains, localized downdrafts and other such perturbations would have forced some of the insects onto the ice.

Based on our findings, the insects must have been interred in huge numbers. We hypothesized that they had been washed by summer meltwater into the crevasses some 300 yards above us. This initial process had not been possible in the glaciers that we had studied in previous years, as these bodies of ice generally lacked the size and topographic variation to form numerous crevasses (except for the third Grasshopper Glacier, and perhaps well-preserved insects will be the reward if and when someone finally accesses the main body of ice). As the ice flowed down the mountain, the crevasses closed and entombed their contents. The frozen creatures were carried over the ice fall formed by the rock outcropping above us and were then brought to the surface by the turbulent flow at the base of the cascade. It was like casting a fishing lure in the still water above a log dam, allowing it to be swept over the waterfall, and then seeing it bob to the surface in the churning water below the cascade.

Charlie and Craig had determined from their work that the glacier was flowing at about six and a half feet per year. So, if our inferences were correct, it should have taken about 150 years for the bodies to travel the 300 yards from the crevasses to where they were found. Months later, our radiocarbon dating placed the time of deposition between 100 and 200 years ago. Given the remarkable sequence of events that ensured both the preservation of the bodies deep within the ice and their return to the surface, perhaps it was not surprising that we'd failed to find well-preserved remains until now.

The thigh-burning trudge back up the glacier, over the pass, and back down to camp at the end of the day was as grueling as ever, but the pain felt strangely good. That night, as Larry brought water up from the stream and Craig and Charlie fixed a dinner of rehydrated jumbo shrimp on a bed of rice (an absurdly decadent meal that they'd snuck into the food boxes in anticipation of a celebration), I dissected one of the few males that we'd collected. Tearing into the body would destroy the integrity of this rare and valuable specimen, but I had to know what we had found. By the hissing, white light of a Coleman lantern, I teased apart the abdomen. The hardened cingula and epiphallus clung weakly to the soft, decomposing tissues within the shriveled abdomen. These were the surviving structures of the internal genitalia, the feature that Theodore Hubbell had found to be so powerfully informative decades earlier. A field microscope provided enough magnification to eliminate any doubt. We'd found the Rocky Mountain locust.

After dinner, I took the dishes down to the stream for washing. Usually, my job was cooking, but tonight I'd begged off in order to conduct my dissection and ensure that our celebration was in order. Scrubbing the plates by moonlight was peaceful. My hands were soon numb in the icy water, which soothed the cuts and scrapes that had come from working on the jagged ice.

Over the next few days, we collected 250 bodies from Knife Point Glacier and Bull Lake Glacier, an adjacent body of ice separated by a shared lateral moraine. Many were too crushed or dismembered for definitive identification, but about 100 had the distinct thoracic spine that gave the subfamily its common name of "spurthroated" grasshoppers. Amid these, there were 14 males with well-preserved abdomens and genitalia, all of which were unambiguously the Rocky Mountain locust.

In the months leading up to our expedition, Larry had invented the "locust body bag," a contraption for concentrating insect remains embedded in blocks of ice. The device had a folding aluminum frame that supported a thick, black plastic bag—very much like a five-gallon body bag—in which a block of frozen remains was placed. The bag was then sealed and the apparatus set on a sunny rock, so the intense sunlight would heat the bag and melt the ice. A few small holes in the bottom of the bag allowed the meltwater to drain out, and in just a couple of hours the contents were reduced to a soggy mass of jumbled body parts. With his simple invention, we reduced five-pound blocks of frozen detritus to a few ounces of valuable specimens (DNA and the other diagnostic biochemicals are fairly stable for short periods, and we kept a small portion of the samples frozen just to be sure). Although everyone carried their maximum load back to camp each afternoon, Larry's strength and fortitude made him the human packhorse at the end of the day. So nobody was more pleased than he with the effectiveness of the "locust body bag" during the 1,300-foot climb back up and over Indian Pass.

Based on our collections, the sex ratio of the swarms was markedly biased toward females, which outnumbered males by slightly more than three to one. Nowhere in Riley's studies was this preponderance of females noted. I speculated that this phenomenon might have been characteristic of freshly emerging swarms in the Rockies. If swarming was a survival strategy for *spretus,* then it makes sense that females would comprise more of the migrants. Let's face it, if we were sending a rocket into space to establish a colony on a distant planet, it would make a lot more sense to stack the manifest with female colonists. We also know that when swarms of other locust species proceed across the landscape they become increasingly dominated by males, as mature females drop out of the migration to lay eggs. So, perhaps a newly forming swarm—such as would have been blown onto the glacier—would be biased toward females to compensate for their loss on the journey.

As the sun melted the blanket of snow covering the upper reaches of the glacier, a most remarkable pattern was revealed in the ice. Hundreds of parallel, curved lines stretched across the width of the glacier. Like growth rings in a tree trunk, these darkened bands marked annual deposits. Each winter, the snow created a fresh layer on the glacier, and during the short summer that followed, dust, pollen, and insects would form a thin organic layer on top. This two-toned annual deposit would then be slowly incorporated into the surface of the glacier, creating a distinct record of the year's events. Trekking up this stratified section of the glacier was like walking along the edge of a gargantuan stack of plates, with the newest plates at the top of the stack. By carefully inspecting each of the darkened bands, we were able to determine the time line of locust deposits on the glacier. These strata did not include whole bodies of locusts, but there were plenty of legs and mandibles. And with Scott's forensic method for identifying mandibles, we were able to determine that all but one of the strata contained the remnants of *spretus.* The only other deposit was, not surprisingly, composed of the remains of *sanguinipes.*

We meticulously sampled a continuous series of bands, representing three centuries of history. Of course, not every stratum had locust remains. From Riley's reports we knew that the average interval between outbreaks of the locust across the Rocky Mountain states was six and half years, with a rather wide variance. The average number of bands between those that contained locusts was six and three-quarters, a remarkable match. It seemed that the glacier provided an incredibly effective and accurate record of major outbreaks. Given that the outbreaks originated in the lands just to the northwest of these glaciated peaks and that the prevailing winds were from this direction, perhaps it is not altogether surprising that the glacier managed to trap a sample of the passing swarms during each of the plagues.

These findings meant that the pattern of locust outbreaks that was documented in the mid-nineteenth century had been ongoing for at least 300 years. Changes wrought by European settlers were not the cause of, and did not increase the frequency of, locust outbreaks. Our analysis also revealed that the temporal pattern of locust remains was random. There were no apparent cycles or regularities in the distribution of swarms. A similar lack of pattern was found when we analyzed Riley's records of locust outbreaks. If outbreaks of the Rocky Mountain locust were driven by the weather, then randomness made sense; within a span of a few centuries, the occurrence of mid-continental droughts is highly irregular.

On the next body of ice beyond Bull Lake Glacier, Larry found no insect remains but plenty of evidence that another scientific expedition had recently passed through. Indeed, just a few weeks earlier, a team from the U.S. Geological Survey—Hayden's old outfit—had taken ice cores from Upper Fremont Glacier to study its history and predict its fate. Through Craig and Charlie's connections we contacted the federal scientists and let them know of our study. Months later, they sent me a single tibia that they'd extracted from a core 315 feet below the surface. I determined that it was the leg of a grasshopper or locust, and after radiocarbon dating it became the oldest evidence of what we assume was a locust outbreak in North America. When this swarm of Rocky Mountain locusts was preparing to sweep across the Great Plains in the twelfth century, Genghis Khan and his Mongol army were sweeping across the steppes of Asia.

On the last day on the ice, we set up a drift net in one of the rivulets pouring down the face of the glacier. A drift net is commonly used to sample stream insects. It comprises a metal frame that is anchored to the substrate, in our case by means of ice screws. Attached to the frame is a long, fine-mesh net through which the water flows. Whatever is drifting in the current is caught in the net, and the flow of the water prevents it from being washed back out or otherwise escaping. By extrapolating from our sample catch, we estimated that the remains of at least 4 million locusts were washing out of the glacier during a typical summer's melting. And according to Charlie and Craig, the terminus of the glacier had receded 250 yards since 1963.

A vast storehouse of biological specimens, representing centuries of natural history that could only be viewed through this window of ice, was being flushed down the valley. Perhaps a small portion of the lighter fragments would make their way into the Wind River and be carried into the agricultural fields along with irrigation water. I like to imagine that the Rocky Mountain locust might in this way return to the crops of the western farmers, completing its centuries-long journey, but taking nothing from the verdant fields. If not thanked for providing a bit of humus to the soil, at least its arrival is no longer cursed.

In recent years the rate of melting apparently has accelerated so that immense mounds of decomposing bodies have begun to pile up alongside the receding ice. According to Jonathan Ratner, an environmental consultant and avid hiker in the Wind River Range, hundreds of acres were covered in two to six inches of the rotting peat-moss-like remains of locusts in the summer of 2002. Based on our back-of-the-envelope estimates, the heaps of material included 20,000 cubic yards of corpses, enough to fill 1,200 dump trucks.

On our final day of the expedition, we packed early because the horses were supposed to show up by mid-morning to take us back out. The wrangler, stringing only four horses, appeared in camp just after lunch. He muttered an excuse for his tardiness but offered no explanation for why there was only a single riding horse other than his. We loaded the three packhorses, gave Charlie the remaining mount, and resigned ourselves to making the twenty-five-mile hike. The last few miles were traversed in moonlight. Gary and Sue offered us profuse apologies for the wrangler's lack of planning. Although it was nearly midnight by the time we'd unpacked, Sue prepared a meal featuring melt-in-your-mouth sirloin steaks and butter-slathered baked potatoes crowned with dollops of sour cream. After days of eating rehydrated macaroni and semicrunchy rice dishes (at 12,000 feet water boils at 190 degrees, which made it difficult to fully cook food), the dinner transformed annoyance into deep satisfaction. We bid our hosts farewell, and looked forward to working with them again the following year.

The next year's expedition featured a cruel ice storm that generated a couple of tense hours during which hypothermia became a real possibility. The rest of the trip went well, with many more whole bodies recovered from the ice. It would be our last collecting trip to the Wind River Glaciers.* Funding sources tightened their belts and presumably found projects that kept species alive to be more important than supporting grave robbers.

The grasshoppers that we brought back to the laboratory from Knife Point Glacier provided valuable material for more refined analyses than had been previously possible. As fate and fortune would have it, we had discovered neither fool's gold nor twenty-four-carat gold nuggets. Perhaps the best metaphor would be a treasure map, hinting at a solution to our mystery but not quite being the answer itself.

Although the proteins in the bodies were too degraded for comparative studies, other molecular features were remarkably well pre-

---

*On this venture our wrangler was more reliable but no less moody. However, we could never have imagined that his dark mood would turn homicidal a few weeks later. Responding to a call from concerned friends who had been unable to contact Gary and Sue Weiss, the sheriff found their bodies about a mile from the Ponderosa Lodge. Evidence of a struggle indicated that they had been shot inside the lodge and their bodies dragged into the woods. Three days later, police found Ken Nickodemus, our sullen wrangler, asleep in the Weiss's stolen truck. Piecing together the rest of the story becomes extremely challenging, as the case devolved into a hotly contested effort on the part of the courts to keep the proceedings secret despite adamant claims by the press that an eighteen-year-old being charged as an adult is not protected by the state laws that shield minors from public hearings. It appears that the troubled young man was convicted, and he is presumably serving his time at the state prison.

served. And Dick was the ideal collaborator on the analysis, being as skilled in the laboratory as he was in the field. Dick was still working for the USDA's research laboratory on campus, and he'd taken personal leave to join the second expedition to Knife Point Glacier. His administration was not fond of his open-ended curiosity and scientific meanderings outside the laboratory's circumscribed boundaries of vector biology. Unlike many government scientists, Dick had a hard time being a good "company man." He was a harsh critic of bureaucratic bungling and self-aggrandizing scientists; he did not suffer fools gladly, and he found no shortage of buffoons within the agency.

Dick began working for the USDA when they maintained a honeybee laboratory in Laramie, and he'd switched to studies of biting gnats when the feds reorganized and created the Arthropod-Borne Animal Diseases Research Laboratory. In his initial research on bees, he'd used the chemical profiles of the waxes that coat the bodies of insects as a means of distinguishing between the gentle European honeybees and the homicidal Africanized honeybees. Being small, insects are highly prone to desiccation, and they protect themselves from water loss with a veneer of wax, not unlike our use of paraffin as a means of sealing jars of jelly to prevent them from drying out and to keep molds from getting in. Dick had worked closely with Dave Carlson—a USDA colleague and the pioneer of this analytical method. Dave had discovered that there are hundreds of different lipid molecules that insects mix together to create their wax layer, and the particular blend forms a chemical fingerprint for each species. During Gurney's work on the taxonomic status of the Rocky Mountain locust, this diagnostic feature was not known, and in any case, the sophisticated analytical instruments necessary to separate and identify the lipid cocktails were not readily available to entomologists at that time. So in an effort to close the book on the identity question, Dick, Dave, and I collaborated on a project to determine whether *spretus* and *sanguinipes* had different types of waxes.

We dribbled a few drops of a solvent down the legs of museum specimens of *spretus* to extract the surface waxes. The same procedure provided wax samples from museum specimens of *sanguinipes* along with locust remains from our first Grasshopper Glacier expedition and from Knife Point Glacier. The *spretus* and *sanguinipes* samples provided distinctly different blends of lipids, each having more than a hundred different hydrocarbons. The extracts from Grasshopper Glacier were frustratingly ambiguous, lying somewhere between our two known blends. The recession of the glacier and the consequent exposure of the insect remains probably led to the slow deterioration of the surface waxes, much as one might expect from an 800-year-old candle. To our delight, however, the samples from Knife Point Glacier, having been entombed deep within the ice, provided a much higher-quality chemical fingerprint. There could be no doubt that these specimens matched those of *spretus*. But the search for DNA—the ultimate chemical evidence to establish both the taxonomic standing of *spretus* and the identity of the glacial remains—would not be so simple.

Bill Chapco is a bespectacled, always-happy-to-see-you professor from the University of Regina in Saskatchewan. This warm and authentic fellow is also the world's foremost grasshopper geneticist. For years he has worked on methods for extracting and analyzing the DNA from grasshoppers, which, as it turns out, is no mean trick. In 1993, I sent him some of my treasured locust mummies from Knife Point Glacier, knowing that if anyone could eventually tease the genetic code out of these creatures it would be Bill. And I was right, although I had to wait nearly a decade for his deliberate and systematic efforts to bear fruit. In reality, he had developed effective methods some time earlier, but knowing the rarity of *spretus* specimens, Bill wanted to be absolutely certain of his technique before applying it to the Rocky Mountain locust.

In November 2002, Bill presented his first findings on the genetics of the Rocky Mountain locust at the national meeting of the Entomological Society of America. Somewhere around 3,000 entomologists converge each winter to share their findings on every imaginable—and a few unimaginable—aspects of insects. Using museum specimens representing a wide range of species, along with the material from the glacier, Bill showed that the standing of *spretus* as a valid species was fully supported by key regions of their DNA. Much to everyone's surprise, neither *sanguinipes* nor even *femurrubrum* shared the greatest genetic similarity to the Rocky Mountain locust. Rather, the nearest living relative was *Melanoplus bruneri,* a species with a catholic diet and a propensity for irregular outbreaks in the mountain meadows of the United States and Canada. Bill's work also left no doubt that the museum and glacial specimens of locusts were the same species. Indeed, much to my delight, the genetic material from the glacial specimens had suffered substantially less degradation than that obtained from the dried museum specimens.

Molecular analysis can also shed light on the events leading up to extinction. If there was a detectable loss of genetic variation in the Rocky Mountain locust—a genetic bottleneck—this change would indicate if and when the species began a gradual decline leading to its final extinction. Such a narrowing of genetic diversity occurs when a species engages in a high degree of inbreeding in fragmented or reduced populations. We all have a small proportion of abnormal and adverse genes acquired from one of our parents, but the corresponding traits are often not expressed because the alternative, healthy form of the gene from our other parent masks or dominates the deleterious form. So there's a good reason why we frown on brothers marrying their sisters—and, perhaps, why evolution has predisposed us to find our siblings lacking in sexual desirability. The children of such matings are much more likely to receive a double dose of these rare, harmful genes and to manifest the associated deformities and illnesses. All of this genetic change would have made for an exciting discovery, except the molecular analysis provided no evidence of a bottleneck in the museum specimens from the turn of the last century relative to the older, glacial specimens.

While Bill had been working on his molecular methods, we had been taking meticulous measurements of glacial and museum specimens looking for evidence of a genetic bottleneck through a trait called *bilateral asymmetry.* Most animals exhibit bilateral symmetry, meaning that if we were to slice them in half longitudinally the two pieces would be near-mirror images of one another. Of course, this pattern is not found in creatures such as sea stars, which have radial symmetry. Even in bilaterally symmetrical animals, like humans and grasshoppers, the two halves are not perfectly identical. However, in genetically healthy organisms, the degree of symmetry is much greater than in organisms arising from inbreeding. Our measurements of tibial lengths and counts of tibial spines from the right and left hind legs consistently failed to show any differences between Rocky Mountain locusts before and during their decline to extinction. The locust's breeding pattern during the last few years of its existence was not unusual; no evidence indicated that there were several generations of abnormally diminished or exceptionally isolated populations leading to inbreeding. Our findings agreed with Bill's—these insects had not been in a prolonged decline.

The late 1800s were not the last gasp of a dying species. Rather, it seemed that the extinction happened suddenly and without warning to a normal, healthy species. It appeared that the Rocky Mountain locust had been decimated throughout its range within a matter of a few years in an entomological Armageddon. But what sort of force could act in such a manner without leaving evidence of its presence spread across the West?

13

Pioneers on Trial

THE FIRST COURSE THAT I TAUGHT AT THE UNIVERSITY of Wyoming was in the fall of 1986. During the summer, I prepared intensively for my first solo venture into academia, amassing a file drawer of journal articles, reviewing texts, and compiling more than 200 pages of lecture notes. On the first day, I was ready to plunge into the wonderful world of "Insect Population Biology" with a class of graduate students from entomology and zoology and a smattering of senior-level biology students. I had prepared like a football team readies for the Super Bowl, but the students were in preseason form. The experience was traumatic for all concerned.

I had assumed a far greater grasp of mathematics than the students possessed, so that my early lectures were a source of confusion, fear, and borderline outrage—rather than joyful enlightenment—for my students. Eventually, we reached an academic truce that had the hallmark of a classic compromise—nobody was entirely happy. They stretched beyond their comfort zone, and I backed-off from my expectations. Having survived my first teaching experience, I set about revamping the course to make the cabalistic field of population biology compelling to the students.

The virtue of teaching for a professor heavily engaged in research is that being effective in the classroom requires one to take a far more comprehensive view of a subject than might be normally the case for a research scientist. Preparation for a course requires a substantial expansion of one's reading into areas that are tangential, even seemingly unrelated, to the central focus of a typical research program. But in my experience, there is a great chance of happening upon a new perspective, concept, or method that is applicable to one's research. And although I manage to work my various research projects into my lectures whenever possible, I have gleaned more exciting and creative ideas from teaching for use in my research than vice versa.

Over the years, I have found a number of fascinating examples of changes in insect populations that served as relevant starting points for the more detailed and abstract principles that formed the infrastructure of my course. Perhaps the best-known and most dramatic display of insect population dynamics in North America is the migration of the monarch butterfly across the continent. Not only would the ecology of this butterfly turn out to serve as a case study for my students, but the life history of this creature also would provide the clue that allowed me to break the case of the Rocky Mountain locust's mysterious disappearance.

Each spring, monarch butterflies move northward from their overwintering grounds in Mexico. In late March they appear in the southernmost parts of the United States, extending into the central region of the country by the end of April. The children of the Mexican population of butterflies pass through the larval stage in about two weeks—longer if the weather is cool. Then the larvae attach themselves to plants and enter the pupal stage. Upon emerging as adults, this generation continues the northward journey into much of eastern North America.

The life cycle is repeated in late spring or early summer, giving rise to the grandchildren of the Mexican population. These monarchs extend the range of the species into southern Canada. In summer, the adult butterflies survive for a month of hedonistic activity, dividing their time between mating and sipping nectar. By mid-summer the great-grandchildren appear, and in late summer the great-great-grandchildren make their debut. However, this last generation is a radically different population. In response to cooler temperatures and shorter days, the adults alter their physiology and behavior. They are like overtrained athletes; their reproductive organs fail to mature and their libido is suppressed. These insect Olympians stock up on high-energy nectar and then begin the long, arduous return migration to Mexico. After four generations, the population of monarchs has grown tremendously, but the 2,000-mile journey takes a brutal toll. More than 200 million butterflies may begin the return migration, but just 1 in 100 makes it to the wintering grounds. How they find their way back to the home of their great-great grandparents remains a mystery.

The winter sanctuaries of the monarch were not discovered by scientists until 1975, although local villagers had known the butterfly's secret for many years. The monarchs spend the winter in patches of fir forest west of Mexico City, clustering at perhaps a dozen small sites on the southern slopes of the mountains. Imagine having 35,000 monarchs in an area the size of your living room. Hang 700 decks of playing cards from your ceiling, walls, and furniture if you'd like to get a better impression of these aggregations.

For five months, these butterflies remain virtually immobile, blanketed by the cool, damp forest and insulating one another from the rain and snow that leaks through the canopy of trees. During the long winter at nearly 10,000 feet they rely almost exclusively on their fat reserves. Predators often take one in ten of the butterflies overwintering in a colony, but a harsh winter is perhaps the greatest threat, with as much as 80 percent of a colony succumbing to a bitterly cold, wet storm, as happened in 2002. With the spring thaw, the butterflies stir and begin their northward migration. The population again begins to grow at a phenomenal rate, individual females laying 400 or more eggs.

Monarch population dynamics are reminiscent of a roller-coaster ride. In recent years, the population dropped precipitously, a change that triggered great concern for the future of the butterfly. Conservationists have sounded warnings regarding large-scale alterations in the monarch's habitats. It doesn't bode well for a species whose only food—milkweed—is, after all, a weed. As roadsides are increasingly mowed and sprayed, the monarch's larder is depleted. There remain, however, large untended tracts of milkweed, so the decline of this plant doesn't represent an imminent threat to the butterfly. Likewise, the environmental alarm over the contamination of milkweed patches via genetically engineered crops now appears to be rather premature.

Although continental-scale hazards afflict the monarch throughout the summer, most entomologists have focused on the time and space in which the species is most vulnerable—the ecological bottleneck of its overwintering sites in Mexico. In 1986, a Monarch Butterfly Biosphere Reserve was created to protect the butterfly's roosting grounds. However, this decree simply mandated protection without offering the local landholders, who are economically dependent on logging, any alternative or compensation. Not surprisingly, deforestation in this area has continued, so that nearly half the original forest habitats that harbor the butterflies have been lost since the reserve was created. To make matters worse, the quality of the remaining forest is rather poor from the insect's perspective. The economic demand for low-quality wood to produce particle board means that loggers take the young trees that can be readily converted into wood chips. The result is an excessively thinned forest that provides little protection against the weather for the overwintering monarchs.

But as grim as the prognosis may be, the situation could be even worse. The butterflies are concentrated into a dozen or so colonies that occupy only a tiny fraction of the forest during any winter. Between November and March, the quiescent colonies are extremely vulnerable to disturbance. If, by chance or malevolence, the loggers were to cut down the groves being used by the overwintering monarchs, the results would be devastating. Just three dozen loggers armed with chain saws could destroy the entire population of monarchs in the course of a single winter. North America would be left with only a small western population of monarchs that primarily winters along the California coast and comprises about 5 percent of the total.

The take-home lesson for my students, in addition to the various implications for mathematical modeling, is that a population is only as safe as its weakest link. An ecological bottleneck can spell disaster for a species if the compression of its numbers occurs in a time and place where human disturbance is likely to occur. If twenty-second-century textbooks in insect ecology recount the disappearance of the monarch butterfly, the story will most likely center on a small tract of forested mountainside in Mexico—not in the fields and roadsides of the North American continent.

For some people, epiphanies arrive on bolts of lightning, forever changing how they view the world. Religious transformations are among the most spectacular of these changes. The classic story in this regard is the conversion of Saul, who is now better known as Saint Paul. While riding to Damascus, where he was intending to obtain authorization from the synagogue to arrest Christians, Paul experienced the most unambiguous of epiphanies. The poor fellow was struck to the ground, blinded by a heavenly light, and heard the voice of God cry out, "Saul, Saul, why do you persecute me?" His attendants, who also heard the Almighty, led him the rest of the way to Damascus, where the voice said he would receive further instructions. And the rest is history.

I can't recall that there was an astonishing moment of "Eureka!" or a sudden realization of an impending breakthrough in the case of the Rocky Mountain locust. I do, however, remember long hours of meandering conversations with Larry DeBrey in the cab of a Chevy pickup crossing the austerely beautiful steppes of Wyoming in the course of our summer research on grasshopper outbreaks. And one of our mobile discussions has crystallized in my memory as the turning point in the investigation.

The otherwise unremarkable afternoon involved a coffee-infused discussion that took place in Old Blue—the peeling, rattle-trap truck that we still use in the field. The conversation—in equal parts intended to keep me awake at the wheel and to pass the time pleasantly—wandered around one of our favorite topics, the case of the locust's disappearance. We talked on and on, sipping bad-but-free coffee from the gas station in Medicine Bow and touching on elements of Western history, pioneer agriculture, grasshopper ecology, and other cases of extinction, in no particular order. Somehow, the conversation began to swirl around the embattled status of the monarch and the final retreat of the locust. What had been an erratic flitting of loosely connected ideas circled toward a point of mental illumination. Given that I was driving at about eighty miles an hour, it's probably good that the epiphany was more like a slowly unfolding dawn than a rapturous bolt of lighting.

"What if," I asked, "we've been looking at the wrong scale for all these years? What if the locust died out in the same way that the monarch is likely to disappear?"

"Yeah, could be." Larry replied, not being one to be knocked from his horse by epiphanies—either divine or secular. "A few pioneers might've done a lot of damage by logging, mining, and farming in the locust's Permanent Zone."

"When we get back," I went on, "dig into the library and see what you can find on European settlement in the Rocky Mountains. We need to figure out what the pioneers were doing when the locust was declining."

"They may not have been the sharpest crayons in the box," Larry replied, "but I'll bet they must've headed to the river valleys, where there was water and decent soil." He penciled a reminder to himself in the ragged notebook that he kept on the dashboard.

"Smarter than Laramie gardeners, eh?" I replied. We had both tried to grow vegetables back home. Although he was far more successful in this venture, we had a running joke that at 7,200 feet on the high plains of Wyoming, the only things standing between us and our bounty were water, soil, and heat.

"Ah, hell," he said after a contemplative pause.

"What's wrong?"

"I forgot to tell Deanna to water the tomatoes. They'll be shriveled like an Eskimo's scrotum when I get back."

Our conversation digressed into various aspects of gardening, women, and life in Laramie. The road wasn't leading to Damascus.

The epiphany was simply tucked away for consideration after we were back on campus. Sometimes a revelation comes with a flash of heavenly light and a booming voice—and sometimes it is jotted in a sun-bleached spiral notebook.

Between the tattered leather covers of the first three reports of the U.S. Entomological Commission lie 1,258 pages of text, tables, and drawings concerning almost every imaginable aspect of the Rocky Mountain locust. There are weather charts detailing the prevailing winds, average temperatures, and typical rainfalls; there are lists of outbreaks subdivided by states and years; there are tables of locust body measurements broken down by locations; and there are woodcuts of locusts, their natural enemies, and various contraptions meant to control these pests. Scattered throughout the pages are dozens of plates, illustrating everything from the histology of the brain, to the cellular structure of the gut, to the rectal tissues of the locust. The appendices are filled with detailed accounts of the locust's invasions from across the nation, all meticulously rendered in hundreds of pages of seven-point font. Best of all are the gorgeous maps, including a color-coded, six-panel foldout map in the Second Report that covers an area of thirteen square feet. Supplementing these tomes are Riley's annual reports to the state of Missouri preceding the commission and various reports that he made to the U.S. Department of Agriculture following the work of the commission.

These volumes are packed with information, the overwhelming majority of which pertains to the biology, ecology, and management of the locust during its outbreaks. This, of course, makes perfect sense. We are captivated by stories of heroes and wars, corporate giants and cataclysmic deluges. Who would write a book about mild personalities or minor battles, and who would want to read a report of a typical business or an average thunderstorm? I had been reading accounts of the locust with the eye of a thrill seeker, relishing the dramatic descriptions of swarms and ensuing battles. But now my goal was precisely the opposite.

While Larry was digging through Western history, census figures, and government reports, I began to scour the entomological archives for evidence of the locust's life between outbreaks. Rather than trying to picture the locust at its peak of vitality, I set out to glean the information necessary to reconstruct the life of this creature at its most vulnerable, when the insect was confined to its sanctuaries in the Permanent Zone. Ironically, this time of recession probably accounted for 80 percent of its life history, but only a small fraction of the texts was devoted to how this creature spent its life in the land for which it was named.

The modern world is drowning in information. We have more data than we can possibly use regarding nearly every picayune matter of society, economics, and politics. Science has contributed to this tsunami of facts and figures, but Riley's reports demonstrate that the tidal wave of minutiae is hardly unique to our time. In every age, the challenge has been to move from information to knowledge. And the value of experts lies in their capacity to extract meaning from the reams of facts. Rather than being swamped by raw data, the connoisseur, artist, craftsman, engineer, clinician, or scientist is selectively and self-consciously blind. Knowing what to ignore, recognizing what is extraneous, is the key to deriving pattern, form, and insight.

A meticulous rereading of the various reports and documents from the late 1800s concerning the lives of locusts and humans initially unearthed only scattered clues, but soon the puzzle pieces began to link together and form a clear picture. From the evidence that could be gleaned from these yellowed, crumbling pages, a single startling conclusion emerged. The unmistakable identity of the locust's killer slowly took shape—and the perpetrator of the most spectacular extinction event in the continent's history had not even been a suspect in the century following the locust's disappearance. Making such an audacious case in the court of science would hinge on three essential lines of evidence. Just as in a criminal trial, I would need to show that the accused had the opportunity, the means, and the motive to perpetrate the killing.

THE OPPORTUNITY

According to Frederick Jackson Turner, a noted historian, the quality of America that distinguished the nation from its European cousins was the process of settling the frontier. A little more than a century ago, one of the greatest migrations in human history was coming to a close. Nearly 2 million people moved to the western prairies and mountains in the 1870s. In modern terms, this would be equivalent to seeing Colorado, Idaho, Montana, Nevada, New Mexico, North Dakota, South Dakota, Utah, and Wyoming grow from empty lands to their current populations. That many folks streaming into a region in a matter of ten years would have tremendous ecological and economic repercussions.

With the financial panic of 1873, thousands of people had been thrown out of work in the East, and the promise of free land and a new start drew homesteaders to the West as surely as locusts poured out of their crowded and dwindling montane habitats during a drought. The industrialists were delighted, as the western migration drained the unemployed from the restive cities. Many folks believed that the rain would follow the plow or the trains. Respectable scientists (such as Harvard's Louis Agassiz), less than credible professors (such as Nebraska's Samuel Aughey), and disreputable journalists explained that the aridity of the plains would be converted into lush fields because "the concussion of the air and rapid movement produced by railroad trains and engines affects the electrical conditions of the atmosphere." Within little more than a decade after the locusts declined, the populations of Colorado and Nebraska doubled, and those of Montana, South Dakota, and Wyoming tripled. Between 1870 and 1900, as much land was settled and brought into agricultural production as had been transformed in the previous 250 years of North America's history.

As the surge of settlement extended westward from the Plains states, the land became increasingly dry and unwelcoming to prospective farmers. But the mountains promised riches for another kind of prospector. Mining communities sprang up along the spine of the Rockies, and with these ramshackle towns came the need for food. The miners, freighters, and merchants represented a lucrative market for farmers. The land could not produce as profusely as the tallgrass prairies to the east, but the mountain valleys had decent soils, water for irrigation, and—most important—a hungry population that had no time or inclination to grow its own crops. And at least on average, there was far more money to be made in grain than in gold. Between 1880 and 1890 the number of farms in the eight Rocky Mountain states and territories doubled to almost 50,000. Even so, production of cereals, potatoes, and vegetables in the Boise Valley and similar communities could not keep pace with the demand, so they were forced to import food. Indeed, crop production in the Rocky Mountain states was less than half that of Kansas. From a national perspective, the farmers in the montane valleys were entirely negligible. Or so the country believed. In the end, what mattered to the breadbasket of the nation was not the pitiable amount of food grown in the Rockies. Rather, history was shaped by the ecological changes that took place as a consequence of these picturesque and profitable—but not terribly productive—farms.

When Larry DeBrey came into my office a few weeks after our fateful discussion regarding monarch butterflies and locusts, I could tell that he'd struck gold. He'd found a map showing the western lands under cultivation in 1880. The blotches representing croplands in the Rocky Mountain region were squarely within the Permanent Zone—the overlap was nearly perfect. The vast, windswept steppes of Idaho, Montana, and Wyoming were bare of wheat, corn, and hay fields. The pioneer farmers were courageous souls, but they were no fools. They avoided the alkali flats and sagebrush steppes, settling in the montane valleys. High above, the snowpack fed the perennial streams that cascaded down the flanks of the Rockies, joining together in the foothills to sculpt broad, sandy river courses that trapped fertile soil in their meandering bends.

But even with this coincidence of locusts and humans in time and space, the coarse scale of the map couldn't reveal whether these ancient adversaries had actually collided. Was it possible that the locust population that gave rise to the swarms that blanketed two-thirds of a continent could be so concentrated as to succumb to the invasion of a few thousand pioneers? Surely even the most worn-out laggards of the plague from the 1870s would occupy far more land than a ragtag bunch of farmers could destroy. However, I'd learned that what seemed obvious was not always so.

It was time to let the numbers speak for themselves. How much land would the Rocky Mountain locust be likely to occupy between outbreaks? To begin, our best estimate of the peak population of the locust during a typical outbreak was somewhere around 10 trillion insects. The challenge, however, was to work backward from this population to estimate the number of individuals that would have been lying low between outbreaks. Based on the fecundity of the locust and natural mortality rates, it was safe to say that these creatures had the capacity to increase their numbers by 10- to 100-fold in each generation of an outbreak. So, let's assume that the population had increased at these rates over the course of three generations, which was the typical period from the onset to the apex of an outbreak cycle. Given this range of reproductive rates, the result would have been 1,000 to 1 million times more locusts at the peaks than in the valleys—both mathematically and geographically. Working backward, then, we can estimate that a plague of 10 trillion locusts originated from a population of 10 million to 10 billion individuals.

From what we know of modern-day locusts, grasshoppers are a sensible surrogate for the solitary phase of *spretus*. And so, if we assume that the Rocky Mountain locust in its recession areas lived in a manner similar to that of existing rangeland grasshoppers, we can generate a reasonable approximation of the land area required to support a few million or billion creatures. On productive pastures and grasslands similar to those occupied by *spretus* in the Permanent Zone, grasshoppers typically occur at a population density of about one individual per square yard. Much higher densities are found during outbreaks, but we're interested in the mundane times between these biological spectacles. Thus, a population of 10 million locusts would have required an area of about 2,000 acres, and a population of 10 billion locusts would have needed a couple million acres. With this line of reasoning, we can estimate that the actual habitat of the Rocky Mountain locust during its recession periods was as little as 3, and as much as 3,000, square miles. In other words, all of the individuals would have comfortably fit into a circle of land between 2 and 60 miles in diameter. Of course, this is quite a range, and we know that the montane river valleys were not laid out in neat circles, nor were the locusts uniformly distributed. However, no matter how we parcel out the locusts and their habitats, the implications are the same—this species was squeezed into a tight ecological bottleneck.

The startling conclusion that emerges from these mathematical extrapolations is that the Rocky Mountain locust was extremely vulnerable to even small-scale human disturbances. But this inference suggests that the locust was far more concentrated than would be apparent from maps of the Permanent Zone, shown to cover parts of five states and provinces. Further ecological evidence gleaned from the historical record supports the notion that the insect was restricted to very particular conditions within the region—habitats that corresponded with the arable lands.

I was not the first to recognize that the immense swaths of land representing the Permanent Zone on Riley's maps were an extremely crude depiction of the Rocky Mountain locust's habitat. In 1959, when Ashley Gurney was struggling to explain the locust's disappearance, he noted, "Within the [Permanent] Region, *spretus* did not breed everywhere, but instead it did so in favorable places. River bottoms, sunny slopes of uplands, and subalpine grassy areas among the mountains were considered to be favored egg-laying sites." But Gurney was seeking an ecological change on a continental scale, so this clue was set aside without his recognizing that it was crucial to solving the mystery. Norman Criddle also harbored suspicions about the actual hideouts of the locust within its montane distribution. Although in 1917 he was still of the opinion that the creature was lurking about, it was clear that he didn't believe that the locust would be found just anywhere in the Rockies:

> At present, however, the insect seems to have vanished completely. Indeed, there are some who would place it with the Passenger Pigeon as an object of the past. It seems almost incomprehensible, however, that such can be the case. More probably the real permanent breeding grounds are more restricted than was supposed, and the locust will yet be located either by the discovery of its real haunts or by a new invasion following favorable weather conditions for breeding purposes.

Riley drew the maps of the Permanent Zone with a very broad brush, and it was not until delving into the particulars of the insect's biology that I found the keen observations for which he was so highly acclaimed. He narrowed the ecology of the locust somewhat in describing it as "a denizen of high altitudes, breeding in the valleys, parks and plateaus of the Rocky Mountain region of Colorado, and especially Montana, Wyoming and British America." But this panoramic allusion was too vague for a natural historian with Riley's acute sense of ecological detail. And the more specific his description, the more intriguing this line of evidence became. His attention focused explicitly on a crucial landscape:

> The insects hatch in immense quantities in the valleys of the three forks of the Missouri river and along the Yellowstone, and, when fledged, they move on from there in a southeast direction at about the rate of 10 miles per day. . . . Prompted by that most exigent law of hunger—spurred on for very life—it rises in immense clouds in the air to seek for fresh pastures where it may stay its ravenous appetite.

Riley was not the only scientist to note that the locusts were highly restricted to particular habitats. In August 1882, another renowned entomologist was leading a scientific expedition into the Permanent Zone. Lawrence Bruner, the namesake for the Rocky Mountain locust's nearest relative, *Melanoplus bruneri,* was working his way across Montana in an effort to track down the locust. He'd already taken the time and effort to name an imposing edifice near Fort Buford "Riley Peak" in honor of his entomological colleague. As Bruner came across a remnant population of *spretus,* he noted in his journal, "We crossed a vast expanse of nearly level prairie, well grassed, with a loose, sandy, clay soil . . . admirably fitted for the rearing of locust swarms. In fact the entire country . . . is one vast hotbed, calculated to produce the largest and healthiest swarms in America [forming] cradles of the ravaging pest."

In contrast to the effusive claims that would typify economic entomology in the later era of DDT, Bruner offered a most humble interpretation of the power of human ingenuity:

The question now arises, Has there been any plausible and practical means discovered during any of these extended tours by which the locusts can be exterminated? My answer to this, if direct, is *no;* if indirect, *yes.* In the first place we are to make an answer in accordance with the definition of the word *exterminated.* As I understand it, it signifies blot out, and that would require every individual insect o [*sic*] this species to be killed, which would be an utter impossibility. But, by various methods already described in the annual reports of this Commission created by Congress, their numbers could be and will be so killed off from time to time as to bring them under the control of their natural enemies.

The possibility of killing the ravaging pest while it lay in its cradle—the entomological version of the mythical infanticidal Medea—never occurred to Bruner or Riley.

What did occur to Riley was that reproduction was the key to understanding the pockets of habitat that supported *spretus* in the Permanent Zone. He knew from his own observations and the reports of his contemporaries that female locusts were very particular about where they laid their eggs. In various documents he noted that oviposition was restricted to sandy and gravelly habitats, where the soils were firm but not hard-packed. The females avoided very loose so¹ and moist ground. Like insectan Goldilocks in search of "just right conditions, the locusts buried their eggs in the well-drained soils of the montane valleys. The egg beds lay between the overly wet, silty streamsides and the sere, rocky hillsides. During their plundering of the prairie farms, the locusts laid their eggs in soils that mimicked the fertile river valleys of the Rockies.

The well-drained, sandy cradles in which the six-legged mothers deposited their eggs were so essential to the life of the locust that Riley argued for this being the limiting factor in the species' ability to persist in its eastward migrations. It was clear that the Rocky Mountain locust could not indefinitely perpetuate itself in the habitats of the Midwest, but nobody knew why. After "fully digesting all the facts," Riley concluded that the most plausible constraints were the warm, wet weather, which induced a combination of "debility, disease, and deterioration"—and the locusts' evident "need for their native sandy and gravelly soil." *Spretus* was reluctant to lay its eggs in rank vegetation, hard-packed clay soils, and rich loamy fields because these nurseries produced fewer, weaker nymphs.*

The Rocky Mountain locust's initial decline had been part of the natural ebb and flow of the species. Outbreaks typically lasted for three to five years, and so the 1874–1877 plague had essentially run its course and a period of remission was to be expected. The collapse of the locust back into its Permanent Zone in the river valleys of the Rockies was ecologically unremarkable. Rather than a tidal wave of vitality washing over the continent, it had been reduced to a trickle of life restricted to its favored habitats. There were no indications that this recession was a prelude to extinction because we had not paid attention to the ecological bottleneck.

In the Rocky Mountain region, farmers and locusts crowded into the arable and irrigable lands of the broad, fertile river valleys. The opportunity for conflict over this rich habitat was undeniable. However, just because the accused and the victim were in the same place at the time of the murder does not mean that a guilty verdict is certain. A prosecutor also must demonstrate that the perpetrator had the means to dispatch the victim. Did the pioneers have the capacity to drive the locust to extinction, and what ecological weapons could have been wielded by these simple folk to slay the mightiest species on the continent?

---

*In light of our recent studies of grasshopper ecology, the intimate association between soils and locusts is not surprising. Several years ago one of my best graduate students, Scott Schell, conducted a spatial analysis of the environmental factors associated with rangeland grasshopper outbreaks in Wyoming. Although vegetation, climate, and topography were all important considerations, one factor dominated the ecological model— soils. Using computer mapping, he pinpointed the lands that supported the most frequent grasshopper outbreaks based on three decades of survey records. These chronically infested habitats, scattered across eastern Wyoming, had one thing in common, a particular soil with a name that only pedologists could love or comprehend: Torriorthents-Argiustolls-Haplustolls. This is a well-drained, sandy-gravelly soil found on eroding hillsides with sparse vegetation. Most remarkably, this particular soil type is relatively rare, being found in less than 1 percent of the state, but it comprised all of the lands rated as having a history of severe grasshopper outbreaks. We think grasshoppers and locusts are creatures that live above the ground, but in reality they spend more than three-quarters of their lives buried in the earth. It is no wonder that the chemistry, moisture, texture, and depth of soils are so critical to these insects.

THE MEANS

Lawrence H. Keeley is a professor of anthropology at the University of Illinois, and his work focuses on the most human and least humane of all behaviors: warfare. His rigorous analyses of the nature and costs of waging war have yielded some surprising results. Although we might well imagine that bombers, machine guns, and other modern weapons have dramatically increased the death rate on the battlefield, Keeley paints a radically different picture in *War before Civilization: The Myth of the Peaceful Savage*. Taking part in primitive warfare is often far deadlier on a proportional basis than participation in contemporary conflict.

Perhaps the epitome of the modern battlefield was the grand campaign of the Normandy landing in World War II. Between D-Day and the liberation of Paris, a period of seventy-nine days in 1944, about 290,000 soldiers died. Guns, bayonets, grenades, artillery, tanks, bombs, mines, and the other instruments of modern warfare killed about 3,700 men during each day of this campaign. Compare these numbers to the massacres of Tutsis and Hutus in 1994. The killings began with the assassination of the presidents of Rwanda and Burundi on April 6 and continued for ninety days, ending with the capture of Kigali. Although the death toll is not fully known, between 500,000 and 1 million people died. No fewer than 5,000 lives were taken during each day of this conflict. There were no bombers, no cannons, no tanks. Yet 1 out of every 14 people in these two African nations was killed in a matter of three months. The weapons were machetes and sharp sticks, with a smattering of small arms. The capacity of humans to destroy each other—and other species—is not contingent upon advanced technologies.

Recent excavations of fossil and subfossil bones on Pacific Islands have revealed an incredible story of extinction. With the arrival of the Polynesians in the outer Pacific, from Tonga in the west to Hawaii in the east, at least half of the species of endemic birds disappeared. Hopscotching from island to island in single outrigger or double canoes, these first settlers left a record of environmental destruction in their wake. The eminent conservation biologist Edward O. Wilson summarizes this period of human expansion quite simply: "The voyagers ate their way through the Polynesian fauna." For example, on Eua (in present-day Tonga) the colonists were greeted by the squawking and twittering of 25 bird species, of which 17 were permanently silenced. Of about 100 species of birds that lived on Hawaii before the arrival of humans, the native people extinguished half before the arrival of Captain Cook in 1778, and another 15 or so have disappeared since. But islands are not the only landforms subject to the devastation of primitive people.

Shortly after the arrival of humans in North America, nearly three-quarters of the large mammal genera became extinct. Mammoths and ground sloths had flourished for 2 million years, but within 1,000 years of our arrival these creatures disappeared. The story is the same for the largest birds that once roamed the continent. Climatic shifts might have played some role in these extinctions, but the general consensus is that global warming during the Pleistocene was, at best, an accomplice of the human hunters. Chain saws, synthetic chemicals, and hydroelectric dams might be the modern, high-tech weapons in the war against nature, but it appears that canoes, snares, and spears were entirely adequate to the task.

The means of environmental disruption available to the European settlers of the Rocky Mountain region were not much more sophisticated than those of the first people who colonized this land. Wherever the locust might have begun to increase in numbers along the river valleys, the farmers probably employed direct means of suppressing the insect. But from the accounts of the settlers and the records provided by Riley, it appears that such battles were scattered and the skirmishes were minor. Rather, the farmers waged a sort of unwitting guerrilla warfare, an insidious assault on the supply lines and homelands of the locust.

In 1866, General John Pope held out little hope for agriculture in the arid West. The only cause for limited optimism was in the Rocky Mountain region, where, "the streams being more numerous, and the timber more abundant, it is practicable to form settlements and to cultivate the valleys of the streams by irrigation." This glimmer of hope soon became a radiant beacon for the settlers seeking prosperity. A century later, the renowned western historian Gilbert Fite described precisely this course of events: "Whenever possible, settlers located on or near a creek or river in order to have water for livestock and irrigation." By the 1880s, the competition for the West's key resource was becoming downright nasty: "Water was becoming scarce at critical times during the growing season, valleys were becoming crowded, and conditions for newcomers were discouraging."

Irrigation was the lifeblood of agriculture in the Rocky Mountain region. Of the 50,000 farms in 1890, 70 percent were operated by irrigators—about 2 million acres were regularly flooded. A decade later, more than 5 million acres in the Rockies were being irrigated by 70,000 operators. Our most generous estimate of the locust's distribution during its recession periods was 2 million acres in the montane river valleys of the West. In this context, it seems entirely possible that the vast majority of the insect's sanctuary was saturated by pioneer farmers on a yearly basis. But would this have been lethal?

In combating the locust, Riley understood that habitat modifications could have far greater effects than desperate acts of direct confrontation, such as thrashing, poisoning, or crushing the invaders. He advised, "When irrigation is practicable, as it is in some of the ravaged parts of Colorado, let the ground be thoroughly inundated for a few days, and the eggs will lose vitality and rot. . . . Experiments prove how soon they succumb to excess moisture." As he reviewed the various primitive tools available to defend agriculture from these rapacious creatures, he became increasingly convinced of the value of water.

Sixteen years later, in one of his last publications on the locust, Riley remained convinced that irrigation was one of the most economical and effective methods for suppressing *spretus*. By this time, he understood that water represented both life to the farmer and death to the locust:

This [irrigation] is feasible in much of the country subject to locust ravages, especially in the mountain regions, where, except in exceptionally favorable locations, agriculture can be successfully carried on only by its aid, and where means are already extensively provided for the artificial irrigation of large areas. Where the ground is light and porous, prolonged and excessive moisture will cause most of the eggs to perish, and irrigation in autumn or spring may prove beneficial.

But for farmers, the point of irrigation was to grow crops, not to drown locusts. And so we must also consider what was being sown. The plants that were replacing the montane meadows may have been lethal in their own right.

The studies conducted by Charles Brett in the 1940s had demonstrated that alfalfa was deleterious to *sanguinipes*—and perhaps by extrapolation to *spretus*. Bob Pfadt's systematic experiments had isolated this detrimental effect to the period of nymphal development in *sanguinipes*. Recall that Pfadt had questioned the contention that alfalfa was lethal to the Rocky Mountain locust, as Brett had provided no compelling evidence that the locust had actually encountered this plant. Riley's exhaustive list of items eaten by the locust would have been funny, if it hadn't reflected the rapacious appetite of the creature that drove so many pioneers to despair.

The litany of plants consumed by the locust fills several pages in Riley's reports. However, amid this catalog of gluttony, alfalfa is not mentioned. The only reference in this regard is Riley's discussion of the legumes—the plant family to which alfalfa belongs: "Of leguminous plants the pods are preferred to the leaves, which are often passed by. . . . The dislike these insects show for leguminous plants is well known, and a crop of peas will often succeed where they abound, when all else is ruined." Riley agreed with his colleague G. M. Dawson, who suggested that from a Darwinian perspective the relative rarity of legumes among the native plants of the Great Plains might account for the insect's lack of affinity for peas and their relatives. For whatever reason, a creature that greedily consumed tobacco, only to die shortly after from the nicotine poisoning, avoided legumes whenever possible.

Most important, Bob Pfadt had persuasively argued that even if alfalfa had been detrimental, a species with the immense distribution of the locust surely had plenty of options when it came to feeding. Gurney and Brooks also dismissed Brett's alfalfa theory on the basis of eco-logical scale. Alfalfa had not blanketed the prairies, so how could it have had any substantial effect on the locust? Of course, had these sci-entists understood the ecological bottleneck through which the locust was being squeezed in the final decades of the nineteenth century, their dismissal of Brett's argument might not have been so facile.

Most of the land being irrigated in the Rocky Mountain region was devoted to the production of cereals and forage. According to the western historian Gilbert Fite, "Alfalfa became a leading hay crop in most of the irrigated valleys and provided feed for the growing live-stock industry. Practically all the irrigation was for forage in Wyoming and Nevada, where ranching was the main agricultural ac-tivity." Elsewhere in the region, cereal crops occupied one-fifth to two-thirds of the irrigated land. Perhaps alfalfa didn't deliver the lethal blow to the Rocky Mountain locust, but it is clear that this crop may have been an important accessory to murder. In the end Charles Brett might have been much closer to cracking the case than his suc-cessors ever imagined.

Not only was alfalfa apparently distasteful or even harmful to the locust, but this crop would also have conspired with irrigation to cre-ate an ecologically deadly scenario. Alfalfa is one of the thirstiest plants in agriculture, requiring about two-tenths of an inch of water per day. The continuous irrigation needed to grow alfalfa would have made conditions disastrous for the Rocky Mountain locust.

Saturating the soil probably killed off locust eggs in some fields, and patches of alfalfa might have hindered the development of the nymphs that did manage to hatch. But the unwitting pioneers had even more devastating ways of transforming the river valleys from cradles into graves.

The two greatest implements of ecological change in North America were arguably the plow and the cow. Vast tracts of prairie were plowed by farmers using oxen, mules, or horses. The tallgrass prairie once spanned parts of fourteen states, blanketing 142 million acres—an area nearly the size the Texas. Well over 90 percent of this ecosystem was turned under or paved over. The soils of shortgrass prairie or steppe were too poor and dry to support crops, so much of this ecosystem was spared from the plow. Instead, it was consigned to intensive grazing by cattle. Today, two-thirds of the western rangelands are in fair to poor condition, a legacy of abuse and neglect that peaked at the end of the nineteenth century. A few ecosystems suffered a one-two punch both under the moldboards of plows and beneath the hooves of livestock. Such was the fate of the montane river valleys.

An acre is a bizarre unit of measure, but like most English units what it lacks in sensibility, it makes up for in history. To be both precise and obscure, an acre is one furlong in length and one chain in breadth. A furlong is a distance of 220 yards. This value is historically derived from the longest stretch of heavy soil that a yoke of four oxen could pull a plow through before they had to rest. Hence, *furlong* is the shortened form of *furrowlong*. A chain is one-tenth of a furlong— a sort of early capitulation to metric notions. The result of multiplying a furlong by a chain is 4,840 square yards—the area encompassed by an acre. Although a furlong has agricultural meaning, one might reasonably ask why the English nobles multiplied this distance by a chain to derive an acre. An acre turns out to be the area that a medieval plowman was required to till in a day. So, the plow and the acre are intimately related.

Despite the advances in technology between the Middle Ages and the Industrial Revolution, the pioneer farmer in the 1800s could plow no more efficiently than his medieval counterpart. Agricultural engineering had provided some advancements, but the rate at which the sod could be turned changed very little in 600 years. At this rate of work, the 50,000 farmers tilling the soil of the river valleys in 1890 could have plowed 5 percent of the Rocky Mountain locust's habitat in a day—if we use a million acres as the midpoint estimate of the creature's area of occupation within the Permanent Zone.

Plowing and harrowing had opposite physical effects, but in either case the biological result was the death of *spretus*. In his 1877 synthetic distillation of Rocky Mountain locust biology, ecology, and management, Riley endorsed plowing and raved about harrowing: "So satisfied have I been for some time that systematic harrowing of eggs, or their exposure by other means, in the fall, is the best work that can be done, that I have earnestly urged its enforcement by law whenever the soil in any township is known to be well-charged with eggs." Normally lying a couple of inches beneath the surface, when plowed under the eggs were unable to receive the warmth necessary for development. And even if they did hatch, the emerging nymphs would be unable to reach the surface. Harrowed to the surface, the eggs were exposed to predators and scavengers, including everything from hungry birds and skunks to foraging ants and beetles. More important, the eggs were no longer insulated from severe weather by a blanket of soil. Riley found that alternate freezing and thawing—typical of springtime in the Rockies—was particularly devastating to the embryos. If they survived these temperature swings, they would almost surely succumb to water loss. For such tiny creatures as locust embryos, desiccation is the gravest physiological threat—and exposure to the brutally dry winter air of the Rockies would have been lethal. But as deadly as the plow was to the locust, there was an even more destructive force at our disposal.

The ultimate limit of the plow's capacity to transform the landscape of the pioneer was that a hulking creature had to drag it through the soil and a sweating human had to guide its path. This trio of animal, human, and machine constrained tillage to the number of hours that even a dedicated farmer could put into such backbreaking labor. The domesticated grazing animals of the pioneers, however, could work continuously in altering the ecology of the river valleys. Attached to a plow, an ox could only turn over so much sod, but left on its own, a cow could graze the floodplains, meadows, and uplands with abandon.

Between 1870 and 1884, the number of cattle in the western states grew by almost tenfold, from about 450,000 to nearly 40 million animals. In Wyoming, the number of cattle increased during this period from 8,000 to more than 1 million. Cattle outnumbered people by a factor of twenty to one. Within a few years, land that had supported a cow and her calf on five acres had been so overgrazed that more than ninety acres were needed. And cattle weren't the only culprits. In the rush to feed animals on public lands, sheep populations were also bursting at the seams. Steens Mountain in eastern Oregon serves as a particularly well-documented example. By the summer of 1900, there were 182,000 sheep packed into the mountain meadows laced with snow-fed streams. This stocking rate represented 450 sheep per square mile.

The grazing by cattle, in particular, was heavily concentrated along rivers and streams, precisely the habitats utilized by the locusts. Many of the breeds of cattle raised in the West were developed in the pastures of Europe, where water was in abundance. Unlike bison, these were thirsty animals, accustomed to plentiful water. The typical beef cow needed ten to fifteen gallons of water daily, and a dairy cow required nearly twice as much. The aggregation of cattle in the valleys dramatically altered these ecosystems.

Based on modern studies, we know that it does not take many livestock to rapidly degrade riverside vegetation. Cattle may not be the brightest creatures, but they know what tastes good. So while hanging out along the streams, they pick out their favorite plants and leave behind an odd and dysfunctional assortment of species. With the loss of deeply rooted vegetation that anchors the riverbanks, the soil begins to erode. And as the banks collapse into the river, the water becomes shallow and silty. In this manner, the falling banks and rising riverbed generate a self-perpetuating process. Through these mutually reinforcing activities, the structure of the channel degenerates, and the river is freed from its established borders.

Like a feral animal, the deep, calm river is transformed into a wild, churning flood. With chronic trampling by cattle and the acute surges of spring meltwater, the channel erodes into a broad, silty floodplain. This transformation is accelerated by the effects of cattle even far from the river valley. The compacted soils and overgrazed vegetation in the uplands renders the land incapable of absorbing and transporting the spring melt and summer rains. This runoff feeds an already bulimic watershed that binges on the winter snowpack and then purges the spring runoff. Without the capacity to buffer the inflow, a river becomes prone to spectacular flooding. According to Clarence Forsling, who headed the Department of Interior's Grazing Service, the West has been plagued by "disastrous floods since the turn of the century because of overgrazing in the mountains."

Although Riley spent years observing the Rocky Mountain locust and generated thousands of pages on the natural history of this species, he conducted only one set of experiments on the locust—and these related to the effects of flooding on the survival of the eggs. It was clear from his records during that winter of 1876 that Riley was not a research scientist, as his experiments followed no systematic design. He tried a haphazard set of conditions, submerging eggs for various durations and frequencies. His experiments also lacked controls, which is the sort of flaw that would be fatal to a junior-high science-fair project. That is, he failed to keep any of the eggs in natural or dry conditions during the winter to understand what the normal rate of hatching would be without his efforts to drown the embryos. Most of his experiments showed that submerging the eggs in the midst of winter, when the embryos were not developing, had little effect on survival. Of course, flooding egg beds in January would have been impractical, even impossible, throughout most of the locust's range. In the mountain valleys, the rivers would have been frozen over and there would have been no potential for the inundation of the over-wintering eggs.

Riley conducted only a few experiments in the early spring, but these results were most revealing. While locust eggs are in diapause (an entomological term for a state of lowered metabolism and arrested development analogous to vertebrate hibernation), they are not much harmed by flooding. But once development recommences in the spring, the embryos become sensitive to environmental conditions. As many as four-fifths of the eggs that were periodically submerged in March and April failed to hatch. Riley concluded that springtime flooding, when the eggs were near hatching, would be particularly detrimental to the locust. However, he never extended this conclusion to the Permanent Zone. Springtime would have been precisely the season in which the peak vulnerability of the locust coincided with the maximal likelihood of inundation in the degraded river valleys. For the Rocky Mountain locust, the conversion of the serene river valleys into churning floodplains would have been devastating in terms of both the erosion of soils that sheltered the eggs and the flooding of these habitats.

Riley also was confident in the effects of livestock trampling on the locust's eggs. Thinking in terms of the farmers of the Great Plains, he recommended, "In pastures or in fields where hogs, cattle, or horses can be confined when the ground is not frozen, many if not most of the locust-eggs will be destroyed by the rooting and tramping." In fact, locusts were reasonably willing to deposit their eggs in grazed fields, so they would have been particularly prone to this crushing and churning. Surely the eggs laid in the river valleys of the Rockies fared no better under the pounding hooves of livestock.

In his seminal paper on the phase transitions of locusts, Sir Boris Uvarov saw beyond the immediate biological meaning of his theory to its potential application in the realm of pest management. Although Uvarov was a consummate taxonomist and brilliant naturalist, he was firmly grounded in the practical world of agriculture. Toward the end of his 1921 paper, he speculated that suppressing the solitary phase of locusts might be more effective than pouring resources into battling the overwhelming swarms that swept across Africa and Central Asia. Uvarov wrote, "The theory of phases suggests the theoretical possibility of the control of *migratoria* by some measures directed not against the insect itself, but against certain natural conditions existing in breeding regions which are the direct cause of the development of the swarming phase."

He clearly saw that the weakest link in the locust's life history was between outbreaks. The time to strike was when the creature was hiding out in refuges. Uvarov briefly reviewed the situation in the Black Sea basin, where the river valleys had spawned immense swarms of locusts for centuries. After the 1880s, however, these breeding grounds had not generated another outbreak. Uvarov attributed this change in locust population dynamics to agriculture: "This is easily explained by the fact that the valleys of the Don, Kuban and Dnieper [river valleys in south-central Russia and Ukraine] were during the end of the last century more or less cultivated or, at any rate, their natural conditions were entirely changed by the persistent grazing of herds of cattle." The failure to apply Uvarov's insight to the case of the Rocky Mountain locust probably reflected both a mistaken sense of ecology (that studies of the Old World locusts had no relevance to North

America) and a regrettable sense of arrogance (that Russian scientists had little to offer their American counterparts).

It seems that in the waning years of the nineteenth century, in river valleys 8,000 miles apart, the sanctuaries of locusts were being destroyed by farmers who were converting these habitats into fields of crops and grazing lands. The people who had been plagued for decades on the prairies of North America and for centuries on the steppes of Central Asia were simultaneously altering their landscapes in ways that would utterly transform the ebb and flow of life. Perhaps the only difference is that the river valleys of the Black Sea basin were ultimately more expansive than human industry could completely alter, whereas those of the Rocky Mountains were far more concentrated. And so today, while the farmers of the Great Plains know of locusts through the journals of their great-grandfathers, the farmers of Kazakhstan and Uzbekistan still know the visceral panic that comes on a summer day when the sky takes on the queer, dirty yellow hue of an impending storm, whose true nature is revealed by the shimmering flecks of 10 billion wings.

THE MOTIVE

The most difficult element in solving a century-old homicide—or would it be an "insecticide"?—is ascertaining the motive of the killer. Often, dozens of people have the means and the opportunity to have done in the victim, so the case hinges on the element of motive. In the extinction of the Rocky Mountain locust, however, there appears to have been only one suspect present at the time and place of the creature's disappearance and with the means to dispatch the victim. Therefore, pinning the blame on the settlers of the montane river valleys does not depend on finding a motive that separates the farmers from a collection of other suspects. However, we are rarely satisfied with simply knowing what happened. As humans we desperately seek to grasp *why*.

Of course, some events appear to occur randomly with no rational explanation. We don't try to explain why a boulder careens down a slope and crashes onto a passing car or why a meteor smashed into the earth and snuffed out the dinosaurs. These seem to have been natural deaths, although rather tragic (in the case of the people in the car) or cataclysmic (in the case of the creatures at the end of the Cretaceous). Other events appear to originate from intentional acts—the assassination of John F. Kennedy, the serial murders of Son of Sam, the Columbine killings, and the extinction of the passenger pigeons, moas, and dodos. In these instances, understanding the motive helps us make sense of the world, and such insights might even allow us to avoid similar events in the future. The passing of the Rocky Mountain locust appears to fall into this latter category.

Although farmers might well question whether a pest should be protected, in the case of *Melanoplus spretus* we lost a keystone species that affected ecosystem processes on a scale equivalent to that of the bison. The locust was a "living fire" sweeping across the western lands, altering the nutrient cycle on a continental scale; a single swarm metabolically burned 4,000 pounds of vegetation an hour. The normal ebb and flow of energy, carbon, and nitrogen across the plains was lost along with the locust, and the ecosystem may not have yet recovered—given what we've learned about the consequences of altering fire regimes in western forests. What species may have been dragged down or critically weakened with the loss of the locust cannot be known because we have such a poor understanding of the biological diversity of the mountains and plains when *spretus* was thriving.

Conversely, the loss of this ecological lynchpin may well have created explosive opportunities for some species; perhaps this is why the grasshopper outbreaks of the twentieth century were so severe. We can be sure that the structure and productivity of plant communities changed in the absence of the locust, but again, sorting out the winners and losers is impossible without baseline data. What we do know is that many western birds and mammals have been in a long-term decline. A colleague in Montana has suggested that the Eskimo curlew (a migratory bird of the grasslands and tundra that is now on the brink of extinction) may have depended on the eggs of *spretus* to fuel the northern leg of its intercontinental journey—its decline coinciding with that of the locust. We also know that some habitats within the West are hypersensitive to livestock grazing, weed invasions, and erosion. Perhaps these are the legacies of having robbed an ecosystem of one of its vital components. Finally, with the passing of the Rocky Mountain locust we have lost a cultural icon—a reminder that we are ultimately dependent on natural processes more sweeping and eternal than the most clever human contrivance.

The motive underlying the ecological transformations that drove the Rocky Mountain locust to extinction might be expressed in terms of either "hope" or "greed"—depending on one's reading of the past. History is a continuous stream of overlapping episodes, upon which we impose a retrospective system of discrete organization in an effort to interpret the world. And if there is a discrete event that marks the beginning of the end for *spretus*, it would be the Homestead Act of 1862. From the early days of our nation, the federal government wrestled with the disposition of public lands. For years, various groups had called for the free distribution of land to the people, in accordance with Jeffersonian ideals. This policy was opposed by the southern states, as they surmised that it was a thinly veiled approach to stopping the spread of slavery into the territories. With the secession of the South, the notion of "free land" became law. Any head of a household who was at least twenty-one years old could claim a 160-acre parcel of federal land. Newly arrived immigrants, former tenant farmers, single women, and freed slaves found this land grant program to be a gateway to hope. Unfortunately, there was not as much open land as was generally assumed because the federal government had given away millions of acres to the states and the railroads. This tactic stimulated the rapid building of both railroads and financial empires. However, railroad magnates did not become wealthy by building railroads but through selling the land along the rail lines. This acreage was extremely valuable because the trains provided a ready means of transporting commodities to distant and lucrative markets. The combination of homesteader hope and railroader rapacity generated the social motivation that would put humans on a collision course with the Rocky Mountain locust.

A tremendous boom in homesteading was seen along the 100th meridian, the imaginary line defining the Minnesota-Dakota-Nebraska-Kansas frontier. In 1871, there were more than 20,000 homestead entries staking claim to 2.5 million acres of land. According to historian Gilbert Fite,

> Every western state and territory wanted more people. After all, population was the greatest resource for economic growth. Without people the natural resources could not be developed. Not only did the state and territorial governments have a stake in obtaining more settlers, but the railroads could not sell their lands or build up their carrying business unless there was a steady increase in population. Every serious observer recognized the need for both more producers and consumers.

New York financier Jay Cooke bought the Northern Pacific Railroad hoping to convert rails to riches. However, he failed to consider that the land along his rail line from Minneapolis to Seattle was marginal for agriculture—and that it was smack in the migratory path of the Rocky Mountain locust. In the tried-and-true tactic of crass commercialism, Cooke hired a gaggle of publicity men to deceive the public as to the desirability of his lands. False advertising can be a very effective strategy, but it is essential to carefully time one's hasty exit from the scam. When hopeful farmers found marginal lands and marauding locusts, Cooke's duplicity was revealed and his business empire collapsed. The nation's economic dominoes began to tumble. In short order, his investment bank—considered one of the strongest financial institutions in the country—tanked, the stock market plunged, more banks failed, businesses went bankrupt, and jobs disappeared. What became known as the Panic of 1873 was the worst economic depression in the young nation's history. In the cities, hunger and homelessness spread. Unrest grew to the point where the country feared a second Civil War, this time between workers and industrialists.

During the four years of this depression, homesteading became an ever more viable alternative to urban life. Most farmers could provide their own subsistence during this time, so low farm prices were not a matter of life and death. Fite maintained that farmers suffered more from locusts than from the Panic. They had not yet been drawn into the commercialization of agriculture, in which the complexities of commodity prices, rather than the simple production of food, would determine success and failure. Between the 1870s and the 1890s, the face of the West changed dramatically, as Americans sought the independence, security, and stability that came with the ownership of land.

The states conspired with railroads and newspapers to promote immigration, and the cry of "Go West, young man, go West" rang out with a fervor greater than the original call twenty years earlier. By the mid-1880s the Dakota Boom was in full swing, and a land rush was sweeping across western Nebraska and Kansas along with eastern Colorado. At precisely noon on Monday, April 22, 1889, the Oklahoma Land Rush was on—and within days thousands of "Boomers" would claim more than two million acres of land. Entire towns of 10,000 inhabitants were created in a single day.

In the midst of these agricultural transformations, mining was becoming the driving force of settlement in the Rockies. The discovery of gold, silver, and other valuable minerals in Colorado, Idaho, Montana, and Wyoming created the demand for commodities. Just as the fortunes were made by the railroaders in selling land, rather than in owning railroads, so wealth in the mountains would come from selling goods to the miners, rather than from the mines themselves. Plowing the fertile soils of the placid river valleys was more profitable (but less romantic) than panning for gold in the swollen creeks. And so farmers armed with plows and cows found themselves in the midst of their ancient mortal enemy at precisely the time of the locust's greatest vulnerability. The rush of humans to strip the precious metals from the Rockies and the concomitant surge of shopkeepers, hoteliers, tavern owners, shippers, and farmers can be seen as an entangled story of virtue and vice, of hope and greed.

14

What Have We Learned?

THREE HUNDRED YEARS AGO, VOLTAIRE SET THE stage for the modern scientist's reaction to new ideas and discoveries: "Doubt is not a pleasant condition, but certainty is an absurd one." My "habitat destruction theory" accounting for the Rocky Mountain locust's extinction met with keen interest, intense scrutiny, and gradual acceptance. It has become the working hypothesis of this marvelous creature's demise. In science there is always doubt, especially when we are unable to replicate an event. Scientists greatly prefer firsthand observations and definitive cause-and-effect explanations. But in the end, subtle coincidences, qualitative reasoning, and circumstantial evidence proved compelling in the "court of science." A critical and anonymous jury of one's peers renders verdicts in this court. The Entomological Society of America's journal *Environmental Entomology* (the publication, but not the editor, that rejected my first paper on Grasshopper Glacier) published my account of the Rocky

Mountain locust's disappearance, thereby closing the case on perhaps the greatest ecological mystery of modern times.

Of course, the nature of science is such that every case is perpetually open to appeal on procedural grounds or in light of new evidence. This chronic uncertainty is what irritates many of the observers of science—and it is precisely what excites the practitioners. If the judgment of my predecessors had been immune to challenge, we would have settled for a nebulous explanation alluding to vague large-scale forces, and the incredible story of the Rocky Mountain locust would never have been told. Perhaps there are further chapters lurking on dusty shelves, in glacial cores, and within biological molecules, but the gavel has fallen on the case as we know it. And we have been found guilty of causing the locust's demise.

The notion of guilt, however, implies a certain culpability and an admission of responsibility. One of the most trite bumper-sticker phrases in environmentalism must be "Extinction Is Forever." As clichéed as this might be, it touches on an important truth. We can't bring back *Melanoplus spretus*. But what we can't change, we can learn from. The story of the lost locust offers some valuable lessons.

By conservative estimates, typical Rocky Mountain locust swarms contained several billion insects. Such a vast quantity is disconcertingly similar to the current human population. The simplest and most unambiguous lesson that we can learn from this locust is that numerical abundance does not ensure future survival. Having reached 6 billion people, we need only look back at the locusts that blackened the skies of North America to realize that our future as a species is no brighter for our quantity.

But, one might legitimately contend, humans are not like locusts. We are far more clever and adaptable. *Homo sapiens* is the ultimate generalist, capable of rapidly adapting to an immense range of environmental challenges and occupying new habitats. However, the Rocky Mountain locust might quietly remind us that it consumed no fewer than fifty kinds of plants from more than a dozen families (as well as leather, fabric, paper, and wool when hunger demanded), whereas the overwhelming proportion of our diet is derived from just three species—corn, wheat, and rice—found in a single family of plants.

And our mobility is no greater than that of the Rocky Mountain locust, if we account for the differences in size. If we multiply the two-inch locust by a factor of thirty-six, we end up with a six-foot human-sized creature. Now then, we must also proportionately increase the distance that the two-inch locust traveled during its lifetime. Swarms could travel a thousand miles, and extrapolating this journey for our magnified locust yields a distance of 36,000 miles. This is the same distance that our ancestors traveled in the process of circumnavigating and eventually colonizing the planet. It appears that being a highly mobile generalist is no insurance against extinction.

There does, however, seem to be a major difference between our condition and that of the Rocky Mountain locust. Although it could invade vast regions, this species was periodically restricted to limited areas. The serendipitous overlap of human activity and the remnants of the Rocky Mountain locust demonstrates the hazard of such ecological bottlenecks. As with the monarch butterfly, whose populations stretch across North America only to collapse back into a few pockets of overwintering habitat each year, the long-term viability of the Rocky Mountain locust was only as great as its most vulnerable link. A handful of loggers armed with chain saws could eliminate the monarch butterfly across most of North America by destroying its winter grounds in western Mexico—just as a small contingent of settlers equipped with horse-drawn plows and simple implements effectively eliminated the locust across the continent by transforming the fertile river valleys of the Rockies. Industrial pollution, earth-moving machinery, and 3,000-mile swaths of concrete are the modern tools of habitat conversion, but extinction does not require technological sophistication.

For a species to become wholly reliant on a place or a habitat, it must sacrifice other options, accepting the risks of being profoundly and deeply linked to a landscape. When in the course of evolution such an ecological setting is found, the species comes to flourish in this place. For the Rocky Mountain locust, the fertile river valleys of the mountainous West represented a sanctuary, a habitat where it could always find what it needed and persist in the face of adversity.

We have such places, too: churches, mosques, temples, and synagogues, along with hallowed groves, stone monoliths, and forested cathedrals. These sacred spaces comprise less than a millionth of the earth's surface but host three-quarters of the human population each year, and they are vital to our well-being, particularly in these troubled times, when humans increasingly seek solace. Just as the locust was able to find a safe refuge where it could rest and revitalize, we need our sanctuaries.

The concept of the sacred has the same etymological origin as sacrifice, which is an act that engenders holiness through loss, suffering, denial, or pain. Holiness, in turn, is a special condition that is associated with transcendent meaning, so that a place of sacrifice is imbued with importance greater than its physical context. In Western society, sacrifice is usually avoided, as we seek security, comfort, and pleasure. However, the existence of suffering is inescapable, and we continue to struggle with the nature, meaning, and necessity of suffering—the "great mystery of life." And so, our places of worship often reflect stories of sacrifice.

Places of momentous loss often become sacred, such as the battlefields at Gettysburg and Little Big Horn, the Edmund Pettus Bridge in Selma, the North Bridge in Concord, the World Trade Center in New York, or a simple roadside cross adorned with flowers. We also honor places of sanctuary where we have found safety amid a world of turmoil and trouble, such as the hiding place of Anne Frank, Thoreau's cabin site at Walden Pond, or our childhood home. Our most sacred spaces both remind us of suffering and offer us sanctuary. But what of other species? Does sacrifice or sanctuary define the extraordinary places in their lives? Do these spaces need to be consciously and intentionally chosen, or can a sacred space emerge in the context of evolution and ecology?

We are reluctant to call the habitats of other species sacred because their sacrifices are not volitional and their seeking of sanctuary is unconscious. But we did not plan for a grassy knoll in Dallas to be the place to lose President Kennedy; we did not intend for a buck-and-rail fence east of Laramie to be the site where Matthew Shepard would be sacrificed to our fear of differences; and we did not design the basements and attics of the houses along the underground railroad to be sanctuaries for runaway slaves. As self-aware animals, we do what we can to honor and protect our sacred spaces, and, perhaps, we should not deny other creatures their own ways of knowing and keeping deeply valued places insofar as they are able. All species have stories of suffering and sanctuary in ecological and evolutionary times. To have arrived in this world is to have risked, lost, groped, huddled, and grasped, using those capacities that one's form and function provide. These stories and places of loss and triumph are encoded in all beings. Are they less real or less important if they are not maintained by thought or word?

The Rocky Mountain locust, the Native Americans, and the early European settlers of the West found that the serene and lush river valleys provided fresh water, abundant food, and reliable protection from severe weather. Each made sacrifices and struggled to establish their hold on these fertile valleys, and each understood that these havens would provide a sanctuary in times of difficulty. The locust sacrificed the life of the grasshopper—a more stable, safe, and mundane existence—for the chance to reach levels of abundance that we can barely fathom. As with the Native Americans, whose cultures eroded with their displacement from sacred lands, the Rocky Mountain locust could not change fast enough to adapt to changes wrought by the settlers.

The complex and intimate connection between the land and native species is difficult—and perhaps impossible—to express in objective scientific terms, but sacred places are central to the well-being of many creatures. Even with all of the "right" conditions of temperature, light, humidity, and diet, animals often languish in zoos. They are unable to express what is missing, and perhaps we would be unable to understand, unless we, too, had experienced the soul-wrenching loss of being forced from a farm or ranch that had been in the family for generations or being driven from a homeland that defined our traditions, stories, and hopes. Even if we had managed to conserve the last of the Rocky Mountain locusts in a zoo, they would be no more their original species than the condors that can never again know the vast, unbroken expanses of land in the California foothills. Unless these insects could once again blacken the skies, they would, in fact, become the Rocky Mountain grasshopper.

The loss of biological diversity in the world is proceeding at a startling pace. Although the details can be endlessly debated, we are undoubtedly losing species a thousand times faster than the normal rate of extinction. In other words, a species disappears about every thirty minutes. Most of these losses are in the tropics, where humans are destroying vast swaths of forests. From our vantage point in North America, it is easy to shake our heads, cluck our tongues, and mutter about the senseless destruction. How can these people justify exchanging the biological legacy of our planet for a few more acres of crops, which will soon degrade to low-value grasslands? But then, how did our agrarian ancestors rationalize the destruction of species? The answer is the same—there is no justification. Both events are tragic accidents induced by socioeconomic pressures, without the actors having malice or forethought.

The Rocky Mountain locust was inadvertently driven to extinction. The most spectacular "success" in the history of economic entomology—the only complete elimination of an agricultural pest species—was the result of unplanned, uncoordinated, and unintentional human activity. The agriculturalists who arrived in the river valleys of the West managed to drive their most severe competitor to extinction in a matter of a few years, leaving North America the only inhabited continent without a locust species. The capacity of the human species to destroy other life forms has not been necessarily, or perhaps even usually, a matter of intentional or wanton disregard for nature. But, one might wonder, at what point does our species become morally culpable for its actions? When can we no longer appeal to being big, dumb, clumsy beasts bulling our way through yet another display of fine, living porcelain in nature's china shop?

There is a final, ironic connection between the bygone days when the Rocky Mountain locust descended on the pioneers, consuming the hard-earned fruits of their labor to fuel the life of the swarm, and modern times, when industrial agriculture descends upon the land, consuming vast quantities of oil to fuel our system of food production: The discovery of grasshopper bodies surfacing in glaciers was made possible by the rapid melting of these ice fields. Global warming is releasing the locusts from their icy graves. A century ago, human alterations of ecosystems caused the demise of the Rocky Mountain locust. And today, the ghosts of these insects warn us of an even more serious threat to the natural world. As our current environmental crisis exposes our past act of destruction—and as it threatens human populations squeezed into our favored habitats of seaboards, riverbanks, and desert margins—one can only wonder what else we might learn from the Rocky Mountain locust.

Away from the rim of the Grand Canyon of the Yellowstone, the thundering falls and thronging tourists give way to murmuring breezes and teeming grasshoppers. Visitors come to Yellowstone National Park to see the fiery underworld: steaming fumaroles, seething mud pots, and roaring geysers. I had come to find an aspect of nature far more rare and ephemeral, a spark of life that had not flamed for a hundred years. I sought the last vestige of the Rocky Mountain locust.

The U.S. Congress designated Yellowstone as the country's first national park in 1872. The Yellowstone Act called for the preservation of the watershed of the Yellowstone River "for the benefit and enjoyment of the people." The marvel of Yellowstone was its fifty-mile-wide crater and the thousands of geothermal features scattered across the landscape. Six hundred thousand years ago an eruption spewed 200 cubic miles of ash across the continent (a volume 300 times that ejected by Mount St. Helens in 1980). Little did Congress know that Yellowstone was still erupting with explosions of life, spreading locusts over an area larger than that encompassed by the largest volcanic eruption in the continent's history.

Yellowstone National Park was intended to preserve a special place for humans, but it also protected the sanctuary of the Rocky Mountain locust. Within two years of the park's formation, immense swarms of locusts descended upon the pioneer farmers of the Great Plains. And within a decade, Charles Valentine Riley would gain the first inkling that these spectacular river valleys of the montane West were the source of the locust. By then, however, Yellowstone was protected from the ecological ravages of farming, and the last haunts of the Rocky Mountain locust were left intact.

I've taken several ventures into the park hoping to discover the long-lost locust. But I wonder: What if I found a pocket of habitat still harboring these once glorious creatures? Regulatory officials might well advocate their destruction, as the potential for a return to the swarms of the 1800s would be a possibility. Even the vaunted Endangered Species Act exempts pests from protection, so perhaps this remnant population would be accorded the same status as the last vial of smallpox. However, in my fantasy scenario, I like to imagine that in an ironic twist, economic entomologists would hasten to point out that *pest* is a label that can be applied only under appropriate conditions of population density. Surely, they would argue, a population of Rocky Mountain locusts that had not bothered us for a century could hardly be termed a pest.

From the environmental camp, a few voices might call for protecting these insects as important components of a native ecosystem that is struggling to sustain biotic integrity. Advocates could invoke the powerful place of this species in the story of the nation and the folklore of America. There might be some appeals based on the Rocky Mountain locust's capacity to serve as a reminder that we must share this world with other species, even those that we have not tamed or controlled. Along with hurricanes and drought, such creatures serve to remind the industrial world that humility is still necessary.

But in the end, would our decision be any different from that of the loggers in Amazonia or that of the early pioneers, had they realized that their nemesis had finally been reduced to a single locale? If we struggle so mightily with whether we should save the last bits of old-growth forest and the few untrammeled tracts of the Arctic, what hope would a locust have? What have we really learned about ourselves and our place in the natural world?

Among the grasshoppers that I have collected in Yellowstone National Park, I remember one female with spectacularly long wings. Of course females are very difficult to identify, but she was officially recorded as *Melanoplus bruneri,* the closest living relative of *Melanoplus spretus.* I may have been wrong in my classification of that long-winged female, but mistaken identities are sometimes a saving grace for individuals whose existence may not be welcomed. Recently, I captured several similar individuals from a meadow in the park. They also appeared to be *M. bruneri,* although they lacked the distinctive yellow coloration on the underside that typifies this species. I think that I know who they were, so I released them back into the field. Because I did not remove them from the park, their identities and location need not be reported to the authorities.

NOTES

CHAPTER 1: THE THIRD HORSEMAN OF THE APOCALYPSE

There are innumerable accounts of the trials and tribulations of western pioneers, many of which make at least some reference to the hardships wrought by locusts (along with disease, hunger, loneliness, cold, drought, fire, etc.). The stories include both autobiographical journals and fiction-alized tales. A couple of the best first-person accounts are *Old Rail Fence Corners: Frontier Tales told by Minnesota Pioneers,* edited by Lucy Leav-enworth Wilder Morris, and *Mollie: The Journal of Mollie Dorsey Sanford in Nebraska and Colorado Territories, 1857–1866,* by Mollie D. Sanford. For sheer readability and cultural relevance, however, nothing beats Laura Ingalls Wilder's *Little House* series. Among the fictionalized accounts, the most popular contemporary work is Larry McMurtry's *Lonesome Dove.* However, perhaps the writings more relevant to the times and places of the Rocky Mountain locust are works such as Willa Cather's *O Pioneers!,* Maud Hart Lovelace and Delos Lovelace's *Gentleman from England,* and Ole Rolvaag's *Giants in the Earth.* There are few scholarly works that di-rectly address the ways in which locusts impacted the lives of the settlers, but perhaps the best such study is Harold E. Briggs's "Grasshopper Plagues and Early Dakota Agriculture, 1864–1876"(*Agricultural History* 1934, 8:51–63).

CHAPTER 2: ALBERT'S SWARM

The best firsthand accounts of swarms of the Rocky Mountain locust are embedded within the U.S. Entomological Commission's first two reports issued by the Government Printing Office: *First Annual Report of the United States Entomological Commission for the Year 1877 Relating to the Rocky Mountain Locust* and *Second Report of the United States Entomological Commission for the Years 1878 and 1879 Relating to the Rocky Mountain Locust and Western Cricket.* These reports are still reasonably available through antiquarian book dealers. However, the best synthesis of the Rocky Mountain locust's biology is Charles V. Riley's *The Locust Plague in the United States* (1877), but this small treatise is much more difficult to find. There are several sources of information on locust biology and ecology. Perhaps the most readable account is Stanley Baron's *The Desert Locust,* which recounts the massive control programs in Africa in the mid-twentieth century. More technical overviews of grasshopper and locust biology include *Biology of Grasshoppers,* edited by R. F. Chapman and Anthony Joern, and *The Bionomics of Grasshoppers, Katydids, and Their Kin,* edited by S. K. Gangwere, M. C. Muralirangan, and Meera Muralirangan.

CHAPTER 3: THE SIXTH PLAGUE

One of the strangest and most fascinating books on legal history ever written is E. P. Evan's *The Criminal Prosecution and Capital Punishment of Animals,* which not only explores the relationship between human laws and animal actions but also reveals profound moral and religious dilemmas in terms of our relationship to the natural world. There are many sources of information on the history of Mormonism, and these books frequently make reference to the role of the Rocky Mountain locust—and, of course, the Mormon cricket—in the story of the Latter Day Saints. A couple of the more readable, but rather contentious, accounts are *One Nation under Gods: A History of the Mormon Church,* by Richard Abanes, and *The Gathering of Zion: The Story of the Mormon Trail,* by Wallace Earle Stegner. For a Mormon's-eye view of Mormonism, including some interesting references to the role of the locusts in the early days of the Utah settlers, it's worth checking out the *Meridian Magazine* Web site (meridianmagazine.com). The Web site historytogo.utah.gov also has some good information about the Mormon settlers and their insect adversaries. And of course, a reading of the Bible's book of Exodus is sure to set the proper context for an appreciation of Western culture's interpretation of locusts.

CHAPTER 4: HUMANS STRIKE BACK

The best descriptions of the methods used to control the Rocky Mountain locust are found in the U.S. Entomological Commission's reports and various USDA bulletins, such as C. V. Riley's 1891 *Destructive Locusts* (USDA Division of Entomology Bulletin No. 25). These documents are difficult to find, and somewhat more accessible accounts from the early part of the twentieth century describe methods similar to those of the late 1800s. In this regard, A. Gibson's, *The Control of Locusts in Eastern Canada* (Canada Department of Agriculture, Entomology Branch, Circular 5, 1915) is an excellent source, as is C. R. Jones's, *Grasshoppers* (Office of State Entomologist, Circular 13, Fort Collins, Colorado, 1914), which has what appear to be the only photographs of the early locust/grasshopper-catching devices in actual use. A more general and accessible historical source for information on insect pest management is Robert A. Wardle and Philip Buckle's *The Principles of Insect Control* (1923). Modern descriptions of locust and grasshopper management methods (many of which can be traced to the work of Riley et al.) include *Biological Control of Locusts and Grasshoppers* (edited by C. J. Lomer and C. Prior, 1992); *New Strategies in Locust Control* (edited by S. Krall, R. Peveling, and D. Ba Diallo, 1997); and *Grasshoppers and Grassland Health* (edited by J. A. Lockwood, A. V. Latchininsky, and M. G. Sergeev, 2000).

CHAPTER 5: POLITICIANS AND PESTS

Without a doubt, the most thorough and interesting historical review of the sociopolitical repercussions of the Rocky Mountain locust can be found in Annette Atkins's *Harvest of Grief: Grasshopper Plagues and Public Assistance in Minnesota, 1873–78.* Her work and interpretations contributed immensely to my own ideas concerning the place of the locust in American history and culture. For readers with a penchant for historical sleuthing, absolutely fascinating discussions of how politicians perceived the locust and the proper role of government can be found in the *Congressional Record,* especially the second session of the Forty-third Congress (December 1874 through February 1875), the first session of the Forty-fourth Congress (May 1876), and the first session of the Seventy-second Congress (June 1932). The text of the letters from General Ord and Major Dudley can be found in the Senate's record of the second session of Forty-third Congress (Executive Document No. 5, "Ravages of Grasshoppers"). And the dramatic accounting of the military food and stores provided to the settlers can be found in the House of Representatives' record of the first session of the Forty-fourth Congress (Executive Document No. 28, "Relief of Grasshopper Sufferers"). To see what the federal government has been doing in regard to grasshopper control in recent years, check out the USDA's Web site at sidney.ars.usda.gov/grasshopper/.

CHAPTER 6: LORD OF THE LOCUSTS

Although there is no definitive and complete biography of Charles Valentine Riley, his story is told in various places. A series of articles have appeared in the *American Entomologist,* including "Darwin, Walsh, and Riley: The Entomological Link" (G. Kritksy, summer 1995) and "Charles Valentine Riley: The Making of the Man and His Achievements" (E. H. Smith and J. R. Smith, winter 1996). The Entomological Society of America's 1991 compendium, *Progress and Perspectives for the 21st century* (edited by J. J. Menn and A. L. Steinhauer) includes a chapter, "A Tribute to Charles Valentine Riley: American Entomologist," by L. V. Knutson. A biography published more closely in time to Riley's life was written by F. G. Summers (vol. 19, no. 4, 1925) in the *Missouri Historical Review* and was titled "Charles V. Riley, Benefactor of Agriculture." The most compelling firsthand insights into Riley's character come from the autobiographical retrospective of his assistant (and successor) Leland O. Howard in *Fighting the Insects: The Story of an Entomologist* (1933). Howard also included many intriguing perspectives on the early days of economic entomology and the personality of Riley in *A History of Applied Entomology* (Smithsonian Miscellaneous Collections, vol. 84, 1930).

CHAPTER 7: THE TRIUMVIRATE

There are no detailed biographies of Cyrus Thomas or Alpheus Packard, but a genuine appreciation of these men's lives can be gleaned from Arnold Mallis's *American Entomologists* (1971) and *History of Entomology* (1973), edited by R. F. Smith, T. E. Mittler, and C. N. Smith. As in the "inside scoop" on Riley that L. O. Howard provided in his *History of Applied Entomology* (1930), there are many interesting anecdotes that he provides with regard to Thomas and Packard. An especially valuable perspective on the life of Thomas, his intriguing associations with nineteenth-century luminaries, and his contributions to the field of anthropology was assembled by Jon Muller of Southern Illinois University's Department of Anthropology and can be accessed at siu.edu/~anthro/muller/Thomas/Thomas.html. Some of Thomas's most important scientific works have been reprinted and are available but a bit hard to find. For the serious scholar or intensely curious reader, Packard's papers (including letters, lectures, and sermons) are conserved in Bowdoin College's George J. Mitchell Department of Special Collections and Archives. Packard's *Lamarck: The Founder of Evolution; His Life and Work: With Translations of His Writings on Organic Evolution* was reprinted in 1980 and is reasonably available along with some of his natural history works that also have been reprinted at various times.

CHAPTER 8: THE LOCUST DISAPPEARS

I must admit to having relied on a Web site for the majority of my biographical information about Norman Criddle and his family, but what a Web site! The Canadian government's Digital Collections Program has conserved local histories, and Criddle's story can be explored at collections.ic.gc.ca/wawanesa/E/people/criddles/criddles.html. Grasshopper outbreaks in the twentieth century are not collated in any coherent manner, although accounts of particular events can be found in A. Gibson's "The Control of Locusts in Eastern Canada" (Dominion of Canada's Department of Agriculture Circular No. 5, 1915); H. C. Severin and G. I. Gilbertson's "Grasshoppers and Their Control" (South Dakota State Agricultural Experiment Station Bulletin No. 172, 1917); W. W. Henderson's "Crickets and Grasshoppers in Utah" (Utah Agricultural Experiment Station Circular 96, 1931), R. C. Smith's "An Analysis of 100 Years of Grasshopper Populations in Kansas" (*Transactions of the Kansas Academy of Sciences*, 57(4), 1954), and C. Wakeland's, "The High Plains Grasshopper" (USDA Technical Bulletin No. 1167, 1958). The best overall synthesis of grasshopper biology, ecology, and management—including information on *Melanoplus sanguinipes* and *femurrubrum*—is unquestionably R. E. Pfadt's "Western Grasshoppers" (*Wyoming Agricultural Experiment Station Bulletin* 912, 3rd edition, 2002, with an online version at sdvc.uwyo.edu/grasshopper/).

CHAPTER 9: A WOLF IN SHEEP'S CLOTHING

A rich source of information on Sir Boris Uvarov is the *Biographical Memoirs of the Fellows of the Royal Society* (Vol. 17, 1971). Uvarov's seminal works were the two volumes of *Grasshoppers and Locusts: A Handbook of General Acridology* (1966 and 1977). His revolutionary paper on the phase theory of locusts was published as "A Revision of the Genus *Locusta*, L. (= *Pachytulus*, Fieb.), with a New Theory as to the Periodicity and Migrations of Locusts" (*Bulletin of Entomological Research*, 12[2],135–163). Faure's efforts to transform *M. sanguinipes* are reported in "The Phases of the Rocky Mountain Locust *Melanoplus mexicanus*" (*Journal of Economic Entomology*, 26, 706–718, 1933). Brett's corresponding work appeared as "Interrelated Effects of Food, Temperature, and Humidity on the Development of the Lesser Migratory Grasshopper, *Melanoplus mexicanus mexicanus*" (Oklahoma Agricultural Experiment Station Technical Bulletin T-26, 1947). My morphological analysis of the locust appeared as "Taxonomic Status of the Rocky Mountain Locust: Comparisons of Morphometric Values of *Melanoplus spretus* with Solitary and Migratory *Melanoplus sanguinipes*" (*Canadian Entomologist*, 121:1103–1109, 1989). The paper by Gurney and Brooks that set the modern taxonomic standard for the Rocky Mountain locust is "Grasshoppers of the *mexicanus* Group, Genus *Melanoplus*" (*Proceedings of the U.S. National Museum*, 110:1–93, 1959).

CHAPTER 10: BEAUTIFUL THEORIES AND UGLY FACTS

The alfalfa theory was initially debunked in R. E. Pfadt's "Food Plants as Factors in the Ecology of the Lesser Migratory Grasshopper, *Melanoplus mexicanus*" (Wyoming Agricultural Experiment Station Bulletin 290, 1949). Cantrall and Young's bison theory was put forth in "Contrasts in the Orthopteran Fauna of Grassland, Forest and Transitional Areas in Southern Indiana" (*Proceedings of the Indiana Academy of Sciences*, 63:157–162, 1954). Riegert's initial version of the bison theory appeared in "A History of Grasshopper Abundance Surveys and Forecasts of Outbreaks in Saskatchewan" (*Memoirs of the Entomological Society of Canada*, 52:5–99, 1968). For an excellent coverage of bison ecology, one can do no better than to read *The Bison and the Great Plains* (Animals and Their Ecosystems Series), by J. D. Taylor and D. Taylor (1992), and the definitive examination of the bison's demise is surely A. C. Isenberg's (2000) *The Destruction of the*

Bison: An Environmental History, 1750–1920. An outstanding and absolutely authoritative synthesis of the ecology of the Rocky Mountain West is D. H. Knight's (1994) *Mountains and Plains.* There are innumerable books on ecology that are pertinent to the Rocky Mountain locust, and although there are many recent writings, one of the most compelling, provocative, and readable works remains T. F. H. Allen and T. W. Hoekstra's (1992) *Toward a Unified Ecology.*

CHAPTER 11: SECRETS IN THE ICE

My findings from the first three glacial expeditions are presented in a series of coauthored papers: "Grasshopper Glacier: A Vanishing Biological Resource" (*American Entomologist,* 36:18–27, 1990); "The Preserved Fauna of Grasshopper Glacier (Crazy Mountains, Montana): Unique Insights to Acridid Biology" (5th Proceedings of the International Meeting of the Orthopterists' Society, *Boletin Sanidad Vegetal,* 20:223–236, 1991); "Preserved Insects and Physical Condition of Grasshopper Glacier, Carbon County, Montana, U.S.A.," (Arctic and Alpine Research, 24:229–232, 1992). Intriguing early descriptions of Grasshopper Glacier can be found in: M. W. Rivinus's "Grasshopper Glacier" (*Frontiers,* Vol. 15, 1952); W. C. Alden's "Grasshoppers on Ice" (*Nature* Magazine, June 1930); R. E. Hutchins's *Grasshoppers and Their Kin* (1972); and my personal favorite, F. J. Farnsworth's *Cubby Returns* (the relevant passage is on pp. 113–115, 1935). An exceptionally timely and well-written account of the ongoing recession of glaciers in the Rocky Mountains is D. Fagre and M. Hall's "Modeled Climate-Induced Glacier Change in Glacier National Park, 1850–2100" (*BioScience,* 53:131–140, 2003). For a more complete understanding of my idiosyncratic compulsion to understand the lives of grasshoppers, the reader is referred to my collection of essays, *Grasshopper Dreaming: Reflections on Killing and Loving* (2002).

CHAPTER 12: THE MOTHER LODE

The scientific papers that my colleagues and I authored concerning our finds on Knife Point Glacier are "The Preserved Insect Fauna of the Wind River Glaciers (Fremont County, U.S.A.): Insights into the Ecology of the Extinct Rocky Mountain Locust" (*Environmental Entomology,* 23:220–235, 1994) and "Preserved Grasshopper Fauna of Knife Point Glacier, Fremont County,

Wyoming, U.S.A." (*Arctic and Alpine Research*, 23:108–114, 1991). Our work on the cuticular hydrocarbon profile of the specimens extracted from the glaciers and comparisons to museum specimens of the Rocky Mountain locust was reported in "Cuticular Hydrocarbons of Glacially-Preserved *Melanoplus*: Identification by GC/MS and Comparison with Hydrocarbons of *M. sanguinipes* and *M. spretus*" (*Journal of Orthoptera Research*, 5:1–12, 1996). Some very well-written views on particular aspects of molecular genetics include Matt Ridley's *Genome* (2000; focused on the human genome but highly readable); James Watson's *DNA: The Secret of Life* (2003; a fascinating mixture of both science and the author's views of modern genetics); and Lynn H. Caporale's *Darwin in the Genome: Molecular Strategies in Biological Evolution* (2002; also focused on the human genome—rather than that of grasshoppers—but with a rich interpretation of genetics and evolution that makes an excellent counterpoint to Watson's views).

CHAPTER 13: PIONEERS ON TRIAL

There are many excellent historical accounts of the history, politics, and sociology of the American frontier. Perhaps the book most relevant to the time and place of the Rocky Mountain locust's extinction is Gilbert C. Fite's *The Farmers' Frontier, 1865–1900* (1966). For a more complete coverage of the places and events that shaped the continent beyond the 100th meridian, Geoffrey C. Ward's lavishly illustrated *The West* (1996) is an unbeatable read. The biology, ecology, and conservation of monarch butterflies are the subject of many children's books, but fortunately there are a few excellent works for adults as well. Two the most engaging perspectives on this insect are *Chasing Monarchs* (1999), by Robert M. Pyle, and *Four Wings and a Prayer: Caught in the Mystery of the Monarch Butterfly* (2002), by Sue Halpern. As for ecological connections between grasshoppers and habitat qualities (particularly vegetation and soils), two papers that I coauthored with Scott Schell are somewhat technical but accessible to the scientifically literate reader: "Spatial Analysis of Ecological Factors Related to Grasshopper Population Dynamics in Wyoming" (*Environmental Entomology*, 26:1343–1353, 1997) and "Spatial Characteristics of Rangeland Grasshopper Population Dynamics in Wyoming: Implications for Pest Management" (*Environmental Entomology*, 26:1056–1065, 1997).

CHAPTER 14: WHAT HAVE WE LEARNED?

My final synthesis of the Rocky Mountain locust's extinction was coauthored with Larry DeBrey and published as "A Solution for the Sudden and Unexplained Extinction of the Rocky Mountain Locust, *Melanoplus spretus*" (*Environmental Entomology*, 19:1194–1205, 1990). Portions of the locust's story were told in my essays in *American Entomologist* (Vol. 47, 2001), *Orion* (Summer, 2002), *Wild Earth* (Spring, 2002), and *High Country News* (February 3, 2003). Compelling views on the value of biodiversity include Norman Myers's *The Sinking Ark* (1979), Paul and Anne Ehrlich's *Extinction* (1981), Edward O. Wilson's *Biophilia* (1986), Al Gore's *Earth in the Balance* (1993)—and the least scientific and most pleasurable read in this genre, Douglas Adams and Mark Carwardine's *Last Chance to See* (1992). My efforts to understand the moral standing of insects and the natural world can be traced in a series of papers: "Not to Harm a Fly: Our Ethical Obligations to Insects" (*Between the Species*, 4:204–211, 1988); "Competing Values and Moral Imperatives: An Overview of Ethical Issues in Biological Control" (*Agriculture and Human Values*, 14:205–210, 1997); "Agriculture and Biodiversity: Finding Our Place in this World" (*Agriculture and Human Values*, 16:365–379, 1999); and my upcoming collection of essays, *Sacred Steppes: Finding Meaning in the Grasslands*.

ILLUSTRATIONS

CHAPTER 1

Photograph of a wagon train in 1882 (from the Union Pacific Historical Collection).

CHAPTER 2

Drawing of the egg-laying behavior of the Rocky Mountain locust, by Charles V. Riley (from C. V. Riley, A. S. Packard, Jr., and Cyrus Thomas, *First Annual Report of the United States Entomological Commission for the Year 1877 Relating to the Rocky Mountain Locust* [Washington, D.C.: Government Printing Office, 1878]).

Title page from W. Kirby and W. Spence, *An Introduction to Entomology* (London: Longman, Brown, Green, Longmans and Roberts, 1859).

CHAPTER 3

Image of a swarm of the Rocky Mountain locust descending on a farm community (from a lithograph made of a sketch by Howard Purcell in 1874).

CHAPTER 4

Drawing of the Flory Locust-Machine in operation (from C. V. Riley, *Destructive Locusts: A Popular Consideration of a Few of the More Injurious Locusts [or "Grasshoppers"] of the United States, Together with the Best Means of Destroying Them* [Washington, D.C.: Government Printing Office, 1891].

CHAPTER 5

Drawing of General Edward Otho Cresap Ord (from the History Central Web site).

CHAPTER 6

Photograph of Charles Valentine Riley (from Arnold Mallis, *American Entomologists* [Rutgers, N.J.: Rutgers University Press, 1971]).

CHAPTER 7

Drawing of a trio of settlers battling the Rocky Mountain locust with nets (from *Frank Leslie's Illustrated Newspaper*, September 1, 1888, vol. 67, p. 37, with permission of the Minnesota Historical Society).

CHAPTER 8

Photograph of Norman Criddle studying at a table (from Canada's Digital Collections Program, Industry Canada, Ottawa).

CHAPTER 9

Drawing of the molting process of the last nymphal stage into the adult of the Rocky Mountain locust, by Charles V. Riley (from C. V. Riley, A. S. Packard, Jr., and Cyrus Thomas, *First Annual Report of the United States Entomological Commission for the Year 1877 Relating to the Rocky Mountain Locust* [Washington, D.C.: Government Printing Office, 1878]).

CHAPTER 10

Map showing the Permanent, Subpermanent, and Temporary Zones of the Rocky Mountain locust (from C. V. Riley, A. S. Packard, Jr., and Cyrus Thomas, *Second Report of the United States Entomological Commission for the Years 1878 and 1879 Relating to the Rocky Mountain Locust and Western Cricket* [Washington, D.C.: Government Printing Office, 1880]).

CHAPTER 11

Photograph of the Grasshopper Glacier lying above Montana's Black Canyon, by Larry D. DeBrey (with permission of the photographer).

CHAPTER 12

Aerial photograph of Knife Point Glacier, Wyoming (U.S. Geological Survey).

CHAPTER 13

Postcard photograph of Bennett Avenue, Cripple Creek Colorado, 1912 (by permission of Ruth Zirkle).

CHAPTER 14

Photograph of the author on Knife Point Glacier, Wyoming, by Larry D. De-Brey (with permission of the photographer).

INDEX